LOOKING UNDER STONES

Fair Day on Main Street, Dingle.

LOOKING UNDER STONES

ROOTS, FAMILY AND A DINGLE CHILDHOOD

JOE O'TOOLE

THE O'BRIEN PRESS
DUBLIN

First published 2003 by The O'Brien Press Ltd,
20 Victoria Road, Dublin 6, Ireland.
Tel: +353 1 4923333; Fax: +353 1 4922777
E-mail: books@obrien.ie
Website: www.obrien.ie

ISBN: 0-86278-842-0

British Library Cataloguing-in-Publication Data
O'Toole, Joe
Looking under stones
1.O'Toole, Joe - Childhood and youth
2.Ireland - Social life and customs - 20th century
I.Title
941.7'082'092

1 2 3 4 5 6 7 8 9 10
03 04 05 06 07

Editing, typesetting, layout and design: The O'Brien Press Ltd
Front cover photographs: (top) courtesy of The Irish Image Collection;
(bottom and on page 2) from the Ó Muircheartaigh Collection,
Muckross Research Library, Muckross House, Killarney, Co Kerry
Back cover and flap photographs: Moya Nolan
Printing: CPD Books

DEDICATION

To Joan, a wonderful partner.

ACKNOWLEDGEMENTS

I have many people to thank:

Teresa for her motherly, non-judgemental eye over five decades.

Max & Phil Webster for their supportive encouragement.

Four tremendous sisters, Mary Sabrina, Anita, Phyllis and Grace, for not panicking about this. Phyl Moriarty for her help, stories and photographs; Ita Moriarty for her openness and courage.

Patty Atty Moriarty for uninhibited information on the early Moriartys; John Moriarty and John Benny Moriarty; Hanora Moriarty. Mollie, Fergus and Karl O'Flaherty for their accuracy; Mazzarella and Norella for their story.

Peadar and Murielle O'Toole, Lettermore; Lena O'Toole, truly a fount of knowledge. Oliver and Annie O'Toole; Clare and Geraldine O'Toole. Tomás, Síle and the Tourmakeady O'Tooles for completing the family tree.

Micheál Ó Móráin for his stories.

Fr Kieran O'Shea.

Pat Neligan, Donal Ó Loingsigh, Thomas Lyne for remembering.

Austin Corcoran for his research.

Micheál Ó Cuaig, Cill Chiaráin, *don taighde áitiúil.*

Ciarán Cleary, graduate of Barry's forge, for describing another Dingle.

Mary Webb for her effective editing, positive advice and sheer professionalism.

FOREWORD

This is a story. It is neither a social history, a local history nor a family history.

Mentally revisiting, questioning, querying and trying to understand anew things which were the norm growing up has been a real challenge. The research, the talking and the writing were thrilling for me. I have learned more and come to understand more about myself and my background during the writing of this book than at any other time in my life. The uniqueness of a Dingle childhood and the constant provocation and catalyst of interesting relations, friends and neighbours re-emerged.

I have also been awestruck in admiration of the zest for life among my O'Toole and Moriarty ancestors, how they dealt with hardship, tragedy, success and change, and most of all how they could still laugh at themselves and live life to the fullest. The more I got to know of them, the more interesting I found them.

Surprisingly, I have found that all those things that I enjoy in my own life, including teaching, politics, writing, boating, haggling and a love of islands, are all there within the clan experience. I have also grown to a fuller appreciation of how those life experiences moulded me.

No one contributed more to the way I turned out than my father, Myko, whose influence and open, tolerant philosophy continues to give me a sense of direction. I hope that this book is a testament to his tutelage more than any other. It may be a strange thing to say about one's father, but it was a great privilege to have known him and shared in his constant optimism and ever-ready good humour. His great lesson was that every day is worth living, and life, with all its challenges, is also an entertainment.

For me this has been an exhilarating and fascinating voyage through my gene pool. My hope is that the reader, as a fellow traveller, will share some sadness, joy and discovery with me and that my account might also induce the odd smile.

Joe O'Toole, September 2003.

CONTENTS

CAST OF CHARACTERS

The Moriartys

Daddy Tom: Great-great-grandfather

Old Johnny: Great-grandfather

Seán the Grove: Grandfather

   Born 1885. Married Bridgy Fitzgerald, 1913.

   Children: Patrick (Patty Atty), Mollie (married Paguine), John (Foxy John), Thomas, Teresa (my mother), Jonathan (Jonty), Phyl, Ita, Benny, and Jimmy

The O'Tooles

John O'Toole: Great-great-great-grandfather

John O'Toole: Great-great-grandfather

Pat (Kruger) O'Toole: Great-grandfather

Joe O'Toole: Grandfather (also his brother Henry, my granduncle)

   Born 1884. Married Margaret O'Boyle, 1905.

   Children: Patrick, Mary Clare, Twins Michael (Myko – my father) and Jack, and Plunkett

The joining of the clans:

Teresa Moriarty married Myko O'Toole in 1946

Children: **Joseph (b.1947)**, Mary Sabrina, Anita, Phyllis and Grace

There have been Moriartys in Kerry for as long as history records, but the first one of whom I heard stories was Daddy Tom, my great-great-grandfather. And by all accounts he was not the kind of behavioural role model we would be inclined to hold up to our children. He had a reputation as a bit of a rake; the kind of man a father would be reluctant to leave alone with his daughter.

Daddy Tom married another Moriarty, a distant cousin, thereby reuniting two sides of the family. His wife, Síle Óg, was from below the hill in Mullach Mhial, a beautiful and remote place tucked in under the Conor Pass, on the Cloghane side. The Mullach Mhial people had a centuries-old track worn into Dingle, across the hill, through Camaois and down by the Glens. Daddy Tom called into Mullach Mhial regularly enough. It was always expected that he would marry Mary, the eldest girl; they were promised to each other. But Tom's eyes wandered. He was distracted by the younger Síle, and soon it was himself and Síle Óg who were becoming great with each other.

It wasn't a situation approved of by Síle's father, who did not trust Tom for either of his daughters: 'By God but weren't we privileged to have had his company again today! He is too fond of the drink and mad for the other thing, that fella. I'm telling you, you'd be better off keeping far away from him. Young O'Donnell is far steadier. Tom Moriarty might be clan but he has a dangerous, wild streak in him.'

Síle was well aware that James O'Donnell was steadier. Wasn't he a neighbour and didn't she know him all her life. When he called to the house you wouldn't notice the difference; he was just like the rest of her family. And he would marry her in the morning. Everyone expected it. James was safe, secure … and dull.

Tom Moriarty was a rogue. He *plámásed* her mother, drank with her brothers, challenged her father, laughed at the world and worried little. He was exciting. Never a *pátrún* day or fair did he miss and he would never leave a ball before morning. And she had heard about him and the women. But she wanted him around and wanted to be with him.

One fine summer's day, when it was time for Tom to leave, Síle walked with him up the path to the top of the hill where, no doubt, the stunning views of the north and south sides of the Peninsula were the last things on the minds of two healthy, handsome youngsters. As Breandy Begley put it, 'They went at it so hard that Tom left the print of Síle's arse on the side of the track!'

Nature took its course, and with a baby on the way the couple did what they were expected to do and got married. And as for a honeymoon, a learned local historian told me once, 'What honeymoon are you talking about? In those days the honeymoon after the wedding was a day in town and a night in bed.' While the young lovers settled in to the married state, it is said that Daddy Tom did not let marriage completely change his rakish ways. 'Seven or eight at home and a few more around the parish,' was his answer to an enquiry as to the size of his family. Tom took to heart the great biblical imperative 'Go forth and multiply' and made it a personal mission.

The story of Daddy Tom and Síle was an entertainment, and the generational distance in time made it safe to tell. But these two people represent the beginnings of the family tree and, as such, they evoked a great curiosity. As it happens, the old track from Glens through Camaois into Mullach Mhial is extant. Little or nothing has changed and, apart from the presence of a power line with its string of poles, the view today is the same as it would have been for Tom and Síle.

Two centuries later I retraced their journey over the hill track down into Mullach Mhial. I started off lightheartedly enough, driving the Glens road out of Dingle and turning right at the Droichead Bán. Leaving the car behind when the road ran out, I crossed a gate and headed up into Camaois. As children growing up in Dingle, Camaois was the back end of nowhere. It was the place of threatened banishment if we were bold. How age matures, I thought, as I soaked in the sheer beauty of the place. How could I have missed this loveliness on my boyhood visits? It reminded me now of the Scottish legend of Brigadoon, which emerged magically out of a drab valley once in every century. Had I stumbled on Brigadoon? Or maybe the real truth of Brigadoon is not that it reappears every hundred years, but that it is only visible to the enlightened and the ready?

Striding up the gentle incline I kept a sharp lookout for the imprint of the posterior of my libertine great-great-grandmother, Síle. I have to report that, sadly, I did not find it. But following in the footsteps of the young lovers, I could almost picture them skipping up the hillside on that warm August day. Now that I was surrounded by the almost spiritual beauty of the place, their story took on a new meaning. The crude, simple telling seemed inappropriate. No sense now of a bawdy, superior enjoyment at their expense. This was a place meant to inspire romanticism and love.

And when you think about it, where could young couples go to be alone in those times? There were no secluded corners in nightclubs, no 'Come up to my apartment'. It was only to be expected that in their desire for each other they would have been loathe to part when it was time for Tom to go. Wasn't it the most natural thing in the world that Síle would walk aways with him? And when they reached the summit they would see the glory of West Kerry spread out in front of them, with the point of Cruach Marthain puncturing the sky and dividing the panorama between the distant Blaskets to the west and Skellig Mhicíl to the east. Breathless after the climb, and cocooned in the dry heather, they would rest before saying their goodbyes, delaying the inevitable parting by surrendering to passion in the most natural and, as it turned out, fruitful coupling.

So there it was, the place of conception and the source of my maternal gene stream. From this pair, through four generations to me, and it continues.

As for Síle Óg and Tom, it could be that as the years passed their love faded and their passion for each other cooled, but it would appear that the older Tom became, the more of a '*stail*' he became. Many years after Síle's death and with his family well reared, Tom was living with a son and daughter-in-law. His son's wife was a decent, caring woman, who put up with the antics of her father-in-law. One night as she was sitting at home, there came a loud and demanding knock at the door. It would be rare enough for anyone to knock; neighbours just lifted the latch and came in with a 'God save all here' greeting. It was rarer still for someone to come to the front door, which had very little practical function in those times, apart from the welcoming of a new bride or the taking out of a coffin.

By the time she had sconced a candle and got to the front door there was no sign of anyone in the dark outside. Thinking that the visitor had gone round the back, she was about to shut the door when she saw a basket on the ground. Wrapped in it was a tiny, newborn baby. Practical woman that she was, she knew it was 'returned goods' to her father-in-law. And soft woman that she was, her heart went out to the little mite. She took herself and the child to bed and the word was put out that she was having trouble with a premature birth. A day or two later she produced the child. She called him Tom and he was reared in the house as their own.

As a young man, Tom felt the call to the priesthood and he was duly accepted as a seminarian in Maynooth College. At the time there was an arrangement that seminarians could be ordained after five years rather than the usual six if they agreed to serve a ten-year stint in Australia. Tom chose that route, and records show that he graduated from Maynooth with high honours in 1903. He loved his time in Australia, where he was held in great esteem by his community. When the ten years were up he was so comfortable with his parish that he opted to stay there, despite the offer of returning to a parish in his native Kerry. The people of his Australian parish were so delighted that they presented him with a sidecar and a pair of white horses. A month later he was driving in the sidecar to one of the outlying parishes when a woman by the roadside raised a large umbrella. The horses took fright, reared up and took off at a gallop. Father Tom could not get them under control. The whole contraption turned over on him and the poor man was killed. All that happened near Melbourne, in the diocese of Ararat, where he had served as priest in some beautiful-sounding places, such as Warnambool, Koroit and Casterton.

By all accounts Father Tom was a kind and generous man who always took an interest in the family back home. But if he had had his way, this book would never have been written and the union of the O'Tooles and the Moriartys, still a long way off, would never have happened.

When my grandfather, Seán the Grove, and Bridgy Fitz got married, Father Tom strongly advised them to come to Australia where he guaranteed them a good start. Interestingly, it was a route that my other ancestors, the O'Tooles, were to take a generation later – one of the many coincidences I was to discover in the story of the two families. Anyway, back to the Moriartys – the young couple decided to take him up on the offer and he sent over the price of the tickets and money for the journey. All was organised, and after the farewells were done, the pair headed for the ship in Queenstown, now Cobh harbour, outside Cork City. As Seán the Grove told it, ' We had everything packed and ready to go, but when Bridgy saw the ship she bolted and refused to go another inch. We turned on our heels home again for Dingle.' Though he relished the telling of the story and laying the blame on Bridgy, it always seemed to me that he was not unhappy with the outcome. He was a reluctant would-be emigrant at best.

Bridgy never changed her mind about emigration and as she would say herself, signs on, only one of her own family later emigrated. After one row too many, her son Jimmy, the black sheep of the family but her pride and joy, decided that Dingle was too small for her and him. When his mother heard that he was about to board a US-bound plane in Rineanna, as Shannon Airport was then called, her comment was, 'The green distant grass makes an ass of the ass.'

From what I heard, Father Tom did not hold it against them that they changed their minds about Australia. Indeed, every story I was ever told about him suggests that there was a man of goodness if ever there was one, and there is no doubt that as a priest he was loved and respected for his caring and commitment. The irony is that if Holy Mother Church had even suspected that Tom was illegitimate he would never have been accepted as a seminarian. The rules of the Catholic Church at the time were unwavering on this matter: 'Bastards can't be priests.'

Makes you wonder, doesn't it?

It is almost certain that Tom himself lived and died in ignorance of his true parentage. It raises a very fundamental question: should he have been told? Certainly he had a right to know, and nowadays we would be in no doubt that he should have been made aware of his biological parents, for all kinds of reasons, including family medical history. But that was the way it was then, and many a child grew up not knowing that the woman they called 'Mammy' was in fact their grandmother or some other caring relative. But it is interesting to speculate as to what direction young Tom's life would have taken if Daddy Tom had been made to face up to his responsibilities.

◼   ◼   ◼

Great-great-grandfather Daddy Tom was described to me by one seanfhear as '*Fear mór leathair, feoil agus ceoil*' – a great man for sex, meat and music. '*Leathar*' was commonly used in Corca Dhuibhne to describe matters sexual: '*Bhíomar ag stracadh leathair*', literally meaning we were tearing leather, or indeed the more graphic '*Bhíomar ag bualadh bolg*' – we were banging bellies. Nothing left to the imagination there. The colloquial Gaeilge for sex was direct, expressive and rich in imagery and the euphemism is often starker and more vivid than the real thing. An enquiry into how far things had gone went straight to the point: '*Ach ar fhágais ann í?*' – but did you leave it in her?

It could be that English was the language of Puritans.

The fact that drink wasn't listed in the description of Daddy Tom's attributes should not be taken to mean that he was a teetotaller, far from it. Drink was such a given that it wasn't necessary to mention it. Indeed, there was a kind of a view in those times that whiskey was a great pickling agent that prevented the breakdown of organs. And in Daddy Tom's case, it seemed to have worked; he lived hard and died at the ripe old age of 105 years.

It was Minnie the Brewery, when I was a young lad, told me about the death and dying of my great-great-grandfather. It was the simplest of accounts.

'I was there. He got up out of bed, went down to the chamber and did his business. Then he went in to bed again and died for himself.'

A few questions elicited more detail of the events.

'Was there anyone with him?'

'You can be sure that *all* his family were around him when he died. None of them were going to lose out.'

Apparently, whenever any of the family came to see him and he had established that things were going well for them, he would counsel them: 'Never be short of money.' For emphasis he would take his stick and rap hard on the locked chest he always kept under his bed. That chest became the stuff of dreams and the source of wild speculation among the family. How much was in it? What would they do with all that money when he was gone?

But the door would be firmly locked whenever he opened the famous chest and nobody was allowed to see its contents. 'You'll have plenty of time for that when I'm gone,' he'd say.

The chest and its prospects became a bonding that kept the family together and attentive to the old man. He was well looked after and never wanted for anything. The estimated value of the chest was well spent on him over the long years until he finally died with his wits and family about him.

It goes without saying that the beneficiaries could hardly contain themselves; before the body was even prepared for the habit they had hauled out the chest and opened it for the share-out. It was stacked full of small, heavy, bulging bags. These were quickly emptied and, one after the other, they discharged their contents onto the floor – small stones, little bundles of *cipíní*, buttons. There wasn't a single item of any value. Not a brass farthing among the lot of it.

'Well, the old bollox!'

And I have no doubt but that the old *cladhaire* was breaking his sides laughing as he looked down on his family searching in vain for his 'insurance cover'.

A wonderful image and a parable for all parents: the family that hopes together, stays together!

'Sugar spilt is profit lost.'

My grandfather, Seán the Grove, had a cautionary tale, if not a parable, for every little incident. He would carefully tip the last few grains of sugar from the large scoop into a strong brown-paper bag on the scales. It was one of those old-fashioned balances with the pound weight on one side and the bag of sugar on the other. Finally the sugar would have the measure of the weight and would gently seesaw itself downward as the weight went upwards, until they were in perfect balance. Granda would stop the flow of sugar exactly on the mark.

'Don't do the customer and don't do yourself.' And then would come the question. 'How many should we have?'

'Half a hundredweight is fifty-six pounds. There should be fifty-six bags.'

'Good. Good. You're not wasting your time up there with the Brothers. Now we'll count them, to be sure.'

There would be a restatement of the lecture during the count.

'Don't waste. Be honest. Give every man his due.'

Of course there wasn't the slightest need for him to be filling bags of sugar. There was plenty of help around if he wanted it. But he undertook the task for a number of reasons. Firstly, few things irritated him as much as spilt sugar. The sound and feel of grains of sugar underfoot grated on him to an irrational degree. Taking charge of the sugar himself ensured that it would not be spilt. Secondly, it kept him in the centre of things and it meant that he wasn't idle. Also – and this was important – it wasn't hard work. I don't think I ever saw him break sweat.

In fact, Seán the Grove had a great lack of confidence in the potential of people with the reputation for being hard, physical workers. He held the view that they would never get much further than where they were. A great believer in exploiting and making the best of any given situation, one of his better moves was to acquire the heart disease angina in his late middle age. He minded it and nursed it for about thirty years and at any moment would explain to you the importance of 'minding the ticker'. Mind it he did, and it improved the quality of his life. When he finally died, in his late eighties, it was not from angina but ripe old age.

He was a most successful businessman, but he rarely took his hands out of his pockets. What he excelled at was buying and selling. He would purchase quality at a bargain and sell at a profit and all parties in between would be treated fairly. He made money without making enemies. There was nobody he did not have word for, he was a great talker and his popularity was legendary. The people he did business with tended to trust him and become his friends. Commercial travellers warmed to him. One of them, Denis Guiney, asked him to become a partner in acquiring a substantial drapery business. My grandfather declined. Guiney went on to build his business, Clery's, into one of Dublin's great department stores. A very rare missed opportunity for Seán the Grove.

My grandfather was born in 1885, or so he told me, and christened John Moriarty. As often as not he was called Jack. He acquired the name of Seán the Grove from the name of his farm, The Grove, just on the edge of Dingle town under Cnoc a'Chairn, where he had been born, and to distinguish him from all the other Moriartys. It is hard to describe his daily activity in a manner which reflects his success. Every day he would walk up to the farm in the Grove and look around. I can never remember him to work on the farm, but he would question Uncle Benny, or give directions. In the shop, which was quite small, he would talk to the customers while my grandmother did the work. All he ever seemed to do was to sell men's shoes and caps and to weigh and pack the loose sugar and tea. I have no doubt but that he was given the task of fitting the shoes because my grandmother, who was spotlessly clean, refused point-blank to be subjected to the olfactory onslaught from feet and socks just released from the hot and sweaty confines of heavy leather boots or rubber wellingtons. In fact, my grandmother would regularly advise people with smelly feet that the best cure for them was to bathe them regularly 'in your own morning water'. I never tried it myself, but I know that 'morning water', that first urination before breaking fast, was commonly advised as a cure-all for things like chilblains and other foot problems. Anyway, grandfather sold footwear to all, smelly feet notwithstanding. Nothing pleased him more than the customer who walked in in a pair of shoes, stuck one big foot on the small footstool with the request, 'Same again, Jack, size eleven.'

'You got good value out of them,' he'd reply, 'they're a great shoe and they'll last forever if you keep them soled and polished. Clark's make them well.'

'I've no complaints, Jack. I wore those shoes at every Mass, funeral, wedding and races these last five years.'

Every night he would call down to our house. Every night he would play cards with us and every night there would be political talk. Seán the Grove loved politics. Even though they held differing political views, he got on great with my father, Myko. The happenings of the day would be recounted and lessons drawn from them. He mixed general advice on living with specific advice on playing cards: 'Trust every man if you must, but always cut the cards,' or the caution, 'The two worst payers are the one who pays beforehand and the one who does not pay at all.'

No two nights were ever the same. The card game that was played in our house was '31', the West Kerry version of '25', with the best trump being worth eleven. It was a game in which every deal was a test of judgement, skill, cooperation and survival tactics. The decisions were complex; it was not just a matter of winning a 'trick' and it was not simply about winning out. There was also the consideration of whether or not it would be better to allow someone else to win in order to prevent the leading player from getting out. But in allowing another player to take one 'trick', you had to question whether your own trump card was good enough to take the next one. We were required to take the broad view. Seán the Grove expected you to make judgements on the quality or potential of a player's hand from the early tricks and plays.

My moves came under particular scrutiny. Every mistake I made would be analysed during the next deal. 'If you had held back the knave until the following trick you could have taken the last two and Myko wouldn't have won.' 'Only a fooleen would have led with the Ace of Hearts. Didn't you know the Five was still in play? If you had waited you could have taken two tricks with a sporting chance of the last!' At the time it was humiliating, but in reality it was no more than learning and teaching through the group method and typical of my mother's people, the Moriartys. For them, everything was a lesson to be learnt. Each day's experience layered on yesterday's. I can still hear my grandfather's voice when I had made some mistake. Shaking his head in mock sadness, he would sigh, 'Níolagan wouldn't be such a fooleen, John Pheadaí would be cuter.' This was a pointed reference to two of my schoolmates, Pat Neligan and John Francis Brosnan. If the truth were known, they were two of the easiest-going of all the gang and would be horrified to think that they were being held up as examples that would show me to disadvantage. They are the same and every bit as decent today.

Myko would relate the latest views and happenings from his colleagues in Tralee Garda Station, the 'experts and the philosophers' as he always referred to them. Many of the stories originated with District Justice Johnson, who also sat in the Dingle

court. He had a wry sense of humour and was forever trying to
unravel pub brawls, fair-day fights and neighbours' quarrels about
rights of way. Whereas the protagonists were introduced to the court
by their full baptismal names, the oral evidence from witnesses in the
box would refer to people by their pet names and nicknames, so, for
example, Mr Patrick James Coffey became Red Padger in the telling.
The defendant might have been baptised John Savage, but nobody
ever heard him called anything but Daggers. Confusion reigned.
Blank looks on the faces of witnesses. Lawyers trying to relate
nicknames to official names. On these occasions the good judge was
in the habit of interrupting the proceedings and cross-examinations
with a plea to the lawyers that they 'read out the cast in order of
appearance' so that he might interpret the evidence by knowing their
names both as 'players and characters'.

No doubt his experiences in the courtrooms of Kerry provided the
inspiration, but Justice Johnson went on to write a play called *The
Evidence I Shall Give*, which was popular among amateur dramatic
groups around the country for many years.

Our house was across the road from the courthouse, so we were
right in the middle of the excitement on the Wednesday court
sittings. As children, we often managed to slip past the garda on the
door and sneak in to the back of the courtroom to listen to local
scandals and see justice being doled out. We shared that space with
every layabout from the town. They were all there to glory in the
discomfiture of publicans who served after-hours, the 'found-ons' as
the illegal drinkers were officially termed. This was all the stuff of
meaty gossip later in the evening, none more so than fair-day fights
and rights-of-way disputes.

My first visit to a dentist was at approximately five years of age and for some reason, which has been long forgotten, it was Seán the Grove who brought me. All that remains in my memory is the pain of the experience and the soft, patient voice of the dentist, Michael Fitzgerald. My grandfather was a firm believer in the importance of young people minding their teeth and constantly cautioned against losing them, as he himself had done. That was quite forward-thinking at that time inasmuch as dentists were still seen as a sort of modern-day luxury and convenience. People would do anything rather than attend at the dentist. Every conceivable method to kill the pain of toothache was tried, from whiskey and *poitín* to witch hazel and cloves, and it was only when all else failed that the dentist was brought into play. Even then it was never to save the tooth, but to 'pull the damn thing and give me some peace'.

The accepted wisdom was that by middle age we would all be losing our teeth, to be replaced by dentures, or 'false teeth' as we called them. People used to take pride in their perfect false teeth and show them off. It was the introduction of school medical examinations that brought a new education and awareness to a generation as to the importance of dental health and hygiene. Seán the Grove made sure that his own children appreciated the importance of good grinders. Teresa always insisted that we brush our teeth at least twice daily and with Euthymol toothpaste, which at the time could only be purchased in a chemist's. That confirmed for her that it was the best!

My recollection of that first dental visit is that it was occasioned by a minor playground accident, which resulted in an injury to my front teeth and gums. Eventually, three of my upper front teeth were extracted to allow adequate space for two adult teeth to come down. And indeed the two buck teeth did eventually make their appearance. My grandfather insisted on weekly reports as to how the new teeth were doing. They did fine. For a quarter of a century after that he would ask me, 'How are Michael Fitz's teeth?' They gave no trouble for over forty years, at which point it became necessary to crown one of them. They are still grinding. And when the time came, Michael Fitz always voted for me in elections. Two victories at age five.

◈ ◈ ◈

Being a practical man, Seán the Grove gave great consideration to the future employment of his family and his grandchildren. Any of his family who were interested in getting into business could count on him for a hand-out. At one stage four of his children, including my mother, had thriving businesses around the town and another had the farm. My grandparents were unusual for their time in that they made very little distinction between sons and daughters; they each got their opportunities, regardless of gender. Third-level education was an option for all of them, even though he would prefer to see them in business. My mother, Teresa, insists that the week she matriculated and was set on doing pharmacy, he convinced her to change her mind and gave her the shop on the Mall, which he had just purchased.

Although he was certainly a practising Catholic, Seán the Grove never struck me as being particularly religious and he tended towards the iconoclastic. One of his daughters, who was a qualified and practising pharmacist, surprised us all by joining a religious order and becoming a nun. My grandfather did not appear best pleased, but said very little. He would be the kind of man who, after investing significantly in her qualification, would feel cheated that the Medical Missionaries would get all the good of it. It was not that he was mean. He was not. But he was thrifty and practical and liked to enjoy the results of his investments.

Previously, this aunt, Aunty Ita, had been in a relationship with and on the point of engagement to a most interesting man who had been a bank official but had given it all up to become an artist full-time. They were committed to each other and it seemed as though they would marry and spend their lives together. They never did. She felt the call of her religious vocation around this time and she answered it. It was the most difficult decision.

As a nun, she spent almost all of the rest of her life in Africa, returning only when she was well past retirement age, while the former bank official went on to become the leading and most celebrated Irish artist of his day. The week of his death the newspapers carried various reports and obituaries. In one of the accounts it was reported that as a young man, Tony O'Malley's heart had been broken by a woman whom he loved, but who had rejected him, asking, 'What would she be doing with a man who had given up his steady job, had only one lung and a few old paintings?'

The report was upsetting, untrue and unfair to Aunty Ita. As far as I can establish, the statement was made, but never by her. It was Seán the Grove who apparently said it. Why? Not from any animosity towards the man himself, but no doubt because of a concern that his daughter might not be provided for by a husband in seemingly indifferent health who had given up a secure job for a precarious profession. Those were different times, when neither the State nor all of its citizens had matured to an appreciation of the contribution of art to the community.

So the pharmacist and the artist split up, but each went on to make a significant contribution in their different areas. Still, throughout our lives we have derived great pleasure from some of the early works of the young Tony O'Malley, which he gifted originally to Aunty Ita and which hang to this day in my parents' house.

One of Seán the Grove's great heroes was his uncle, his mother's brother, Fr John Martin. For some reason, within the family he was always referred to as Fr Martin rather than as Fr John. Fr Martin was a scholar and linguist, well-versed in the Classical languages and in German. He had travelled through the Continent and had been a curate in Lancashire as a very young priest. In the first decade of the last century he was appointed parish priest of Tarbert, north Kerry. Immediately prior to that he had been a curate in Cahirdaniel, in the southern end of County Kerry. As a curate he had established a reputation for taking a great interest in the affairs of the community and the welfare of the people. In fact, in an effort to stabilise prices, each Sunday he would read out, at Cahirdaniel Mass, the average prices of food by the merchants in the neighbouring towns of Sneem and Cahirciveen so that parishioners could decide in which town to spend their money that week. Clearly he had no Moriarty blood in him. The Moriartys would have been best friends of the merchants. Having no interest in wealth for himself, it was said that he left Cahirdaniel without even the travel cost to Tarbert. On his elevation to PP it was important that his new status be reflected in his trappings. As a gift for his uncle, my grandfather bought a horse in Dingle and rode all the way to Tarbert, a journey of about sixty miles, to deliver the animal. When he arrived at the presbytery, wasn't there a trade-union picket, placed by the Irish National Teachers' Organisation (INTO), outside the priest's house!

Apparently, when Fr Martin arrived in Tarbert there was a vacancy for a teacher in the local school. A very popular local teacher expected to be offered the job, but Fr Martin had a different idea and he was the school manager. Sure, he knew a mighty good teacher from Cahirdaniel who was available and came highly recommended. Her family were the best of people. He duly proposed her for the job. Clearly the poor man wasn't very political. There was outrage.

The school principal and the teachers were incensed, as was the community, that a runner-in would take a job earmarked for the local and said that they would oppose his proposal – no light undertaking in those days when the clergy's word was law. Fr Martin was determined to stamp his authority on them and insisted on having his way. There was an immediate strike.

Seán the Grove was allowed through the picket line to his besieged uncle, who told him how he had made the choice of the Cahirdaniel girl above the local. He finished his story by asking, 'What would you have done, Jack?' My grandfather, who knew that all business is local, replied that, if it were up to him, he would have 'given it to the local girleen'. Fr Martin had no doubt been expecting the full moral support of his nephew, and snarled, 'Well, maybe then you should go outside and walk up and down with that crowd!'

Seán the Grove loved telling that story and would finish it by saying, with more than a degree of satisfaction, 'and in the end he had to give in and give it to the local'. Things obviously improved after that first *contretemps*, as Fr Martin spent the rest of his priestly career in Tarbert, which he grew to love. He became popular and respected. He also had the support of a very loyal housekeeper and there was a whispered family rumour, never proved, that perhaps the relationship was more than platonic. But then those were the days when it would not have been unheard of for a parish priest to ask his housekeeper to go up and warm the bed for him. It would be an easy and understandable thing to get so cosy and comfortable that she might still be there when the priest arrived in the bedroom.

When eventually he died, Fr Martin was buried in the graveyard beside the church in Tarbert. If you are driving past, it is easy to pick out the grave by the Celtic high cross that marks its location, to the left, at the very back of the cemetery. I find it very ironic that, while his headstone stands authoritatively and imposingly at the back, anyone wishing to visit it must first walk past the first grave to the left of the entrance gate. It is the last resting place of a former INTO president, Brendan Scannell. Brendan was a larger-than-life character and a friend of mine. He would have appreciated the quirk of fate that has him providing a perpetual picket to the man who did battle with the INTO and who was my great-granduncle.

Seán the Grove was always looking ahead and planning. One day, when I was a young child, he asked me what I would like to be when I grew up.

'A bishop or a carpenter,' I answered innocently and enthusiastically, sure that my choices would satisfy him.

'Not bad. Not bad.'

But before I could bask in the afterglow of his approval, he astonished me by advising me to become a parish priest. He claimed it was the best job of all. My childish protests that prayers and praying did not really appeal to me were dismissed as being utterly irrelevant. This had nothing whatever to do with religion. He did not even bother to explain that a bishop was also a priest, a linkage that had clearly escaped my assessment of career options. The point about being a PP was that it was a well-paid and respected position that brought with it much influence and a good house. Nobody could order you about, not even the bishop. In fact, in his estimation it was better than being a bishop, who was answerable to a number of layers of higher power. Times have changed somewhat on this one, the bishops have wised up and nowadays parish priests have to sign a contract with the bishop before being appointed. However, long before that alteration had occurred, my mind was made up that a clerical life was not for me. And Seán the Grove knew that well.

My grandfather's world was one of farming and business, and if he had his way that's where he would have wanted to see all of us. Sometimes he took a mischievous delight in presenting himself as being a bit naive. 'Tell me now, girleen,' he said to Joan the first time he met her, 'are ye in business or have ye land?' When Joan explained that, yes, her father had a farm, but that she was the youngest in a family of four boys and four girls and had no entitlement or expectations in that direction, he completely dismissed her protestations. 'It does not matter, girleen, some of it will fall to you.' Dingle friends loved that story. And indeed, maybe he was right. Joan's father very generously gave us the site on the farm where we built our house.

※　　※　　※

Seán the Grove always maintained that any young lad could learn a lot from being given a ten-pound note and a map of the world and told to come home in five years. He felt that every new experience should fit into a steep and continuous learning curve. I remember being with him at the Dingle races when he took me to see the 'Trick o' the Loop' man. This particular gent operated out of sight of the police. He carried with him a small wooden box on which he placed a cloth of green baize. Taking a longish, soft leather belt, he brought the two ends together, put a pencil in the resulting loop, then wrapped the doubled belt around the pencil and laid it on the table for all to view. I could clearly see the pencil in the loop.

He kept up a great chit-chat all the while.

'Now, keep an eye on the pencil. Nothing could be easier. Keep your eyes open and make a fortune. Don't ask me why I do it, but I've given four half-crowns away in the last half-hour.'

On removing the pencil from the loop he most foolishly offered the audience an even-money bet against them returning the pencil to the correct loop. He even showed us how easy it was, by holding the pencil, pulling the belt straight and, sure enough, the pencil was trapped in the loop. No wonder he was losing money, I thought. It was simple, anyone could do it.

'That man is going to lose more money foolishly, Granda.'

The bet was offered again. A man who was not a local placed a bet and won a red ten-shilling note. The Trick o' the Loop man looked worried.

'You're making a poor man of me!' he protested. 'But I'm going to give you one more chance.' Carefully and in full view he rolled up the belt again with the pencil in the loop.

'I'm going to leave the pencil in the loop so you can all have a look. Now, any bet?'

Sure, you couldn't lose. It was money for nothing. My grandfather finally conceded to my earnest requests for money and granted me a loan of half-a-crown. I rushed forward to make my fortune.

'Are you sure, young fellow?' he said doubtfully, looking around when I handed him the half-crown. I never noticed my grandfather nodding to him.

Taking the pencil from the foolish fellow I stuck it in the obvious loop with more certainty than anything I had previously done in all of my young life.

'You can still change your mind,' said the Trick o' the Loop man.

Hah! He knows he's lost and is trying to talk me out of it. 'No, it's this one. This is the right one,' I said smartly.

'All right, young fellow,' he conceded. He pulled the belt smoothly. It came clean; the pencil was outside the loop. Someone shouted, 'Guards.' In one simple movement he lifted my bright half-crown and ran off with his table, muttering 'damned Peelers' under his breath.

There I was, bereft of fortune and naked in my scarlet embarrassment; the object of much comment and ridicule from the passing public.

There was not a day during the following month nor a week during the following year when my grandfather did not find some reason to refer to my foolishness at the races – losing a 'lorry wheel' to the Trick o' the Loop man. The story became a parable to the younger generation. As a learning experience I would have to concede that it was a far more impactful lesson than a puritanical lecture on the evils and dangers of gambling.

As soon as I was old enough – and that might have been before the legal age – I was deputised to drive Seán the Grove to funerals in the estate car belonging to his son, Foxy John. These were never dull outings. Burying the dead with due respect was important and was a co-operative effort. It was done in Dingle in the same manner as the biblical civic responsibility. Attendance at funerals was much more than a mere political or business-related drudgery. Certainly, it was discharged out of a sense of duty, but it was also genuinely part of neighbourliness and community. It would be unthinkable not to attend the funeral of a neighbour, and 'neighbour' was a loose term that actually meant anyone in the locality. Contradictory as it may sound, dying was an inexorable and inevitable act of living. It is a purely logical fact that one has to be alive to die.

As youngsters we saw death being greeted as a natural part of life. We were never shielded from it. Young children would be brought gently to the coffin of their grandparent and spoken to in a soft voice.

'We'll say goodbye to Granny.'

Even the use of the colloquialism relaxed the tense and timid child.

'Goodbye, Granny.'

'Do you want to give Granny a kiss?'

A step too far, maybe. A slow shake of the head.

'That's all right, *a ghrá*. Say a small prayer.'

But sometimes there would be no demurring when the mother, holding the child's hand in her own, would quietly reach across and in the most natural way in the world place both their hands on Granny's. Curiosity satisfied and fear banished. It was a learning experience.

There always had to be a report on the funeral for those who were unable to attend. It was a reckoning of popularity; a noting of surprising absences, or perhaps surprise attendances; a naming of extended family and far-out relatives, particularly arrivals from overseas.

'Was it a big funeral?'

'The cars were stretched back around Milltown Bridge and up the High Road. In fairness, all the nephews and nieces came back for it. They gave him a fine send-off.'

Most aspects of Dingle life were competitive, and this included funerals. The language had to be carefully chosen. 'That was the biggest funeral I can remember' would be all right to say to a family member or relative of the deceased on the day, but if it were said to neighbours it could easily put them into the position of having to defend family honour by reminding the listeners of the huge gathering at their last funeral.

Because they were such a common feature of our lives, funerals did not tend to be very sad occasions. All the good done by the dearly departed would be recalled and celebrated and any bad would be hidden away. 'Never speak ill of the dead' was a given on these occasions. As a sign of their grieving and as a mark of respect to the dead, close family relatives would wear a black cloth diamond sewn on the upper arm of their jackets for a mourning period of months. Afterwards, life went on as normally as circumstances would allow.

Tommy McCarthy was a neighbour and lifelong friend of Seán the

Grove's. They grew up together. They met at the fair. They talked in the snug and they were business competitors. Their friendship never wavered. Tommy's eldest daughter, Sheila, married Seán the Grove's eldest son, Patty. The friendly rivalry of youth continued between them through life. Tommy was a publican, farmer and bakery owner. The bakery had a strong cultural impact on our lives. Normally it supplied two types of fresh bread on a daily basis – the ordinary *builín* or batch loaf and what was called the basket loaf. This was smaller in size and had a curly design on the top; my recollection is that it had a sweeter, richer taste. At Hallowe'en it produced rich, curranty, treasure-filled barm brack. Just before Christmas, McCarthy's bakery also provided an extraordinary bread called butterloaf. This was a big loaf and had different flavours; it was baked in a cooler oven, but was particularly memorable for the fact that it was a seed loaf, with copious amounts of caraway seeds mixed into the bread. As children we hated it for the appearance, taste and smell of the seeds; we thought they looked like mice droppings. As we grew older we grew to love that bread. My search of bakeries through the years has failed to yield similar bread anywhere, and to this day my mother looks forward to receiving by post, from Tommy Devane, an annual pre-Christmas gift of a Dingle butterloaf, though nowadays it is baked in Castleisland. It's as appetising as ever and stays fresh for days and days, like long ago.

The day of Tommy's funeral, my inclination was to be a little bit more deferential towards my grandfather. There was a sense of loss and sadness about him and he was quiet for a long time. The normal chat about business and family stories was missing. But by the time we were back in the town and had the car parked he had come to terms with it. We were rounding the corner from Green Street into Main Street when, with a glint in his eye, he turned to me, straightened himself to his full height, which was not that high, and said, 'Do you know, I'm the oldest man in the town now.'

Something gained out of the day. Age was venerable in Dingle.

After the funeral of Seán the Grove's sister, we were leaving Kildrum graveyard, at the end of the Long Road outside Dingle, when he took a good look at the family tomb. There was a bit of a crack in the side of it. He turned to me and said, 'I'll be next in there. I'll give you a red ten-shilling note if you come back next week and fill in that crack. I hate damp.'

The family tomb was a large, plain affair, most unattractive. The story was that Old Johnny, my great-grandfather and a son of Daddy Tom's, bought the plot when he felt he was coming to the end of his life and built the tomb himself. When he had finished it he went home and took to the bed, which he didn't leave for the remaining six months of his life. My uncles recalled a revolting habit he had of keeping a container of rancid butter beside his bed from which he would take a dollop to drop into his mug every time he was having tea. Maybe that was what killed him.

My uncle Patty Atty, the eldest of Seán the Grove's eleven children, told me that every time a new child was born into the family, Old Johnny would call to the front door of the shop in Main Street. He would rap on the red-and-black floor tiles inside the door for attention. Having ascertained whether it was a boy or a girl, he always made the same comment: 'A poor man can't have too many of them.' Eventually, Patty Atty plucked up the courage to query his daunting grandfather about this. Old Johnny explained that where there was a small family, the children were inclined to stay to inherit the property. When the wealthy man had a large family, they would all stick around disputing the wealth, contributing nothing, protecting their own interests, and there would be endless feuding and fighting. However, when the poor man had a large family, what little they had was shared in their rearing, there was nothing for them to stay for or fight over, so they tended to leave and fend for themselves. In all likelihood, if they did well for themselves they would be generous towards their parents and would be happier and friendlier towards their siblings. It was the type of explanation regarding the inclination towards good or evil of humankind that one might expect in the ruminations of Hobbes, Locke or Rousseau, but it came from Old Johnny and probably had a wealth of experience behind it, not to mention the lubrication of rancid butter!

CONNEMARA
ROOTS

John O'Toole had spent his life on the move. He and his young wife were tired of it and wanted to settle down and start a family. As he sailed through Cill Chiaráin Bay in south Connemara, north of Lettermore Island, and along by Inis Treabhair, he saw a small shallow island off his starboard side. There was no house on it, no sign of life. It was nowhere more than ten feet above sea level, and not much growth on it either. Guiding his boat around the lee side, he dropped anchor in the sheltered spot between it and a larger island.

The small island John O'Toole had found was called Laighean and shortly before 1800, he built a small house on the shore of the adjoining, larger island, Eanach Mheáin; there was only nine or ten yards between it and Laighean; the house would be protected from the south-westerlies and it was possible to walk from one to the other at most times of the tide.

Not much has changed physically in the two hundred years since. But today the two islands are joined by an attractive stone pedestrian bridge, courtesy of the local golf club, whose course extends over both islands.

John's eldest son, also called John, was born on Eanach Mheáin around 1800. Young John O'Toole was my great-great-grandfather. In time he met and married Kitty Browne from Cross and they reared the next generation there, the eldest of whom was Pat 'Kruger' O'Toole, my great-grandfather.

How did the O'Tooles, traditionally a Wicklow clan from the east of Ireland, come to be in Connemara at all? On these matters the clan history is well documented. Dunlong was the first O'Toole to settle in Connaught. His grandfather was a nephew of Saint Laurence O'Toole. Dunlong went west in AD1325 to marry a woman of the O'Malley clan who was gifted the beautiful island of Omey as a wedding dowry. No bad deal that, whatever her looks. Omey is one of those offshore islands that are usually surrounded by the sea on all sides but are accessible across a causeway at low water, in the manner of Mont St Michel in France.

The O'Tooles settled happily on Omey for ten generations, until 1586, at which time Theobald O'Toole of Omey was the head of the family. He is described in the Annals of the Four Masters as 'a supporter of the poor and a keeper of a house of hospitality'. But the good die young and there were hard times ahead. In 1586 Theobald was hanged by Sir Richard Bingham and a party of English soldiers. Not only that, but his estates were confiscated to the Crown. The family were routed and penniless. Some remained in the area, but the rest were scattered to the four winds.

Theobald O'Toole's grandson, Connor, made a name for himself fighting for King James at the Battle of the Boyne in 1690. He survived the battle and settled afterwards in Kilcogny in County Cavan. Most of the others tried to re-establish themselves around the Galway-Mayo coast by claiming pieces of poor land along the shore. They are still to be found on many of the islands, but Inishturk more than any other place became their home.

Because of the nomadic nature of their existence, it is impossible to track the precise movements of the various branches of the family during the following hundred years as they tried to scrounge a living, battling for survival. But it was in those circumstances that John O'Toole ended up on Eanach Mheáin.

'Kruger' O'Toole, my great-grandfather, was born in 1843, just before the Great Famine. It was a terrible time in our history as a nation, a time when we lost more than half our population. The smell of death was everywhere. When I began looking into our history, I expected to discover that Kruger's family had suffered badly during that time.

The soil where they lived was very shallow, and even where there was some soil it was wet, boggy and infertile. Eanach Mheáin, the Middle Wetlands, lived up to its name. There was not enough soil for root crops and it was highly unlikely that they could have got potatoes to grow there. But, to my astonishment, I discovered that the Famine had little or no impact on the O'Tooles of Eanach Mheáin. The census of population for the area is more or less the same in 1851 as it was in 1841. The simplest explanation is probably the most correct. Kruger's family were only two generations ashore and were fishermen; most of their food would have come from the sea. And because the waters around the island were richly stocked, the terrible hunger that afflicted so much of Ireland had little impact on Eanach Mheáin. They would have eaten well in those desperate times.

Since most of the O'Tooles had moved on a few miles to Lettermore over the last century and a half, I did not expect to have too much luck when I went searching for the exact location of that original island dwelling, but I looked anyway.

'Sure I know where it was,' was the immediate response of my first cousin, Peter, when I told him of my difficulty. 'Hop into the jeep and I'll show you,' he offered, before I could get around to asking him.

In five minutes we had crossed from Lettermore to Eanach Mheáin and turned into the island. We continued through the golf course and down to the far end until we could see Rosmuc straight across from us.

Peter stopped and pointed: 'There you are.'

Right beside the sixth green were the walls of an old *fothrach* or ruin, about ten feet high. No roof, no anything except the walls, which had been recently pointed by the golf club. There, in a beautiful location at the water's edge, with Rosmuc just over a mile across the water and the imposing presence of Cill Chiaráin rising up in the distance over Inis Treabhair, was the source of my paternal gene stream. And it's now in the middle of a golf course, for God's sake.

Kruger's first wife died in childbirth and the child did not survive. He later remarried, by which time he had built a house beside the bridge in Lettermore, about two miles west of Eanach Mheáin. His second wife was Mary McDonagh, who came from a remarkable family, the McDonaghs of Crappagh and Gorumna islands, just across the bridge from Lettermore. Mary was one of twenty-three children, most of whom did not survive beyond childhood. Her brother, Tomás Reamonn, established the mighty McDonagh business empire and dynasty in Galway City. They became merchant princes and made a lasting impression on the business and social history of the west of Ireland. Some of those early McDonaghs in the late nineteenth century were, I regret to say, no friends of workers or trade unions, and there were many clashes over wages and conditions of employment.

Another of the McDonagh sisters married Nicholas O'Connor and thus created the one-hundred-and-fifty-year-long relationship and friendship between the O'Connors and the O'Tooles in Lettermore. The first son of each generation was named Nicholas, and in a remarkable coincidence, more than a hundred years later, when I was elected to the Senate a newly elected colleague was Senator Nioclás Ó Conchubhair from Lettermore. Our great-great- grandmothers were the McDonagh sisters.

A third sister, Sabina McDonagh, opened the famous Hotel of the Isles in Tierney, across the Lettermore bridge. In those days it was the only hotel in the area and was a magnet to many well-known people of the era, including Roger Casement and Eamon Ceannt. Much of the building is still intact and is nowadays part of a hostel.

Kruger O'Toole lived a long and full life. He enjoyed himself and he liked his comforts. Having retired just before 1910, he lived on for another twenty years and was touching ninety when he died. By the end of his life he had become something of a local institution and he certainly played up to the role. He would regularly visit his widowed daughter-in-law, my granny. It was less than a mile from his house to Granny's and the horse and cart would be harnessed to take him over. Kruger found the cart a bit uncomfortable and insisted that his armchair, with him sitting in it, be loaded up on the cart. They would then proceed to Granny's, with Kruger saluting or waving regally to anyone going the road. In his *báinín* suit, big hat and pipe, and sitting on his 'throne', he could have been the Pope, or some great African chieftain. The local people talked about it for years afterwards.

▨   ▨   ▨

'Daddy, why has Uncle Henry got a funny hand?'

I knew that I should not, under any circumstances, ask this question in front of Uncle Henry, but I was bursting to know and blurted out the question as soon as Myko and I were alone.

Though my grandfather was long dead by the time of my birth, his brother, my granduncle Henry, was in Lettermore during my summers there. Henry lived life to its limits and enjoyed himself. He was Kruger's youngest son and the oldest O'Toole that I had met. Henry used to fish under the Lettermore–Tierney bridge, but sometimes – not having the traditional fisherman's patience – instead of using a fishing rod and line, Henry opted for sticks of dynamite. The method was to light the fuse on a small stick of dynamite and then drop it into the water, where it exploded. The shockwaves of the explosion killed or stunned the fish, which would then float belly-up in the water, to be netted and landed. It was quick, economical and productive. Conservationists will, predictably and with some justification, be appalled. But that was then, and that was the way of things. Dynamite was barely regulated and was an essential tool for opening foundations or clearing the rocky fields of Connemara. There was no shortage of it.

Henry, like many young men, was a little careless. One time when he lit the fuse and went to throw the stick of dynamite, the fuse wire got entangled in the buckle of his jacket. With the fuse burning down rapidly, he desperately tried to free it. By the time he got it loose there was nothing left in the fuse. It exploded in his hand and blew it off to above the wrist. There was no doctor is the area, but his niece, Mary Clare, was a student nurse. With the blood pouring from poor Henry's arm, someone ran for Mary Clare. Luckily, a van belonging to Corbett's of Galway came along and it was flagged down. Henry was lifted into the back, and with Mary Clare trying to staunch the wound, they headed for the hospital in Galway.

Henry wasn't given any hope of surviving, but thanks to his strength and Mary Clare's endeavours, he pulled through. His hand and wrist and part of his forearm were gone, but he did not let it stop him. Indeed, he married, had a family and lived until 1983, when he was in his late eighties.

I remember Henry as being a pleasant man, with a word and a joke for everyone, but I will never forget my first meeting with him when I was a little fellow. I had never before seen anyone with an artificial arm and I just could not take my eyes off the plastic hand. Myko and Henry were in convulsions at my reaction.

Henry was not the only one of the O'Tooles to lose a hand. Dick O'Toole had property both in Lettermore and on Eanach Mheáin. Probably because of connections to the St George family, who owned the ground rents in the area, the family went hunting and shooting. While out one day with a new double-barrelled shotgun, Dick neglected to ensure that the safety catch was engaged. The gun accidentally discharged and he lost his hand.

The unlikely handless hat-trick is completed by my father's first cousin, Dino Keyes. While still at primary school, Dino was brought to Galway City one day. This was during the troubled times of the early 1920s when guns were commonplace. The forces of law and order were edgy and shootings were not infrequent. Dino, who was a mischievous lad, curious and inquisitive by nature, went exploring around Eyre Square; taking everything in, missing nothing. His attention was drawn to a large building in the corner of the square, opposite the Imperial Hotel, near the junction with the Dublin Road. There was a marked military presence about the place. Soldiers everywhere. It was a magnet to the child.

It was a bright, sunny day. Dino wondered what was inside, but the sun reflecting off the glass dazzled him and he couldn't get a clear view into the guardhouse. He put his hands against the window to shade his eyes from the sun. As he raised his little hands to the glass, their shadow was magnified and projected onto the bright wall of the room inside. The nervous young soldier on guard duty panicked. With one instinctive movement he whipped around and discharged an automatic volley at the window. Both of Dino's hands were hit. One of them had to be amputated completely and he was left with only two fingers on the other. It was a tragic accident, but he showed great courage in coming to terms with it. As a child and as a man, Dino was a great favourite with all the family. Popular and good-humoured, he never let his injury become an obstacle to his advancement. Myko loved him and regularly presented him as a role model to any of us who thought we had a problem in life. He was successful in getting through school and then graduated with a Law degree from University College Galway. He established a thriving legal practice in Galway and eventually became Chief State Solicitor for the county.

These adventures seemed to me to prove that the O'Tooles were more devil-may-care than the Moriartys. The Moriartys made a virtue of minding their own business and keeping out of harm's way, but the O'Tooles tended towards the centre of the action, sometimes with unfortunate consequences.

However, it was a common approach of both families to look forward towards the next generation rather than back at the last. They did not hold with the notion that parents were the responsibility of their children. What we learned was that the past was the past and the real responsibility was to look after the next generation. 'You owe us nothing. Look after your children,' was the exhortation. I can see this now as a fundamental strategy for survival and the regeneration of the species. It could well be articulated like this: what we received from our parents, we owe to our children. That's the payback.

This paradigm very effectively passes on the values of one generation to the next. Not only does it maintain the species and the line but it also protects and transmits a culture. Put it in the context of a well-developed gene pool, which determines so much of the course of our lives in aspects as diverse as health, intelligence, fertility and creativity, and it is difficult not to conclude that, far from being discrete, independent beings, we are in many ways the creatures of our ancestors, following a well-trodden, pre-programmed path through life. So, how much free will do we really have? Do we influence our own children more than our long-dead ancestors do?

Any general assessment of our children seems to show that the outcome of our rearing is far more transmissive of our own innate cultural values than it is transformative in the creation of a new and different generation. And, when you think about it, society in general supports that notion in its attitudes and expressed expectations. How often have you heard someone comment: 'I cannot believe he did that; he comes from such a good family.'

That sort of remark makes no sense unless we believe that the family is more influential than our so-called free will. All the indications are that we are born already possessing strong instincts and innate directors. It may well be that our whole learning and education experience, far from preparing our life's path, is merely a liberation of those innate instincts to follow the well-trodden route of our ancestrally moulded genes. It could be that none of us has ever had a fully original thought, or come to an unprecedented conclusion about anything.

This might be a deeply discouraging notion, but it concurs with a conviction of Seán the Grove's that people remain fundamentally unchanged through the course of their lives. Could it be the case that the core truth of that belief stretches back much further and earlier than a person's life and flows from the family generational gene stream? What it would seem to indicate is that when we are assessing situations and coming to conclusions, our thought processes are not nearly as independent as we might think. It may be that we follow a pre-determined logic, guided by our genes and developed through the experiences of our predecessors.

░ ░ ░

On all sides of my family were busy people. Both my great-grandfathers had three jobs at the one time. Kruger O'Toole had a farm and a business, in fact, he owned the local Post Office and was also the Congested Districts Area Officer, from which position he eventually retired with a pension. In addition to his business, Old Johnny Moriarty was a rent and rates collector, as well as having a substantial farm. This was a tradition continued in their turn by both my grandfathers and it was a source of great amusement and private entertainment to me when I was regularly and publicly accused of being a 'double-' or 'treble-jobber' myself. That was at the time when I was both a politician and also running a trade union, as well as being involved in a myriad of other things. But it was bred into me to be doing things.

Hard workers and busy people are not synonymous; indeed they are very different from each other. Keep me away from the hard workers. Even though they are well regarded in the community, in truth 'hard workers' usually have a very narrow focus and are too deep in the trenches to see beyond the now and the job in hand. Their chief characteristics seem to be that they are always breathless, rushing, and with never a minute to do anything. Rarely have they a moment to think. On the other hand, the busy person who is involved in many different projects feels and develops a synergy between them and transfers experience from one to the other as well as maintaining a freshness of approach. People with a number of different jobs tend, because of a broader set of experiences, to be more interesting and more likely to add to the community's general productivity, creativity, commitment, energy and excitement.

In many ways these two categories of people define the difference between a strategist and a tactician. The strategist identifies projects, thinks things through, plans the way ahead and anticipates the difficulties in achieving the objectives. He will recognise a number of routes to that objective. The hard-working tactician can't wait to get started, jumps straight in and then finds himself facing obstacles that could have been avoided if he had taken time to first plan his course.

The philosophers in Flaherty's snug in Dingle have an allegorical tale that sums up the difference in a rather earthier manner. It is about an old bull and a young bull standing on a summer hillside, looking down at a bunch of attractive young heifers ruminating in a riverside field, with the warm sun on their backs.

'Let's charge down there and do a heifer each,' said the hard-working, hormonal young bull.

'Ah no, no,' counselled the strategic, busy old bull. 'Let's stroll down and service all of them.'

Perhaps crude, unsophisticated and inappropriate, but somewhere in there is a moral.

My ancestors tended towards the strategic in their business affairs, but were less tactically disciplined in affairs pertaining to the joys of life.

THE EMIGRANTS'
RETURN

The young couple made their way down the gangplank to the dockside. She was hugely pregnant and he tried to shield her from the pushing and jostling of the excited crowds rushing to the familiarity of solid ground.

'Ye had a long, hard journey. But thank God, *tháinig sibh slán. Fáilte go Australia.*'

Glad as they were to see the familiar faces from home, the young couple barely heard the welcome from his two sisters in the noisy and sweltering surroundings of the port of Fremantle. It was all so bewilderingly different.

'God Almighty, what were we thinking of, to leave Connemara?'

A journey to Australia was a major undertaking a hundred years ago. The hazards of a long and debilitating boat voyage were a major concern. Still, many adventurous young took the risk in search of their fortunes. In those days no return was ever contemplated and the wrench from home, family and culture took extraordinary determination. The finality of the leave-taking was such that it had the moroseness of a wake.

As soon as they were married, my grandparents, Joe O'Toole and Margaret O'Boyle, headed off to Australia to his two sisters, Agnes and Sarah. It was a mighty voyage, including a passage through the Suez Canal. They located in Geraldton, north of Perth, where they worked in Agnes's husband's hotel. Every opportunity was open to them; the world was at their feet in a new and developing country and they were being sponsored and helped by a wide circle of friends. Their first son, Patsy, was born there shortly after they arrived.

They had everything they could have wished for, but Joe missed home. It was something he couldn't put into words. Surrounded by wide-open spaces of flat, traversable terrain, all he could think of were those rickety stone walls enclosing impossibly irregular, tiny patches of rocky ground in Connemara. Those walls that he had cursed so often when repairing the gaps, he missed them now. Basking in the comfortable climate of south-western Australia, his thoughts turned to the rain-laden prevailing south-western winds blowing off the Atlantic onto the Galway coast. An emigrant is never at home. Every week was a torture; no matter how he tried, no matter how much he was reassured, he could not settle away from his native place. Less than a year after their arrival, they turned for home, this time with their tiny son.

Back in Galway, not exactly destitute but with very little in the way of material things, they took a lease on a pub in Merchants' Road and optimistically started all over again. That first day back, Joe went to check that there had been no hindrance or objection to the transfer of the liquor license to his name. He had heard that the local sergeant, a recent arrival, was an officious bollox and a stickler for regulations. It would not do to fall foul of him before he had even sold a bottle.

Even though they had travelled a world of distance and seemed an age away, Joe was immediately struck by the familiarity of his surroundings. As he strolled along Merchants' Road, it seemed only yesterday that he had walked the same route. There was the same unchanging sign for Thomas McDonagh & Sons; he could have rhymed it off by heart:

IMPORTERS OF PERUVIAN GUANO
FOR THE WEST OF IRELAND.

PROPRIETORS OF GALWAY STEAM SAWMILLS

IMPORTERS

Of Pitch Pine, Deals, Flooring B ards, Laths, Iron, Steel, Cement, Building Materials of every desc iption, Corrugated Iron, Bangor Slates, English, Scotch, and Steam Coals, Salt Glass, &c,

MANUFACTURERS.

Of Spokes, Felloes, Stocks, Car and Cart Shafts, Fork, Spade and Shovel Handles, &c., from best native Timber,

School, Church, and Household Furniture of every description

He turned into Quay Street on his way to the courthouse. All the faces were familiar; he felt he wanted to tell people that he had been away, but was back now for good. But would anyone care? Certainly the business and commerce of the city had not been disadvantaged by his absence and had no great need for his return.

Every Monday morning was the same at the Petty Assizes: retribution imposed for the excesses of the weekend; drunks, tramps and loiterers waiting their turn, miserable, pitiable and harmless. Be better to leave them off, thought Joe.

One of the assembly greeted him.

'Joe! *Dia dhuit.* I didn't see you for a while. I heard you got married.'

Joe was irrationally embarrassed to have to explain, 'To tell you the truth, I was away in Australia.'

He could see the unspoken comment in the man's eyes: you musn't have done too well over there to come back so soon, with your tail between your legs. But all he said was, 'You didn't find any of that auld gold over there, then?'

'Indeed and I did not.'

'Well, you hardly came back with *pócaí folamha* all the same.'

The clerk of the Assizes, old St George, told him that his case would be processed, without query or question, later in the day.

Joe didn't like the St Georges and they did not like him. They had land and ground rents all around Lettermore, but because their agent, Sabina O'Malley, was married to John O'Toole, the relationship was protected. Joe knew that he could depend on St George.

That morning, the courthouse was busy. When Joe arrived in, a local publican, Nora Healy, was being prosecuted for a breach of the licensing laws.

Sergeant Horgan was well into his evidence: 'Your Honour, as I approached on Sunday evening, I saw a can of porter being handed out through a back door of the pub in Forster Street ...'

Joe had a sudden and vivid memory of making purchases through that same back door in the past.

The sergeant continued. 'There were two men on the premises and two half-empty glasses of stout on the counter–'

Nora was loud in her defence. 'Well, that it might choke you to tell the truth!' she challenged the sergeant.

No doubt she would have continued in the same tone if the chairman had not intervened. 'I cannot allow that kind of comment to a man who was only doing his duty.'

Joe somehow got the feeling that the magistrate's heart was not really in it, and that he had no great love for the puritanical, temperance-driven sergeant.

Nora was undeterred. 'That can of porter was for an expecting woman who was a bit delicate and under doctor's instructions to have a drop of it every day for medicinal reasons.'

According to Nora, the two men 'found on', who were named Hartnett and Joyce, had come in to set rat traps because the place was infested. Sunday was the only day it was safe to let the traps around the place, as there were no customers.

Joe was mightily impressed by her argument; not so the bench. She was fined £5 and a note was put on her license.

'In God's name, sir,' Nora protested, 'the business is not going well at the moment. It's only a small pub – five fivers side by side would cover the whole place.'

The magistrate had heard it all before. 'Next case.'

The pub that was leased by Joe is still in operation in Galway today. It is called 'Padraig's' because it was where Pádraig Ó Conaire, probably the best-known Gaelic writer of his time, was born. His parents owned the pub at the time. But a tenuous O'Toole family connection is still maintained. As my daughter Áine, a student in Galway, told me, 'That's the early house – the first Galway pub to open in the morning. We always go there after college balls.'

I had thought that the pub was the only Ó Conaire link until my friend Austin from Galway asked me, 'Did your side of the O'Tooles, by any chance, have a connection with Pádraig Ó Conaire?' Well, far be it from me to disclaim a family connection with the famous, but this was one of which I had never heard tell. But Austin was fairly sure of his ground. 'There is a clear "O'Toole" reference in the Ó Conaire biography. I'll show it to you tomorrow.'

He did and off I went to investigate. In the biography there was a number of references to a letter that Ó Conaire had written to his cousin, Máire O'Toole, thanking her, as his former teacher, for teaching him his Irish (Gaelic) alphabet and for giving him his love for the language when he lived in Rosmuc.

This was very interesting, but could she really be part of the family? Could Ó Conaire be connected to us? It would be heartening to find that our family had given a kick-start to Gaelic literature at a time when it was seriously in the doldrums. I continued my research and discovered that Pádraig had attended Eanach Mheáin National School. Now that was where my great-great-great-grandfather John had settled and it was from there that the family tree expanded. Eanach Mheáin is next door to Lettermore and the O'Tooles in both places are closely related. The odds of an O'Toole teaching in Eanach Mheáin not being part of the family would be very long indeed. Máire O'Toole had to be one of us. Ó Conaire had said that he was taught by her in 1895, so I checked the dates against the family tree and there she was – Mary O'Toole, born in the 1870s. Mary, or Máire, was one of a family of sixteen, including a sister, Catherine M O'Toole, and thereby hangs a fascinating tale.

▦ ▦ ▦

Catherine O'Toole was Priomh Oide (Head Teacher) in Eanach Mheáin primary school. She was a popular and successful teacher, and when she died suddenly the locality was grief-stricken. To keep the school in operation after the funeral, Catherine's younger sister, Máire, acted as substitute teacher. She enjoyed the role, and the local community, who would all have been O'Tooles or their relations, were happy with her. So they took the pragmatic course. It was decided not to inform the authorities of Catherine's death. Máire would continue to teach and would sign herself Catherine M O'Toole and nobody would be the wiser.

It worked for a few years. It was only noticed when an Inspector's report made reference to the curious fact that the teacher looked at least five years younger than the age given for her in the report of the previous Inspector. Dublin sent the sniffer dogs to do a full investigation. Máire vanished to the United States. Even though they suspected treachery, the authorities never unearthed the full story. They could not trace the teacher and could not piece the jigsaw of clues together. Not surprisingly, local co-operation was not forthcoming. Finally they closed the investigation by issuing a notice withdrawing recognition from Catherine O'Toole and forbidding her from ever again teaching in a national school, little knowing that the poor woman was five years dead and not having a clue as to the real culprit. Máire O'Toole's identity as the teacher was never disclosed.

At the time when Máire was illegally acting as principal in Eanach Mheáin, the young Pádraig Ó Conaire was sent to his grandparents' house in Gairfean, following the death of both of his parents. Rosmuc would have been the local school, but Eanach Mheáin, though thirty miles distant by road, was just over a mile by boat across the narrow eastern end of Cill Chiaráin Bay. It was a huge upheaval for the young lad to be transferred from the busy city to the rural countryside. It would be some compensation for him to be with his relations and acquaintances in Eanach Mheáin, so every morning he was rowed across by currach to the school. If the weather was too bad for the return journey, he stayed with the O'Tooles overnight. His grandparents' house and the O'Toole house were in full view of each other across the water. That was where Máire taught him and introduced him to Gaeilge before she had to beat a quick retreat out of the jurisdiction to the United States. From her he received the great love of Irish that he put to such good use in his later writings.

But the exiled Máire did not stay too long in the US. As soon as was prudent, she returned to Connemara and to teaching. She had a clean record because the authorities had never discovered the identity of the imposter who had posed as the principal of Eanach Mheáin. She was a natural teacher, and the records now show that, despite her unorthodox and illegal entry to the teaching profession, she became the first Head of Gaeilge in Coláiste Chonnacht in Tourmakeady, where she spent the remainder of her career.

All of this story was confirmed for me by my elderly cousin Tomás O'Toole of Tourmakeady, who knew her and who showed me a number of photographs of her, including one with a very bohemian Pádraig Ó Conaire. More pertinently, he lent me Máire's book of notes on the teaching of Irish. Apart from telescoping the generational gap, it was an amazingly poignant feeling to probe through this tangible evidence of the life of a most interesting woman whose fascinating story I had just discovered. It would have been a privilege to have met her, but in her neat notes and guiding principles for teachers I felt a real sense of engagement.

Máire led a full life. She beat the system and then she became the system.

And because of her, walking past the statue of Ó Conaire in Eyre Square, Galway, has never been the same. I'm claiming Pádraig as part of the extended family, and indeed am likely to feel indignant at how little recognition he has received in recent times.

▦ ▦ ▦

It seems extraordinary now, but in those times authority – 'the system' – constituted the opposition and people felt challenged to get the better of them. Beating the system was a constant theme, and for people who had very little, success against the system could make the difference between mere survival and a level of comfort. My innocence in these matters was brought home to me once again during my research of Máire's story. While examining the census returns of the 1891 to 1911 period for the Eanach Mheáin and Leitir Mór O'Toole households, I came across a number of errors in the ages for the heads of households. The census was carried out every ten years, but in 1911 some of the late middle-aged O'Tooles seemed to have aged by more than the decade that had elapsed since 1901. It wasn't just in one case; it was a trend.

I was discussing it with Tomás O'Toole, wondering aloud at the inaccuracy and speculating whether it was carelessness, ignorance or just that the census enumerator, who checked each form, was at fault. Tomás gave me the sort of glance one would normally reserve for a simpleton.

'Well, that's innocent rearing you're getting down there in Kerry,' he declared. 'Wouldn't you think a man of your education would be aware of the major social change that took place in the first decade of the twentieth century?'

I hadn't a clue. What was it?

'The introduction of the old age pension.'

The penny dropped. 'Christ, we O'Tooles had no conscience at all.'

The history book confirmed Tomás's information. Courtesy of Prime Minister Asquith, the Old Age Pension Act of 1908 delivered the goods. More relevant to the times is the fact that the Chancellor of the Exchequer who sponsored the bill through the Commons and the Lords in Westminster was none other than Lloyd George. And it didn't get an easy passage, because the Lords initially objected and only reluctantly relented when he threatened to strip hundreds of them of their titles. We should have seen then that he was no bargain, and would make trouble for us in the end!

But in the meantime, could anyone blame the Connemara folk for making a minor technical adjustment to their official age when it qualified them for a present of five shillings a week from the Crown? It was a blow for Ireland, for God's sake. The O'Tooles were simply getting their reaction in first, even though they could not have known that fourteen years later Lloyd George would sit opposite Michael Collins as head of the British side in the negotiations which resulted in the Treaty. A treaty that partitioned Ireland and started a civil war.

░ ░ ░

For those living in poorer areas of the country, like Connemara, every opportunity that could make life that little bit easier had to be grasped. Tomás gave me a simple example.

'One day, back around the late 1890s, my grandfather was walking the beach on Dinish Island, southeast of Lettermore, as was always done after a bad storm, to check for any stuff that might have been thrown up by the Atlantic. Sure enough, there was a huge block of wood just above the low water mark. It was a magnificent piece of hardwood, and he thought it might be mahogany. It was. A few of the family manhandled it up the beach and eventually carted it home. Then they brought it in to Galway City to the McDonagh cousins who owned a saw mill. They planked, planed and polished the wood. Some of it was sold for good money and the rest was made into a fine table for the house. It was a fine piece of furniture.'

'Fair play to them,' I said, and added offhandedly, 'I wonder whatever happened to it afterwards.'

'Lift up the tablecloth there,' he instructed.

And there it was, more than a hundred years later, sound and well polished, having given a century of great service and still doing the business in the kitchen of the O'Toole household in Tourmakeady. Here was another generation of the family, breaking bread together across the wood salvaged by our ancestors. I found it intensely moving. It is the kind of experience that telescopes history and makes reality of stories.

All the islands off the west coast relied to some extent or another on the materials brought in by the tide. Trees were non-existent, so wood was especially valued. The flotsam and jetsam of unknown ships or wrecks of ships became the tables for the food of islanders. It also became the base of beds on which life was conceived. And in hard times when they could not get ashore, the bed or the table might be taken apart again and reassembled as a coffin to bury the body of a drowned son or husband. In those salty places the sea giveth and the sea taketh away.

But we have strayed away from Granny and Joe on the dock road in Galway. The pub where they set up is right on the docks, looking out at the ships, big and small, local and foreign, that lock into Galway harbour, and it is regularly dwarfed by the giant freeboard of the vessels. From this busy and noisy port, cargo and passenger ships departed for all parts of the world, but especially America. And whether it was to Philadelphia or the Aran Islands, the last pitstop for *deoch a' dorais* before boarding the boat was Padraig's on Merchants' Road. It was a teeming place at that time and the business was quite successful. Margaret gave birth to a second child, Mary Clare, there.

But the pair were country people at heart and city life was unattractive. They missed the familiarity and the reassurance of Connemara. So, when the opportunity arose, they returned to Lettermore and sold their interest in the Galway public house.

At that time, Joe's father, Kruger, was retiring from his position with the Congested Districts Board, and in typical O'Toole fashion he managed to wangle the job for Joe. With his position secured, Joe bought a house and small business from his cousin about half a mile west from Lettermore bridge, on the Lettercallow road.

'The house was only a storey and a half when we came here,' Granny O'Toole used to say.

Those few years were probably their happiest. Joe purchased a Baby Ford and travelled the countryside on behalf of the Congested Districts Board. Margaret kept the business going and their family increased. When the twins arrived in 1915 my father, Myko, was hale and hearty, but his twin brother, Jack, was sickly and delicate. He was not expected to live and Margaret was under such pressure that her mother, Annie, came down from Kilmaine for a few weeks to help her out. She nursed Jack diligently, but with no expectation that he would survive. Margaret had already lost a baby two years earlier; families generally were conditioned to a high rate of infant mortality. While the mother fretted, the older generation and the extended family took a more detached view. A sickly child, no matter how much wanted, or how much loved, was an enormous burden. Usually it was better for nature to take its course. Many believed that to interfere with the natural way was perverting the will of God and could only bring bad luck. Live and let die.

What great-grandmother Annie believed is not recorded, but what is known is that as she nursed and lovingly held young baby Jack, *á luascadh ina baclainn* (rocking him in her arms), she would croon softly and gently to him, 'Maybe in God he'll take you tomorrow.' Harsh words leavened in iambic pentameter.

But it was neither cruel nor heartless. It was driven by survival and concern. It was the way things were. To eke out an existence was a huge challenge on the infertile lands of the west coast of Ireland and the offshore islands. There has always been a question as to whether or not communities took a hand in ensuring the survival of the fittest. While there is no concrete evidence to support the theory, it is certainly true that very few physically disabled persons survived. Was this just nature, or was nature prompted?

In Uncle Jack's case he defied them all, and not only survived, but eventually qualified as a doctor for the Connemara area and is still living, in his late eighties.

The 1916 Easter Rising was over but still fresh in the minds of the people when Joe and Margaret's last child was born in 1920. Granny did as one of her sisters, Annie, asked of her and called him Plunkett, in memory of Joseph Mary Plunkett, the poet and 1916 martyr who had been executed in the stonebreakers' yard in Kilmainham Gaol on 4 May 1916.

Joe in his Baby Ford enjoyed the work and enjoyed the life. He was friendly and affable and easily absorbed into revelry. Unfortunately, he had, as Granny used to say, too much of a '*grá* for the *deorum*' and he loved the *poitín* punch. He was often away from home for days and eventually the drink got the better of him.

He was also, as so many were at the time, involved in republican activities and had to go on the run from the Black and Tans, the notoriously undisciplined ex-British Army force drafted into Ireland in 1920, during the War of Independence. By now his health was deteriorating and the fugitive lifestyle – poor, damp accommodation in 'safe houses' – did not help. Joe never really recovered from this period. His health was broken and it was no surprise that he eventually developed tuberculosis. He died in 1925 at the early age of forty years.

In fairness to my grandfather, he was a man who was practical in business matters, and no doubt seeing how things were going, he took out a hefty insurance policy a few short years before he died. A significant sum of money came to Granny on his death, and it made a huge difference to the young widow.

'It was a sad way to get it, but that was the way it was,' Granny recalled, simply and unemotionally.

She extended the shop and set about building up the business with energy and determination. All distractions were removed, and to give her a break, the twins, Myko and Jack, who were just about ten years old, were sent to their grandmother's house in Ballymartin, just a mile outside the village of Kilmaine. They attended Kilmaine primary school and later went to the secondary school in Ballinrobe. In the meantime, the business in Lettermore, even though it was somewhat off the main road, thrived under Granny's direction. She developed a loyal and regular set of customers. Today, Tí Phlunkett, as it is called, is still busy under the ownership of my first cousins, Peadar and Oliver.

Myko was always loud in praise of Granny. 'By God, she was a hard worker.' He would recall how a pig was slaughtered regularly, mainly for the shop but also for the family. There would be no waste. Some of it was used fresh, more of it had coarse salt rubbed into it and was left hanging from ceiling hooks to cure. Prime cuts were smoked in a smoking shed out the back. Even the pig's head, split and flattened, was eaten, as were the crubeens (feet), with cabbage. Granny would carefully collect the blood from the pig. Then she would extract the intestines from the body and scour them clean.

That was hard work, squeezing the insides clean of excrement and the rest, and then running water through them until they were rinsed clean.

But that wasn't the end of it. With the twins and baby Plunkett running beside her, she would take the intestines down to the little quay across from the house and wash them again in the sea, for the flavouring, seasoning and the preservation benefits of the salt water.

In the meantime, the pig's blood was mixed in a large pudding bowl with a concoction of oatmeal, flour and various other scraps and offal, to be cooked off for hours and hours until nothing was recognisable in the dark, gooey mass. While it was still warm it was ladled into foot-long pieces of intestine. By the time it had cooled it had been transmogrified into the world's best black pudding. Do people ever stop to think what they are eating?

GRANNY AND
HER SISTERS

My granny, Margaret O'Boyle, grew up in a household that had seen its fair share of tragedy. Her little sister, Nora, died as a baby, and as was common practice at the time, the next child was also christened Nora in her memory. There were only two boys in the family; one contracted a virulent scarlet fever and within days the other lad was also infected. They were buried beside each other. Mary lived to adulthood but died giving birth to her first child. The baby also died.

The surviving girls, Margaret and her three sisters, Nellie, Nora and Annie, all chose teaching as a career. In order to get a teaching qualification it was necessary to have a thorough command of the Irish language, so they departed their native Kilmaine for Rosmuc to learn Gaeilge. Rosmuc, with its barren beauty, was a different world to Kilmaine, but they loved it and its surroundings and it seems that from the moment they arrived they felt at home and never really thought of going east again. New friends were made. Their Irish teacher, Sinéad O' Flanagan, shared with them not just her language skills but also the whole panoply of Irish heritage. They were enthused by her telling of the folk tales, the myths, the tales of magic and the tales of Na Fianna. Both the written and oral traditions were studied. The O'Boyle sisters made them their own.

Rosmuc was a gathering place for many young idealists committed to the language. People were drawn to it. A tall young man named Eamon came to spend time in Rosmuc and fell in love with the place, and with the Irish teacher. The year after meeting her in Rosmuc, Eamon followed Sinéad to Tourmakeady where she was involved in the course for young teachers. The courtship continued.

And a romantic courtship it was. Tomás O'Toole told me the story. His cousin Richard had seen the pair together up at Droim a' Droighin, beside the beautiful Gaynor's Bay on the shore of Lough Mask, just about a mile south of Tourmakeady. An idyllic setting. She was resting against a large rock, and her young man was reading her poetry.

Knowing the history of the young suitor, I wondered what class of poetry he had been reading. 'Was the poetry *as Gaeilge*, or in English?' I asked Tomás.

'Sure, it was from Aunt Mary's English poetry book.'

I speculated aloud as to who the chosen poet might have been.

'Well, I can answer that too,' said Tomás. 'There was only the one poetry book in the house at the time and we still have it.'

There it was, *The Poetical Works of Alfred, Lord Tennyson,* with its handwritten inscription: *To Mary O'Toole from Thomas Conroy, December 24 1895.* No doubt a Christmas gift.

What a wonderful picture, I thought. Eamon de Valera, the future President of Ireland, wooing his beloved by the lakeshore, reading the works of an English peer from a book gifted to my cousin Máire by the father of Pádraig Ó Conaire, the future leading Irish-language author. To this day, the rock that Sinéad rested against is referred to as Carraig Dev by the family.

Sinéad and Eamon eventually married and they both went on to make their mark on Irish society. Sinéad developed into a well known and most prolific writer of stories and legends for children, while Eamon de Valera, as we all know, became one of the most influential political figures of the twentieth century. Granny and Sinéad corresponded for many years after they had all left Rosmuc.

▨ ▨ ▨

When the time came for them to seek teaching posts, Granny and her sisters looked west, towards Cill Chiaráin. Annie and Nora were appointed together to the same school in Loch Chon Aortha, a few miles north of Cill Chiaráin; Nellie took up a teaching position in Cill Chiaráin. Her principal, Nicholas Keyes, was an unusual appointment. He had transferred from a position near Maynooth in County Kildare and had no connections whatever with Cill Chiaráin.

Nellie's love of the language was not shared by Nick. She was a soft and gentle person whereas Nick was irascible and forward. Nonetheless, opposites attract. The two became close and nobody was surprised when they announced that they were to be married. They set up home in Cill Chiaráin.

Granny was somewhat separated from her sisters because she was appointed to a job in the national school on the island of Inishbarra. This was just a quarter of a mile off Leitir Mór island, but was on the far side of the mouth of Cill Chiaráin Bay from her sisters. She did not live on Inishbarra but in digs in Lettermore. Each morning she went out by currach to the island school, and on the odd occasion when storms blew up, she was sometimes marooned and had to stay with a hospitable parent of one of the pupils. As a young woman in her early twenties, it was only natural as she was coming and going that she would meet others in the area of the same age. Herself and young Joe O'Toole from beside the bridge met. She thought him a bit wild but nice, she was attracted to him. They married around 1905 and it was then, as we have already heard, that Joe and Margaret decided to strike out and try their luck in Western Australia.

With Joe's death in 1925, Margaret O'Toole was left to rear and provide for five young children. There was little or no free time, but the business was closed on a Sunday, and after attending Mass, doing the books and preparing for the coming week, she would, if the weather was fine, head off to visit her sister, Nellie. From Leitir Mór to Cill Chiaráin was a land journey of more than forty miles, but only a short, though potentially hazardous, sea journey. She would take young Myko with her and some local lads would row them across the mile-and-a-half strait in a currach. They would put ashore at Cooke's jetty, and while she visited with her sister, the crew would head for the *teach tábhairne*. She was always terrified on those journeys. She hated stepping into the skittish currach; she would hold Myko to her when they bounced off the waves, and she prayed as she covered them both from the spray of water that rose over the bow.

It was worse on the return leg with a crew who were by now well fortified by drink. About half a mile out of the quay at Cill Chiaráin the boat left the shelter of land and was at the mercy of the south-west winds, with the ever-present danger of being blown back on to the reefs around Cionlaí and Oileán na Circe. There were some dangerous stretches in the channels between the islands. Some of these could only be navigated at high tide or close to it. If the crew overstayed their time in the *teach tábhairne* and left it late before setting out, then it was risky. Myko would be sent to ask the men to come straight away.

Margaret loved her sister Nellie and made the journey for her. Nellie worried about her widowed sister trying to feed and educate her five children on her own. Margaret felt that Nellie was a little too quiet for her husband, who was a confident, forceful man and who also liked his drink. On those few Sundays, a couple of times a year, they shared their troubles, telling each other just enough to understand their circumstances but never so much that the other would be overly worried. Myko did not look forward to those days; he was a little afraid of his Aunt Nellie's husband, Nick Keyes; the journey was scary and his mother was upset. When the visit was over, his mother and his aunt would cry quietly and softly as they took whispered leave of each other at the jetty. It made him uncomfortable and confused.

Once the rocky passage across to Leitir Callow had been safely negotiated, Margaret would brighten up and do her best to shorten the two-mile walk home to Leitir Mór by pointing out the local landmarks.

'Look out there at Inishbarra. Can you see the old schoolhouse? That was where I got my first teaching job.' A little later, as they passed the little road branching off down to the quay on the southern tip of Leitir Mór island, she would show him where she used to take the currach across to the school.

'Was the sea always rough going across, Mam?'

'No, *a ghrá*. You see, Inishbarra is to the south of us and the quay there is facing us on the north side of the island so there was usually good shelter from the wind. But there were times when I could not get across and times during the winter when I had to stay for weeks on the island. I used to walk in the wind to the west of the island and look across the bay to Cill Chiaráin point and wonder was Aunt Nellie out for a walk over there.'

'Mam, why were you and Aunt Nellie crying when we were leaving. Why were you sad?'

'Nothing to worry yourself about, *a stór.*'

Myko was much older before he learned why the two sisters grieved.

Annie O'Boyle was an attractive and energetic young woman who lived a full life. She loved her little school in Loch Chon Aortha, but she had broader interests too. She was a nationalist and, like all her friends, neighbours and colleagues, supported the IRA's activities at that time. Much and all as she disliked their hard drinking, she admired the involvement of her two brothers-in-law, Nick Keyes and Joe O'Toole, in the War of Independence.

By the time the Black and Tans were sent to Ireland in 1920, Annie was marginally involved herself, running errands for 'the cause'.

Any time the Tans were on their way from Galway to Cill Chiaráin they had to pass the school at Loch Chon Aortha. As part of their strategy to instil fear in the community they regularly checked out the school. It was Annie's responsibility to warn people in Cill Chiaráin that the hated and dreaded Tans were coming. Nick Keyes, in particular, had good reason to keep well out of the way of the Tans.

Sometimes they arrived unseen at the school, and on those occasions Annie would give a pre-arranged wink to one of the older pupils who would absent himself on the pretext of some domestic responsibility. Annie and her colleague, Bridie Cooke, would then delay the Tans to give the young lad a good headstart to get to Cill Chiaráin. At other times she would see them coming through the turn of the road beside the lake and would be away before them. Racing on her bicycle into Cill Chiaráin, she would alert Nick.

'Quick, the Tans are on the road. They'll be here within the half-hour!'

And Nick would send the word out to anyone under threat. Nellie would be cycling demurely out of the village by the time the Tans arrived, and there were never any suspects to be found. When this happened a few times, the frustrated Tans realised that they were being pre-empted. Following a brief investigation, their brutally persuasive methods of interrogation yielded them the low-level intelligence that the person responsible for announcing their arrival was the young teacher, Annie O'Boyle.

They set out to teach the teacher a lesson.

Annie was conducting the junior classes when the door burst open, the window was smashed in and the tiny room was filled with men in the feared uniforms of the Black and Tans. Guns were trained on her.

'Don't move a muscle,' the English accent, strange and foreign in these surroundings, reverberated around the classroom.

Annie froze with fear.

'Away from that desk, you.' Two of them dragged her backwards and pinned her roughly against the wall, knocking over the blackboard and easel.

The pupils screamed.

'Please let the children go out, they're terrified,' she begged.

Even villains and bullies are helpless with children, particularly upset children.

'Send them out.'

'*Siúlaigí amach go rialta anois agus fan sa chlós.*'

The children were released to the schoolyard and Annie's nightmare continued. They asked her, over and over: 'Who is in charge of the guns?'

But she did not know and could not tell them.

They prodded and shook her. With a bayonet pressed to her navel, she was threatened with death. A flick of the blade and her clothing was cut through as she screamed with terror. Then they stripped her.

No doubt they did more, but that was as far as Granny ever told the story. It is impossible to know whether the soldiers sexually assaulted or raped Annie. But whether or no is probably irrelevant, because her dignity and self-respect was obliterated by their taunts, sneers and vulgarities. What they did they did, and then they ran her, stark naked, out of the school, into the schoolyard, and let her go.

I don't know where she finished up that day. It would have been a mercy to have killed her because nobody ever met the real Annie O'Boyle again afterwards. Sure, her body lived, but from that moment her heart and soul died and her mind was dysfunctional.

At a time when modesty was the measure of maidenhood, to be seen naked was a public shame. At a time when victims of sexual abuse were shunned by society, her suffering continued.

Nowadays, when newspapers show acres of naked flesh every day, it may be difficult to understand the enormity of the trauma suffered in those times by a young woman who had been nakedly exposed before the community. For the rest of her life she was tainted and marked. Damaged goods.

She did try. She taught in different places for short periods, before eventually going to live with her sister, Nora. By this time Nora had moved into Galway. The girls' mother was originally a Lydon from Galway City. She still had a house in Eyre Street, just off Eyre Square, which she had given to Nora. Nora convinced Annie to move in with her to escape the memories, and gave up her own teaching career to look after her sister. To maintain an income she provided lodgings for students. Annie wandered aimlessly around the city during the day; her mental health continued to deteriorate. The students were in the habit of leaving their bicycles outside the house. One day, some years later, poor confused Annie took one of the bikes, and acting on a memory of her time in Loch Chon Aortha, cycled west. It was the middle of winter, cold and miserable. After completing the forty-mile journey to Loch Chon Aortha, she arrived, exhausted and confused, at the house of old friends, the Coynes.

By this stage the Keyes had moved into Galway also, so Annie had no relations left in the area. The Coynes took her in and cared for her while word was being sent to her sisters in Galway. That was more or less the end. Within a short period she had been signed into Ballinasloe mental hospital, where, incredibly, she survived, incoherently and vacantly, until the late 1960s.

I knew nothing of the existence of my grandaunt Annie until shortly before she died, but Granny had visited her regularly throughout all those years in Ballinasloe. The visits were disturbing and frustrating; as the years passed, poor Annie no longer recognised Granny as her sister Margaret. Her mind was stuck in the 1920s and she expected her sister to look the same as she did back then. On one visit, Granny was accompanied by her daughter-in-law Lena. Annie mistook Lena for her sister, and, pointing at Granny, said: 'Margaret, who is the old lady?'

When she died, my uncle Plunkett found among her possessions in Ballinasloe an old Post Office book from the 1920s with ten shillings (about sixty cents) on deposit. That was her total estate.

Although the circumstances that brought about Annie's incarceration were unusual, she was one of thousands who were committed to mental institutions in Ireland at that time, and for many years afterwards, and who never left. It was not that nobody cared. This was the contemporary medical advice. The concept of counselling did not exist. Modern cynics enjoy undermining and demeaning the whole industry of psychotherapy, psychiatry, psychology and counselling, and those that practice the disciplines are often the butt of jokes, as 'shrinks', or the ' touchy-feely gang'. But they have the tools to relieve traumatised victims of their pain; to help people help themselves. And, in many cases, they literally put broken lives and spirits back together again.

If society had access to these a century ago there are many lives, such as Grandaunt Annie O'Boyle's, which could have been mended.

Granny and her sisters were tough, adventurous and capable. They had experienced a natural lifetime's expectation of grief before they ever left home and had shed their full measure of tears. No doubt the move to Connemara was an attempt at a new start. Granny O'Toole's life was full of change and challenge. She took on teaching duties not just in the far west of Connemara, where she knew nobody, but in a remote island off it. After marrying Joe she upped sticks for Western Australia, only to return the following year to take over the pub in Galway City, before returning to Lettermore to run the business. Then there was Joe's death and Annie's tragedy. The Lord took one final swipe at her when, eighteen years after her husband's death, she had to bury her only daughter, Mary Clare, her pride and joy, who died of tuberculosis in 1943. At the age of sixty, Granny then took much of the responsibility for the rearing of Mary Clare's young children, Max and Joe.

When I got to know Granny O'Toole she was lively, but had mobility problems, suffering greatly from arthritis of the hip. She relied for support on a stick with a crook on it. Although she could not walk without the stick, she seemed constantly busy and on the go. I was always in awe of her and knew that behind her kindly face was a toughness. It is a pity that she never told me her story herself. Maybe I was too young, or more likely she was too forward-looking to be indulging in the past. But it raises the question: how well did I know Granny O'Toole? I would have said very well, only to find, when I began looking under stones and putting the pieces together, that I never knew the woman at all. The same must apply to many of life's relationships.

How many stories lie undiscovered behind the faces and front doors of those we think we know very well?

My father's third-level experience was brief – he went to University College Galway for a week. But, unquestionably, they were an eventful seven days during which he managed to cram in some interesting diversions, including driving a car over the docks and into the harbour! Fortunately, all survived and it would appear that it was his cool-headedness that saved them from fatalities. However, the consensus was that he needed a more disciplined regime than college life.

His mother made enquiries and he was immediately accepted into the Garda Depot in Phoenix Park, which, as well as being Garda Headquarters, was also the training school for new policemen, and from which he eventually emerged as a fully-fledged garda.

My father's name is Michael O'Toole, or to give him the full moniker by which he grandly introduced himself to my mother – Michael Francis O'Boyle O'Toole, born and reared in Lettermore, County Galway. But he is known to everyone as Myko, probably an anglicised phonic corruption of the Irish *Maidhc Ó*.

Myko was a bit inclined towards mischief. He was a twin and one of a family of five. After the death of his father, in 1925, his mother had her hands full with the family's general store and farm and in true Gaelic tradition, Myko was sent to his grandmother in Kilmaine to be reared for a time. He was enrolled in Kilmaine National School and then spent his early secondary school years at the CBS in Ballinrobe. He finished his post-primary education in St Mary's in Galway.

After completing his garda training, Myko was based in Dublin and billeted in the depot in the Phoenix Park. Myko enjoyed life in Dublin. Among other activities, the young garda took up acting and was reasonably successful. Strong friendships developed over the course of rehearsals and performances and late nights were an essential part of the fun. An O'Casey play was one of the group's most successful offerings and it got a good run at the Peacock. A major party was planned for the closing night of the play, but as can happen at such times, the celebrations became over-enthusiastic and the partying got more than a little out of hand. They were drinking in the Plough bar near the Abbey Theatre, and sure they were only building up an appetite for more when last orders were called. The only hope for more drink was to travel outside the city limits to what was known as a *'bona fide'* pub, where opening hours were much longer, on the grounds that the customers would be *bona fide* travellers. Without doubt, this must have been the most abused piece of legislation in the history of the State.

But how would they get there? As luck would have it, there was another garda drinking in the pub who just happened to be the official driver for the then Minister for Education, Tom Derrig. The poor man had been an IRA gunman in a previous time and was one of many who, as part of a fairly progressive initiative, were rehabilitated into positions in the police force or the army at the end of the 'Troubles'. (Haven't we the mighty tendency towards the euphemistic in Ireland? While we were killing and maiming each other in what every other country would call a civil war, we refer to that period as the 'Troubles'.)

Our heroes, Myko and his mates, organised a few generous measures of drink for the already inebriated driver. Drunk and innocent, the unfortunate man was soon persuaded to hand over the keys of the State car to his new friends, two gardaí and a teacher, Séamus Ó Dúda. The official driver was ensconced in the back seat and the unofficial garda driver took over. Off the lads headed, down the Liffey quays, out past Chapelizod and Palmerstown to The Dead Man's Inn in Lucan. There they stayed and continued the spree, indulging themselves mightily until they were shown the door at a time which was nearer to early morning than late night.

Having made their way homeward, only God knows how, they left the State car in the north city centre, with the key in the ignition and the driver, the former IRA man, sleeping it off in the back seat. Rather than split up, the bosom buddies decided that Ó Dúda should also come back to the barracks. By the time they finally found their way through the Park gates and reached the Garda Depot they were well after the curfew time. You have to remember that this was during the 'Emergency', which, because of our neutrality, was the official Irish euphemism for the Second World War, and gardaí were subject to military-style regulations while in the depot. Needless to say, the merry thespians did not have the required late pass.

No problem; it was Ireland, regulations were flexible, the barracks was small and the sentry recognised them, so he was prepared to look the other way. But these boys were in no humour to do the sensible thing and slip quietly into their billets. No sir! High on alcohol, they were ready for more devilment. They demanded that the sentry fire a volley of revolver shots in the air to celebrate closing night and their safe return. Of course he refused, whereupon they proceeded to relieve him of his revolver and emptied the magazine through the roof of the sentry box, finishing the night with a grand finale.

The teacher, Ó Dúda, who was not known to the sentry, was smart enough to make a run for it. But the other two boyos were in serious trouble. There was the inevitable enquiry, followed by disciplinary proceedings. Amazingly, they escaped expulsion from the force, but within days one of them was transferred to Donegal and Myko was on his way to beautiful Kerry. That was how he came to be stationed in Teresa's county.

Needless to say, I did not hear about this episode from Myko. By pure coincidence, and I suppose because of the nature of my job, three decades later I met that same teacher, Séamus Ó Dúda. He hailed from West Kerry, was as wild as they come and great company. It was he who told me the story of my father's enforced exile to Kerry, a tale that Myko only grudgingly admitted the truth of over the years.

Teresa Moriarty and Michael O'Toole were married on 17 September 1946 in St Peter and Paul's Church, Arran Quay, Dublin. You might ask, why Dublin? Well, with one of them from Connemara and the other from West Kerry it could be said that the Dublin venue was convenient to both the Dingle and Lettermore contingents, but possibly the truth would be that it was a neutral spot. And the Dingle crowd were not at all unhappy with the trip to Dublin – it was All Ireland Final week and they would be travelling anyway.

The Dingle party was based in the Four Courts Hotel, just down the quays from the church. Teresa says that herself and Myko had a bit of a tiff on the night before the wedding and that she was on the point of calling the whole thing off. According to herself, she threatened to dump the wedding flowers over the Liffey wall into the river and not get married at all. Obviously, she thought better of it, so she didn't and they did.

Whatever about the mood of the bride, people generally were in bad humour and Dublin was no place to be that week. It was wet and dismal; the city had been hit by floods and strikes; last-minute wedding shopping was uncomfortable and difficult.

Coincidentally, considering that it would be me who would be leading and managing similar campaigns on its behalf thirty years later, the Irish National Teachers' Organisation (INTO) was in the news, as the political and Church establishments sought to bring to an end its six-month-long teachers' strike in Dublin. Notices of meetings organised by the INTO to inform the general public of the issues involved decorated the lamp-posts. Placarded picketers patrolled each primary school. The media was praising the INTO for indicating a readiness to accept Archbishop McQuaid's offer to act as mediator between the union and the government. De Valera and the government were coming in for criticism from parents' groups and the media for not exhibiting the same willingness. It became the most significant industrial action in the organisation's 150-year history. It politicised the INTO, to the extent that it immersed itself in the next general election, with the union activists aligning themselves with the newly founded Clann na Poblachta Party against the reigning Fianna Fáil government, which had been in power for more than fifteen years. Fianna Fáil was defeated and Clann na Poblachta went into power as part of Ireland's first coalition government.

But that all came to pass over the following couple of years. Back to the wedding and the news of the week, and indeed of the month. That September saw the 'Battle of the Harvest'. The diabolical weather had produced the wettest summer for years, and the harvest was seriously threatened. Much had already been irretrievably lost, and lay rotting in sodden fields. This was at a time in post-war Ireland when food was still being rationed, and people became seriously concerned about food stores for the looming winter. The situation developed into a national crisis. It was a disquieting coincidence that it was exactly one hundred years since the Great Famine, which was still fresh in the folk memory. Everyone was urged to help the farmers. Lorries, cars and buses were organised to transport thousands of city workers out to the farms to bring in the harvest. Predictably enough, they were christened 'the collar-and-tie brigade'.

Some of the Dingle wedding guests were planning to stay on in Dublin to go to the Roscommon–Kerry All Ireland Final at the weekend. Local heroes Gega Connor and Paddy Bawn Brosnan were playing, and more than a few of the guests had stand tickets. The happy couple were also planning to attend. But, true to form, the GAA was not going to be found wanting at a time of real, patriotic, national endeavour. So they put their shoulders to the national effort by postponing the All Ireland for a fortnight so that the country would not be distracted from the essential business of the harvest. For maximum impact, they allowed the public debate of 'Will they? Won't they?' to foment all week before making the announcement on the Friday. Well done, lads!

Never ones to be left out of the 'Big Story', the four Catholic archbishops called for a National Triduum of Prayer as a general act of supplication to the Lord God, seeking a respite from the atrocious weather. The triduum was scheduled to start on Friday, 20 September. Every Catholic was urged to attend. All over Ireland people trooped to the churches and wore out their knees praying. The Litany of Loreto was followed by the Rosary, then Benediction and the Litany of the Saints. The same again on Saturday and Sunday. On Monday, universal thanks was given for the huge support and massive turnout for the triduum.

But in a perfectly mischievous display of precision, irony, or pathetic fallacy, the Good Lord responded the following day with the worst floods of the year. Dublin recorded 2.4 inches of rain, which fell in a fourteen-hour non-stop downpour.

People had to be evacuated from their homes and given temporary accommodation in halls, institutions and colleges, including St Patrick's Teacher Training College in Drumcondra. In a minor media coup, the INTO opened a Teachers' Harvest Bureau in their strike headquarters at the Teachers' Club, Parnell Square. The bureau provided the names of striking teachers who were volunteering to help the farmers with the harvesting. School pickets were reduced in order to provide more helpers and the newspapers carried photographs of the strikers lining up to board lorries to the farms.

◧　◧　◧

Myko and Teresa stuck with their plans and stayed on in Dublin until the weekend, despite the fact that the hard-won All Ireland tickets were now useless. On the Sunday, when they should have been attending the match, they drove west to Mayo. The newly-weds spent the next ten days in the magnificence of Ashford Castle, situated between Loch Corrib and Loch Mask in the beautiful village of Cong, County Mayo. That was considered fairly posh even in those days. The pair enjoyed themselves. Biological and chronological evidence would indicate that I came back from the honeymoon with them. So there it is, a Mayo conception!

It is more than possible that I was the worst footballer ever to come out of West Kerry, but then my relationship with the footballing world started out very badly.

'Jesus, we're going to be late for the match. What in the name of Christ is keeping Hanlon?'

It was the day of the semi-final and the Dingle fans were anxiously awaiting the arrival of local hackney driver, Mr Hanlon. Dingle was enjoying its best-ever decade in Kerry football. We had contested eight and won five county finals in the last ten years, but had not been in the final for the last two years. The blood was up. A good result today and we could be back in the county final, playing John Mitchell's. Dingle against Tralee! The old enemy. And we had a good chance.

The match was taking place thirty miles away, and the transport options were pretty slim in the years immediately after the war. What few private cars there were all had three in the back and two more on the long bench seat in front beside the driver. Moran's, Cleary's and Hanlon's hackney cars had been booked well in advance by the diehard supporters from Sráid Eoin and The Quay, the two Dingle clubs. Most of them had spent the previous few hours in Neligan's, or Foxy John's, or some other pub, illegally fortifying themselves with alcohol for the big event. Now they were gathered on the small bridge at the junction of Main Street and the Mall, waiting for the hackney cars. It was going to be one great day; they had been to Mass, some of them might have a meat sandwich, made from the crusty heel of the loaf, protected in a brown sweet bag and stuffed in a pocket. The talk was of football, and it was confident talk! They did not know it yet, but for some of them their day was about to unravel.

It was Sunday, 20 July 1947 and in a house less than fifty yards away from the bridge, an event that would bring much invective down on the innocent Mr Hanlon had just begun. He was about to get an emergency double-booking. Teresa Moriarty, now O'Toole, already a few weeks overdue on her first baby, went into labour and got into difficulty. She had to be brought to Tralee, and fast.

Myko rushed across the Mall and up the Barrack Height where he hoped to find a hackney, either in Jack Moran's garage or in Hanlon's house. Mr Hanlon was the first he met and he didn't have to ask a second time. Hanlon's big Plymouth hackney car was at the door as soon as Myko. Aunty Phyl helped Teresa to the door and into the car, then she went around the other side and sat in the back with her. Myko was in the passenger seat. They were on their way in minutes. Teresa was uncomfortable and well into labour. Myko asked the driver to slow down going over the bumps on the bridge near Baileristeenig. They picked up speed again through Lispole, Annascaul and up Gleann na nGealt. By the time they reached Camp, and still with ten miles to go, Teresa was sure they would not make it. Poor old Myko was speechless with worry, silently willing the car onward. They got to Tralee and rushed into the Bons Secours Nursing Home. Teresa's midwife was a sister of Ned O'Loughlin, her neighbour in the Mall. More importantly, the gynaecologist, Dr Coffey, had a reputation far and wide as being the best in his field. He had good connections too, in fact, his hands had been blessed by the Pope himself.

It was a long labour and a difficult birth. Teresa, at the best of times not a physically strong woman, was drained and sedated after the ordeal. She would recover, however, and eventually survive four more difficult births, counting down the arrival of my four sisters.

So there I was, Sunday's child. Delivered into the world by good Catholic hands that had been blessed by the Pope. That was Pope Pius XII, who, pictured or sculpted, was almost as ubiquitous as God himself in the homes of Ireland, gracing hallways, mantelpieces and parlours nationwide and easily recognised by his cadaverous expression, Roman nose and gimlet glasses. The Roman nose was unfortunate, because if the little busts fell, the prominent facial feature invariably smashed. Around 1960, the Pope was joined on display by that other great international Catholic icon of the time, John F Kennedy. The both of them, Pope and President, were very big in Dingle. Role models for the 1960s.

After following their separate courses for generations, the two gene streams had finally converged. One from its source at the edge of Cill Chiaráin Bay in Eanach Mheáin through five generations of O'Tooles in Connemara, and the other from the top of the Cam between Glens and Mullach Mhial through five generations of Moriartys in Corca Dhuibhne.

And there I was, leading off the fifth generation since Daddy Tom. Irreverent and iconoclastic as he was, he would hardly have been overly impressed by my kickstart from the Pope.

Apart from the misfortunates who missed half the match because of me, my birth also brought no luck whatever to the Dingle team. In fact, I flattered to deceive; even though they won the semi they were beaten in the Final. Having started out on the wrong foot, so to speak, with the footballing world, it must be admitted that time brought no great improvement. I loved the game, but I was awkward, clumsy and uncoordinated. I played it for as long as it took me to realise that, while my own ineptitude frustrated me, I really enjoyed watching other people play, and I'm still at that.

I was given the name Joseph John after my two grandfathers. Apparently, there was some talk about putting the John first. This would have appealed to my mother, who would have seen it as giving precedence to her side, but the vulgar potential for John Joseph to deteriorate into Jonjo through common usage left it with no chance.

My mother held very strong views about names and to this day has no tolerance for the shortened form of her firstborn's name. Over the years, as I grew through my teenage and early adult period, new acquaintances of mine were often met with the terse and unhelpful response, 'Sorry, there's no Joe in this house; you must have the wrong number,' when they rang home.

Our home on the Mall was at one end of an attractive terrace of four stone houses. Most unusually, the houses are constructed straddling a stream grandly called the Mall River. Starting up above Ballinassig, under Conor Pass, it flowed down through Cuilneach, along by the creamery and the Spa road to the bridge. Before traversing the length of the Mall, it ducked under our terrace and then continued on to the harbour. Pat Neligan, Ruairí O'Connor and myself would drop floats into the river from the small bridge. Then we would watch them, each cheering on his own, until they vanished under Mrs Batt's house. We'd run down along the four houses to check which of the floats would emerge first from the other end, at our house.

Inside the house, the water flowing underneath created an unceasing background sound, very faint during dry periods but quite a noisy little torrent when in flood. Late at night, when the town was absolutely quiet, I would lie in bed and have the sound of the stream as a friendly and constant companion, unlike the monotonous tick-tock of the American clock in our kitchen, which would imperiously interrupt each hour to chime out the time. That tick-tock seemed to infiltrate the whole house late at night. I grew to hate the sound of it.

The house was quite roomy and comfortable. It had three storeys. The ground floor was taken up mainly by the shop, but there was also a living room and bedroom, with a small kitchen and a dining room in an extension built on out the back. On the first floor there were three good-sized bedrooms and a bathroom. The second floor was a large open area. Even though it was fully floored and had a solid stairs and bannisters leading up to it, it had never been divided into rooms because we didn't need the space. We called it the attic and it was used for storage only, which was a pity really because it was an attractive area. As well as a few skylights, it had two windows on the gable-end from which there was the most wonderful view down the Mall and across the harbour to Cooleen. It was my favourite spot in the whole house and it was lovely and warm when the sun shone.

As was the case with most town houses at the time, the front door opened onto the street. The front walls had that very attractive stonework that went out of fashion for years and was often covered over with pebble-dash, but which, thankfully has enjoyed a revival. At the back was a small garden with a number of sheds and a garage area for the car. You could enter the back through a narrow laneway, which we called Púcaí Lane, the Lane of the Ghosts, because it was unlit and spooky. Neither Teresa nor Myko were gardeners, so the only two green features were a large ash tree at the bottom and rambling roses along the stone wall. I'm afraid the clothesline and the trash area where we burned waste created more of an impact. But I did climb and enjoy the tree and Pat Neligan and myself erected a decent swing, with a wooden seat, hanging from the strongest horizontal branch.

It could fairly be said of my mother, Teresa, that in her eyes all her geese are swans. My four sisters and I were as close to perfection as could be expected. While there would certainly be strong criticism of us when we stepped out of line, this was generally well counterbalanced by fulsome praise and encouragement. Both my parents were extraordinarily supportive of us in all our endeavours.

'There is no such word as "can't". Of course you can do it,' they would say.

This confidence-boosting was probably a great entrée to life, but in later years it led to me regularly and optimistically underestimating problems. This level of support is still there and nowadays is also directed at the grandchildren and in-laws. Mind you, my mother long ago made it clear that she had no wish to be addressed as Granny or any synonym of same. All the grandchildren address her as Teresa, and my father, when he was alive, as Myko.

Detail was important in our house: the table would always be fully set or laid, no matter how humble the meal; containers showing proprietary brand names were not welcome; it would be unthinkable not to have a saucer under every cup; there would always be a tablecloth; and we never ate anywhere except in the dining room.

My father was based in Tralee Garda Station, which was thirty-one miles from Dingle. He was a very early riser and would always be washed and dressed, bright, breezy and breakfasted in time for the 7.30am bus. My sister, Mary Sabrina, two years younger than me, and myself would usually be downstairs before he left, which meant that we had at least an hour and a half before leaving home for school, which began at 9.30am. One of us would often wait at the hall door, keeping an eye out for the bus. Myko was a good timekeeper; he would never be late, and whereas the bus driver would certainly wait a few moments if necessary, it rarely happened. Anyone who was late would be sure to get an earful from Billemite, the conductor. In his day, Bill Dillon, to give him his proper name, had been a mighty footballer, winning honours at all levels of the game, including a hatful of All-Ireland medals, but as a conductor he was not known for his patience. Some mornings he would tell me, 'Look out and see is Benny Malone waiting at the bridge.' Benny was a neighbour who had worked in the Dingle railway station but was transferred to Tralee soon after the closure of the Dingle–Tralee line. He was an intelligent and cerebral type of man who had the habit of reading late into the night and he sometimes overslept. Regularly, my father would run up and rap on the door to check that he was up and about. That would be typical Myko; quietly looking out for others was a way of life for him.

As we always had a car, the decision to travel by bus was his choice and was probably influenced by cost. On some occasions he shared the driving into Tralee with Pádraig Ó Siocrú who lived in Burnham, three miles west of Dingle, but who taught in Kilflynn, outside Tralee. Pádraig was a nephew of the writer Pádraig Ó Siochfhradha (An Seabhac) who penned that lasting children's classic, *Jimín Mháire Thaidhg*. The decision to change from car to bus would almost always follow a petrol price-increase in the budget.

The first car of ours which comes to memory was a black Ford Anglia, registration number IN 6393. Around the mid-fifties we changed to Morris Minors (black, of course), which were economical and popular.

My father was still driving a Morris Minor around the time Joan and myself first met. Joan's dismay at being picked up from home by a guy driving a Morris Minor never registered with insensitive me. She was well-known at home for her publicly stated policy of *never* going out with anyone driving a Morris Minor. It just goes to show that general statements often come back to haunt us! Apparently, she received an unmerciful mocking and jeering from some of her brothers and sisters before she got out the door. But worse was to follow. Later that night as we were talking, or whatever, in the car at the gable-end of Joan's home, there was a rapping on my door, which was then opened unceremoniously and a voice demanded, 'What are you at?' Before I had time to reply, Joan leaned across and said: 'It's okay, Richard. This is Joe O'Toole.' Richard was one of Joan's older brothers; there had been some minor pilfering from the outhouses and byres and he was sure that he had caught an intruder redhanded. He knew that none of his sisters would have been involved with a Morris Minor driver!

Teresa worked late hours in our shop and therefore was in the habit of not rising until nine o'clock. Me being the eldest, it was generally my responsibility to make the breakfast. The routine was the same every morning. The porridge, Flahavan's Oatmeal, would have been steeping since the night before. As soon as Myko was away on the bus, all I had to do was to bring it to the boil, simmer and serve to Mary Sabrina and myself. As we got older, Anita, my second sister and the middle child of the family, would be there as well.

'Bring it slowly to the boil,' Myko would caution as he left. 'Don't turn up the electric ring too high or it will stick to the bottom of the pot, and stir it a few times while it is heating.'

While it was simmering, we brought Teresa breakfast in bed. Not that you could call what little she ate breakfast. On a tray with a china cup, saucer and plate, she had two buttered Goldgrain biscuits. The tea was in a silver teapot. She drank her tea 'black', except for the odd time when she would put less than a teaspoon of milk in it. After her breakfast she would have her first wash of the day. She called it 'splashing her face'. It would be followed by a much longer, intense wash at about mid-morning when she had disposed of any heavy work in the shop.

Because I looked delicate and was deemed to be not too strong, cod liver oil was part of my breakfast diet. Most people seem to have a revulsion for the taste, but I quite liked the stuff. My last act before leaving the house every morning was to put the bottle of Seven Seas cod liver oil to my mouth and drink a mouthful of it. It does sound disgusting now.

Because of the amount of time taken up by the shop, there was always, in the colloquialism of the time, a 'girl' employed in the house to look after it and the children. Teresa was never completely comfortable with babies and was far happier to have someone else cleaning, feeding, changing and settling them. According to some of her friends, she could never hold the babies in a properly comfortable way, but Teresa would vehemently dispute that. However, she kept a close eye on the house and would take personal control over and supervision of the cooking. She might have someone else doing the prepping, but she was a good cook. Every day there was a full cooked meal, usually two courses. Typically with Teresa, the second course was always a dessert, never a soup. Sherry or custard trifle were common, with Jacob's Bourbon biscuits in the jelly and the custard top sprinkled with multi-coloured 'hundreds and thousands'. Jelly and ice cream was a regular fall-back and rice pudding or banana pudding were special treats, accompanied by pouring cream.

Sunday lunchtime was the big meal of the week; despite the hour, we called it dinner. The meat would have been purchased from my uncle Patty Atty's butcher shop, opposite the church in Green Street. His meat was always the best quality, but just in case he might be tempted to pass off some of the poorer cuts to family, it was drilled into us to make sure to ask Uncle Patty for 'a very nice piece'. The Sunday roast was usually beef. Easter Sunday would be the start of the lamb season, which would continue until autumn. After the October fair, lamb was considered to be mutton and would be dropped from the menu. Roast pork was a rare treat; served with the crackling, apple sauce and stuffing, it was a taste to die for.

My father worked as a garda clerk in the Superintendent's office in Tralee. He enjoyed and indeed loved his colleagues in the garda station and referred to them collectively as the philosophers. Whatever the story or issue of the week, it was certain that the philosophers would have a view and position on it, and I suspect that if they hadn't he would prompt and prod them until they had. Only very rarely did he ever appear in uniform, and as far as I am aware he never arrested anyone.

He always bristled with energy, always looked on the bright side and was an unshakeable optimist. It was difficult to be in bad humour around him.

Sundays were Myko's day off, and we would all head out for the Sunday drive, an outing that my mother loved. We would go to Ventry, or around Slea Head. She enjoyed every bend, view and scene. In common with all Dingle people, she considers that scenery to be as fine as is to be found anywhere in the world.

'Did you ever see Mount Brandon look so magnificent?'

We were brought up to love our place. West Kerry was and is our benchmark of beauty and everywhere else is measured against it. No matter where I am, my mind will automatically begin the comparison.

On these drives Myko would relate all the latest news from Tralee – the characters, the feuds, the families and the latest dictats from the autocratic Dean of Tralee. Petty crime was always of interest. There was one character, a down and out, who each year, as soon as the cold winds began to blow, tossed a brick through one of the large Tralee shopfronts – Revington's, or The Munster Warehouse – in order to be charged, remanded and esconced in the more comfortable and warm environs of Limerick jail for the winter. Obviously the court system worked more efficiently in those days, because he could time it to perfection!

Or it might be a tale of some major entertainer presenting a show in Tralee. Hypnotists' visits were great gas. Myko told us about a big, lumbering garda on the beat who wandered into the theatre just to check things, as it were, but in reality to get in from the cold street and to see the show. He was totally amazed by what he saw. Then the hypnotist started to select his next set of victims.

'Everyone concentrate on this spinning disc. You are beginning to feel sleepy ... *zzzz*.'

Within minutes our hypnotised garda, in full uniform and with a smile as big as Christmas, was on the stage with the other five from the audience.

'I am going to give each of you a task, starting with you, Garda Griffin. A bunch of green leprechauns have robbed a bank and they are hiding in Tralee. There's one in the foyer of Benner's, in the Imperial and in the Grand Hotel. Arrest them and bring them to the station and lock them in the cells. You will wake up as soon as you lock the cell doors. You will start running after them as soon as I click my fingers ...'

By the time Myko had finished with every detail of his hapless colleague's charge through the hotels of Tralee and into the garda station, carrying his supposed leprechauns, he and we were in tears of laughter.

One of the major stories to emerge from Tralee at that time was the disappearance of Maurice (Mossie) Moore, a farmer from outside the town. It was big news. Pádraig Kennelly, a local photographer, was the only one to have a photograph of him. This was enlarged and displayed in shop windows all over Tralee and North Kerry as the search for the missing man continued. His body was eventually found and the affair later became the subject for John B Keane's *tour de force, The Field.*

But Myko was a stickler for correctness and people's rights before the law and he never conveyed the stories and gossip surrounding the case. It could be that I was the only person of my age in Kerry who did not realise until adulthood the story behind the death and the connection with the play.

On the other hand, I was made very aware of the rules of natural justice and the importance of the concept of 'innocent until proven guilty' in Irish law. He was forever giving legal prompts.

'A lot of people think that for a person to plead "Not Guilty" when they have clearly carried out the act is a lie or perjury. Always remember that that is not the case. When a person pleads "Not Guilty" what they are really saying is, "I am not guilty until and unless this court proves me guilty".' He said it to me once and it was perfectly clear forever. Myko was a natural lawyer; it was a pity he never took it up professionally. He would explain the intricacies and importance of points of law most painstakingly. The operation of the courts and judiciary were of importance to him.

'People should never be convicted on direct evidence alone,' he would say. 'There should also be circumstantial evidence to corroborate.' In his opinion, circumstantial evidence which placed a person with certainty in a particular place at a particular time was far better than the memory or recall of a witness.

'People are always imagining things. How many times have you heard for certain that somebody saw you in a place where you weren't?'

'For instance,' he said to me one day, 'I believe that if we had taken the witnesses in a different order we would have gotten a conviction in the "*Cá bhfhuil sé?*" [Mossie Moore] murder case.' He took great interest in new legislation and would explain its implications in detail, along with his views on its efficacy.

Myko and my grandfather, Seán the Grove, always agreed that circumstances alter cases. 'I have never seen two absolutely identical sets of circumstances around human events. Don't jump to conclusions.' That was a bit of advice that certainly influenced me through my life in the consideration of cases, happenings and events. Myko lived that belief. I don't believe I have ever met a person so non-judgemental.

◆　◆　◆

In church, the priests warned us that pride was a sin against the Ten Commandments; in school, teachers taught us the saying, 'Pride cometh before a fall', but at home the injunction was different. Teresa was always advising us, 'Have pride in yourself.' She was probably right. There is little doubt that many of the old rules and perceived wisdoms have had the effect of controlling young people, keeping them in their place and ensuring that they remained unquestioning. But in our house children were expected to be heard as well as seen. The family would always ensure that we youngsters did not hear any unsuitable conversations, but apart from that caveat we were generally spoken to in an adult fashion and were part of the adult discussion. From a young age we were expected to have views.

A sense of family pervaded all. This was not in the syrupy sense of today's commentators on family values, nor did it have its roots in the religious motto that 'The family that prays together, stays together'. My grandmother would have led the family Rosary every evening in her home, and my mother, somewhat less regularly, in her house, but this was not the cement that bound the relations together. It was more to do with 'clan' and the extended family than the close confines of the immediate family. We had to know our second and third cousins as well as the closer ones. My grandmother would regularly bark at me, 'Do you not know your relations?' when my blank expression was proof positive that I was not recognising the total stranger to whom I had been introduced. It was embarrassing at the time, but it did confirm roots and build my sense of self as part of a wider network.

There was an almost farcical sense of purity of clan. All physical characteristics would be attributed. Good qualities would invariably be assigned to a Moriarty, whereas the less attractive ones would find home with some of the distaff side who had married into the Moriartys. Hence my double chin and jowl are a legacy from the Fitzgeralds, my grandmother's people. The Moriartys were blind to the fact that they were not of great physical stature. Some of my uncles were tall men, which clearly came from the Fitzgeralds. While the O'Tooles were never given credit for my above-average height, they would be blamed for the fact that my complexion tends to be more strawberry than peaches-and-cream. Any of the clan with poor eyesight blamed the Martins, my great-grandmother's family. At the same time, there would be a cautiously complimentary consensus about these families. Mind you, it was based on a belief that as they were smart enough to marry into the Moriartys there must be some good in them!

Those Martins referred to above were from the Lispole side. They were very bright, intelligent people. Two of them, Father Martin and Sister Augustine, were accomplished linguists who had studied in various European universities. Sister Augustine, who was my great-grandaunt, lived to a venerable age; one of my earliest memories is being taken to visit her in Drishane Convent, near Millstreet. I was frightened by her stature, remoteness, reputation and by her nun's habit, and could not wait to get out of the place. But I remember my awestruck reaction on hearing of the distance she and her brother had travelled to complete their education. Teresa, however, was quite dismissive of them.

'Mother's vocations, the pair of them!' she snorted. Harsh, instinctive and judgemental. All that was really wrong was that they were not Moriartys.

My grandmother – a Fitzgerald – sang the praises of the Fitzs and never conceded to the Moriarty supremacy. She looked taller than my grandfather, but whenever I got them to stand back to back, Granda had a trick of stretching his neck upwards for an extra inch and also inclining his head in a manner which seemed to raise the poll of his head somewhat higher. My grandmother was a striking and handsome woman, who took pride in her slightly Roman nose, turning her head slightly to show it off and to give the full profile of her face. She reigned supreme over her family of eleven living children and their partners. Until the day she died, her hair was almost waist length, but she always wore it up, and the only time it would ever be seen down was just before she retired for the night, when she would unclip her locks and give them 100 long brush strokes, fifty to each side. She dressed extremely well, but she was notoriously difficult to please. Being a draper herself, she prided herself on her knowledge of cloth and cut, and one of the most embarrassing experiences imaginable as a young boy was to accompany her to a clothes shop. On one particular day, in a shop in Tralee called Vogue, she drove the assistants demented with her demands. They had every dress in the shop around her and she was still not satisfied. The shade of one or the detail of another was always wrong and she kept looking for the combination which they did not stock. Not only that, but she would be quite critical of them, as if it were their fault. It took some guts to approach her and to suggest that 'this might suit you'. Eventually she would purchase, with bad grace and with every assistant in the shop exhusted. No wonder they always skirmished when they saw her coming.

She was spotlessly clean and insistent that everything and everyone about her be the same. It would be impossible for her to walk into a room without running her fingers along a ledge or a sill to check for dust. That was instinctive. This was a quality that she brought with her from the Fitzgeralds, because in all truth, the Moriartys could ignore a fair amount of untidiness and dirt before they would be motivated to start cleaning. Unfortunately for me, it was the Moriarty gene that found its way to me. When someone relayed to her a comment made by some town girl, 'Those Moriarty lads are good-looking enough, only there is always a smell of carbolic soap from them,' she went mad.

While it was true that she was domineering and difficult, she was also prodigiously hard-working, generous and compassionate. She could be giving you a present of a ten-shilling note while tearing strips off you for losing a shilling in a transaction. The Moriartys were full of contradictions and opposing qualities, but I have always felt that most interesting people are. Predictability is such a boring quality and is usually the defining mark of those who demand that the world be as they are, consistent. Consistency simply adds to the greyness. None of the Moriartys were ever consistent or predictable or boring. They fit in well with the general Corca Dhuibhne psyche of being earthy, bawdy and passionate. They were loud and they were fun. Everything was done to the limit: working, talking, drinking, arguing, laughing, bargaining. They never gave an inch. As a young child I remember having the life frightened out of me by my Uncle Jonty flying off the handle and getting carried away in argument with a dealer.

'By Jesus, I'm telling you, you'll never leave this town in one piece,

I'll bury you,' he threatened, with the fire burning out of his eyes. Jonty maintained that the buyer was cutting inside a deal he was doing with a local farmer for a few heifers. The buyer knew him well and said, calmly, 'You won't Jonty. There'd be nobody left in West Kerry if you buried all you threatened. Come in here to Fred's and we'll sort this out.' And that was the end of it.

'Who is the best-looking man in West Kerry?' roared Uncle Jimmy, his eyes popping and his red hair flaming, as he pinned me, a child, to the floor of my grandmother's kitchen.

'You are, Uncle Jimmy.'

'Are you sure?'

'Yes.'

I escaped in tears as my grandmother made for Jimmy with the wooden spoon, barely getting a swipe across his arse before he bolted in high spirits out the door. There was no controlling him. She used to lock the door at one o'clock in the morning to try and teach him a lesson. But he just came down to our house in the Mall and slept there. By the time I was ten he had had enough of the constraints of small-town life and emigrated to Connecticut, where he is now retired and conservative. I took great pleasure in relating that story to him in front of his wife and son just a few years ago.

⬚ ⬚ ⬚

My arrival was quickly followed by my sister Mary Sabrina. After that came Anita, Phyllis and Grace, so as the eldest and only male I became the white-haired boy who could do no wrong and was spoiled rotten. Our parents never reared us to know our place. 'You can be anything you want,' they always said. We were taught to respect people at all levels, low and high, and to give appropriate deference to authority, but we were expected to feel the equal of all, even those in positions of importance. We were never to be in awe of anyone. Even though it was never expressly stated, Myko and Teresa managed to infuse us with the certainty that high office did not bestow intellectual superiority. The great advantage of this was that we were never cowed and never felt the slightest inhibition in challenging the views or actions of those who might be seen to be our betters.

In fairness to my parents, this attitude worked both ways; we were always to respect the most ordinary of people, and the merest hint of us acting or speaking with any kind of a superior tone was cut down abruptly and immediately.

'Who do you think you are? You'll soon hit a brick wall and learn your lesson.'

Anyone working for Teresa or my grandparents, or for any of my uncles was treated like one of the family and God help any of us who either spoke to them or addressed them without due respect. In fact, when I was very young and a lot of my aunts and uncles were still around, I did not distinguish between family and those who in the Dingle of the time were referred to as 'servant boys or girls'.

Similarly, all of the customers were equally important and were to be treated as such. It was superb preparation for life. It was learning to accept people for what they were rather than for their status or positions and as a result we were rarely overawed by personages, their offices or their titles.

'UNWILLINGLY TO SCHOOL'

At four years of age I was brought, screaming and roaring, to Sister Rose's Junior Infants class up at the convent. The whole idea of school held very few attractions for me. Sister Rose was one of nature's truly wonderful people, universally and justifiably loved. She did her very best to calm me down and to reassure me. 'Aren't you the big boy! Come over here and sit with Pat Neligan.' But Pat Neligan didn't want anything to do with this cantakerous new arrival. From a pocket in her habit she produced a few sweets. 'Look at the lovely surprise I have for you.'

None of this cajoling made the slightest impact on me. But the poor woman was a trier. At the back of the classroom stood a painted wooden rocking horse. It had a leather saddle and stirrups and was a real beauty. 'I know you're going to love this,' Sister Rose said confidently as she lifted me up on its back. But nothing doing, I jumped off and made a break for the door. As she attempted to hold me, I gave the poor nun an unmerciful kick on the shin and ran out of the school, down to my grandmother's, which was only a hundred yards from the convent. There I was received with the support and understanding which only grandparents have and to which I was certainly not entitled. It was not a very auspicious start to a career in education. As for Sister Rose, she forgave me and welcomed me back to the class at a later date.

A few years ago, I mentioned her on a radio programme, adding a gratuitous, 'God rest her'. To my astonishment, some weeks later, on 19 March, I received a card, richly decorated with roses. The inscription was: 'Roses from Sr Rose on your feast day. I'm still around, you know.' Just goes to prove what we always said about nuns – they hardly ever age and rarely die!

Why every child, both boy and girl, began their schooling in the convent is rooted in history. Sometime around the turn of the last century, a regulation was introduced that forbade men from teaching children under the age of seven. This prohibited male teachers, both lay and religious, from teaching the first three classes in primary school. I don't know the reasoning behind the ruling – maybe some long-forgotten educational principle or psychological theory, or perhaps it was informed by some visionary understanding of child protection. This has led to a situation where in many of the towns in Ireland, to this day, children still begin school with the nuns and do not transfer to male teachers until age seven.

After my initial rebellion, it took me some time to settle into school and it is probably fair to say that for me it was always something of an interruption of and interference with other plans. Every day I ate lunch with my grandparents. I was considered to be a somewhat delicate child, so each day I would be sent next door to Uncle Foxy John's pub for a cupful of porter in a neat little whiskey glass. A dessert-spoon of sugar was stirred in and I drank the mixture before my lunch. This went on for most of my primary school years; as time went on I wanted less and less sugar! Decades later, I still get a yearning for sweet porter at odd times, but particularly on the morning after a 'feed of drink'. At that time, porter was a recommended tonic for people in recovery from any debilitating illnesses, and in contrast to current practice, pregnant women were invariably advised to take a glass of it every evening during their pregnancy. Even my mother forced herself to drink the odd drop of porter when she was expecting, although she hated the taste of it.

Drink was very much part of the culture in our family and extended family. In fact, my mother looked with some mistrust on men who did not take a drink. I remember well arriving home on the day of my Confirmation, proudly sporting my Pioneer Total Abstinence Association badge. As part of the Confirmation ceremony, each participant was encouraged to 'take the pledge', in other words, to abstain from alcoholic drink until the age of eighteen. My mother took one look at my badge and remarked witheringly, 'You'll take a drink like your father and all your uncles when you are old enough.' She was right, of course, but I wore that badge for most of my teenage years. I have a clear recollection of the day I stopped wearing it. It was the occasion of my interview for teacher training college in St Patrick's in Drumcondra. At that time, being a teacher was almost synonymous with being an abstemious Gaeilgeoir. It was important to convey the right image from the very beginning. Consequently, the waiting room seemed full of besuited seventeen- or eighteen-year-olds, all wearing a Fáinne, or Pioneer pin, or both. When I saw this, I removed my Pioneer badge and gave it to my father, who was dropping me off. I have not seen it since.

My years at the convent school saw me through Junior Infants, Senior Infants and First Class. Sister Rose and Sister Kevin were wonderfully soft and loving women who made their classrooms bright and welcoming, but we all dreaded the move into hard-hearted Sister Evangelist's First Class. She was strict in the old-fashioned sense, a disciplinarian of the Gradgrind school. Ridicule was part of her armoury, and we were regularly called 'dunces' and 'fools' as she meted out punishments, such as standing in the corner, or facing the wall while wearing a dunce's hat or a girl's skirt. She rarely smiled and offered words of praise and encouragement only to the overachievers. Underachievers didn't matter. Undoubtedly she was a person for her time, and her style would not be acceptable today.

For Sister Evangelist, religion and education were conduits of control, guilt and repression. She did some, but not all of the preparation for First Communion and managed to give us nightmares about possibilities, such as waking up on Communion morning with some of last night's sweets still undissolved in our mouths, thereby breaking the requirement to fast from midnight. In another scenario, our mouths would be so dry on receiving the Sacrament that the host would not melt, or, worse still, our teeth might touch it. It's a wonder we had the courage to approach the altar rails at all.

First Holy Communion was the biggest and most important day of our young lives. We were the centre of attention as we sat up there in the specially reserved front pews of the church. All the girls in the class wore flouncy white dresses and the boys had white suits with red sashes. These outfits were worn on the day and sometimes also on the following two Sundays, but never again for ordinary use. Their only other outing would be the Corpus Christi procession in June. It was a day of lavish, luxurious waste. Canon Lyne was the celebrant. He was a character; he could be strict and unbending at times, and people stood somewhat in awe of him. But not us children; it seemed to me that he was loved more by children than by adults. Certainly, when hearing our First Confessions, he listened attentively to our carefully composed lists of sins, and was warm and kindly to anyone who stumbled or was worried. He shared in our joy on First Communion day; he was happy for us and we were comfortable with him.

The convent in Dingle was built very close to, but not adjoining, the church. Unusually, there was an underground tunnel that connected the sanctuary of the church to the convent. A tunnel was the stuff of fantasy to our young minds and resonated adventure and mystery. And there was some reason to believe that intrigue had happened. On the corner of Goat Street and Green Street stood a substantial house, Rice House, which, we were told, had been built by the Rice family as a refuge for Marie Antoinette during the time of the French Revolution. The story went that a tunnel stretched from the house all the way out to the beautiful cove called Nancy Browne's Parlour, immediately below the lighthouse, at the mouth of the harbour. Now, despite the fact that nobody had ever discovered the tunnel, we firmly believed in its existence and spent many summer days exploring the area around Nancy Browne's Parlour in fruitless search of the underground system. Nothing would convince us but that the nuns' tunnel from the convent to the church was part of the same tunnel system.

There was a historical basis for the Marie Antoinette story, as I discovered through some casual research. Apparently a member of the Rice family, Count Louis Rice, had enlisted in the Irish Brigade and served in Central Europe, where he developed a close friendship with Emperor Josef II of Austria. Marie Antoinette was a sister of the emperor and when she was in danger during the French Revolution, a plan was hatched to rescue her from France. There were to be four Kerrymen, including Count Louis, in the rescue party and they would bring her to a ship of the Rice commercial fleet off the west coast of France, whence she would travel to Dingle and a safe haven. The plans were all in place and ready to go, but Marie Antoinette refused to leave without her husband, the King. But for her change of mind, those gallant and chivalrous Kerrymen could have changed the course of European history. The guillotine would have been deprived of its most famous client. Dingle could have had a royal family, and, who knows, we might all have been reared to eat cake instead of bread.

Anyway, back to the convent tunnel. On the day of our First Communion we had the once-in-a-lifetime chance of visiting the tunnel. After receiving the Sacrament we were ushered importantly inside the church sanctuary, through the nuns' oratory and into the tunnel for breakfast in the convent. It was an opportunity to view the secret areas of the convent which we had never seen before and would never see again. Between keeping an eye out for the ghost of a French queen and getting used to the strange environment, none of us could remember much about the inside of the tunnel afterwards.

As we exited at the convent end, our first sight was of a smiling, radiant and unusually happy Sister Evangelist. Then she did the unforgivable. Before any of our parents had an opportunity of getting near, this tall figure of fear stole the first kiss from each of us. The kiss from a new communicant was considered special and powerful. It was surely an unpardonable abuse of position and privilege by Sister Evangelist to plunder it.

The breakfast was memorable for the taste of the nuns' home-made apple jam, a speciality of Sister Bernadette's. She was a lovely woman, but in the segregated system of the convent she was, for some reason, treated as a sort of inferior or lesser being. It was hinted in the town that the dowry she brought with her was inadequate or some such. Whatever the view of her in the convent, the children and the townspeople loved her. Sister Bernadette treated us royally.

The rest of the day was great. We toured all the relations, showing off our finery and being congratulated and praised, right, left and centre. I received a 'lorry wheel' from my grandfather, Seán the Grove. A lorry wheel was a half-crown coin, worth two shillings and sixpence in old money, nowadays about 15 cent, but in those times it was a significant amount. The half-crowns were beautiful silver coins, impressive, with a mighty horse on one face. Seán the Grove held them in high regard and they were very much his system of calibration and calculation of worth and progress in an unending variety of situations.

'I was down in Daneen the Barber's for a shave and haircut on Saturday night, and he collected a lorry wheel each from nine of us in the hour I was there.' This would be said in a tone of regret that this money was not being attracted in the direction of one of his own businesses.

'I have two lorry wheels put aside for every Honour you get in your

Intermediate examination,' he told me. Given such practical encouragement, study took on a new focus and relevance. I think I collected twenty-six lorry wheels over two Intercerts. Maybe that was why I repeated. Certainly it was an early experience of creating a bond between school and commerce.

On my return from school each day there would be close questioning by my grandparents as to what I had learned. Granduncle Jim, who was blind, lived with my grandparents. In my early days at primary school, Jim would listen to me recite my addition and multiplication tables and he would give me a little spelling test each day, usually managing to catch me out with a tricky one. The last word he ever asked me to spell was 'enough'. When I got it right, he said, 'I think you know *enough* about spelling now.' Jim was full of little cautionary rhymes and advice.

'April and May keep away from the say (sea),

June and July swim 'til you die.'

The only thing that ever upset or worried him in his dark world was a gusting, gale force wind, which, no doubt, left him feeling helpless as it shrieked and whistled through the house. But he had the advantage of us regarding lightning; he did not see it and did not worry about it. He took the time once to allay my fears about thunder and lightning. 'Count slowly from 100 to 104,' he advised. 'That's how long it takes sound to travel one mile. If you start counting from the time you see the lightning, up to the first sound of thunder, you can tell how far away the lightning is. The thunder is only the sound of the lightning you saw a while ago; it might rumble and shake the house, but it can't hurt you.' I never forgot that lesson, and even now my mind automatically begins to count at the first lightning flash.

Having finished my stint with the nuns, I made the big move to the Christian Brothers' school. After three years of climbing up to the convent each morning with Pat Neligan, it was a major change to just walk out the door, cross the street and up the Barrack Height to the Brothers, arriving at school within two minutes. That first day seemed so strange. We were allocated the classroom just inside the door and we sat there nervously and tentatively, unsure what to expect. It was our first time in an all-male class; Celeste O'Keeffe, Geraldine Smith, Ursula Walsh, Rosemary Ryle and the other girls were left behind at the convent. To tell the truth, we were a bit lost and quiet without them. Two sides of the room were composed of partitions – the bottom half wood and the top glass – which separated us from the other classrooms, but could be pulled back to make one big room for some important school event like a concert or a religious ceremony. I was fascinated by the collection of stuffed birds on the window ledges of a third wall; it included a cuckoo and a lapwing. I had never seen a cuckoo previously, nor, despite hearing its distinctive call many times, have I seen one since.

The schoolyard was an unrelieved concrete affair surrounded by high walls. The Brothers maintained strict supervision at breaktimes, patrolling the yard at an almost military pace, keeping step and swinging their arms. The only area that fell outside their visual range was at the far end of the yard, which housed the toilets and the bicycle shed. This was a gathering place for the older lads. Inevitably, any disputes were sorted out there. The fights tended to be quick; by the time three or four blows had been exchanged, the roars of the crowd would have alerted the Brothers. The combatants would be hauled off each other and could expect a few whacks of the *leathar* for their pains. Beside the bike shed was where the tough men smoked their Woodbines; I'm told that on one memorable day, someone produced a copy of the *Daily Sketch* containing a picture of a bare-breasted woman. Unfortunately, us young lads never even got a whiff of it. Not fair!

At one stage the Brothers decided to introduce some form of Physical Education into the school. They invited a local army man to take us in hand. He put us through a regime of squats and press-ups and running on the spot, with a bit of marching thrown in for good measure. He wasn't very strict, and as soon as we felt too tired for any more exertion, we were allowed drop out. The last man standing became the hero of the day, and then it was all over. We thought the whole thing was hilarious. The arrangement didn't last long and we happily went back to chasing and kicking ball.

Needless to say, our religious education was not neglected. Apart from the ritual prayers at the opening and closing of each school day, there wasn't a month in the year in which we did not observe some saint's feast day, holy day or other significant religious event. The class crib was taken down after the Feast of the Epiphany on 6 January; on 1 February we sang out the praises of Saint Brigid, and shortly afterwards we were reminded of our mortality as the Brother intoned 'Dust thou art and into dust thou shalt return' while making the Sign of the Cross on our foreheads with the ashes from last year's blessed palms. Saint Patrick was the main man in March, but vacated his position for the solemn celebration of the ceremonies of Holy Week and Easter. May was the month of Mary and every classroom had a little altar where her statue would be laid on blue satin and surrounded by vases of bluebells. We sang the popular anthem to the Queen of the May every morning before class, 'Oh Mary, we crown thee with blossoms today ...' and were encouraged to attend Benediction in the evening. The blue of Mary gave way to the red of the Sacred Heart in June, but somehow it wasn't as popular. Before we were let off for our holidays in July we were warned that although we were on holidays from school, we were not on holidays from our religion.

'Make sure to get regular Confession and Communion. Don't miss Mass, and avoid occasions of sin.'

Occasions of sin? We should have been so lucky!

November was the month of the Holy Souls, when we were in and out of the church like yo-yos, trying to gain as many indulgences as possible for the possibly-not-yet-redeemed souls of our dead relatives. Then it was time for Advent and Christmas again. We learned the lives of the saints off by heart – those who had come to particularly gruesome ends were the most popular. We were told how Saint Brigid's cloak had miraculously stretched to cover half of Kildare, but oddly enough, the fact that Patrick, the man who had converted us all, was a Brit didn't get much coverage. Eugenio Pacelli, Pius XII, was Pope at the time and there was a very positive spin put on him. No mention of his dubious record with regard to Fascism. Our Catholicism was confirmed and reinforced day in and day out.

I soon found out that the Christian Brothers were a different kettle of fish altogether from the nuns in the convent school. It would be true to say that there was no stage during my primary schooldays when my relationship with them could be described as easy.

That first year I shared a desk with a lad called Paudie. He was the nicest of young fellows, quiet, but friendly and popular; his mother had died when he was young. Paudie never caused or created trouble. At some stage during the first term the Brother accused him of spilling ink on the wooden floor. Paudie answered honestly that he had not. The Brother, we called him Blackie, was not having any of it and demanded that he admit the fact. Eventually, with Blackie shouting into his face and the leather being brought down like a thunderclap inches from his ear, he was frightened into saying he did. Probably our first experience of intimidatory interrogation and the unreliability of confessions.

Blackie was youngish, low-sized, well-built, and with tight, black, crew-cutted hair. A hard man, he went for a swim in Slaudeen every day of the year. He had a nasty streak in him and was in the habit of maintaining our attention by catching us by the short hairs just above the temple. In second class we were still in short trousers, and when sitting in the old, oak, two-seater school desks, our pale white skin showed from the tops of our stockings at the knee up to the reddened, wind-galled bit at the legs of our short trousers. As Blackie strolled up or down the room between the rows of desks he would suddenly dive and grab one of us by the bare skin of our thighs, pinching between his fingertips and the heel of his hand with all his strength, until the quavering 'Please, sir' from his eight-year-old victim won respite and he let go, convinced of his control and superiority and leaving the marks of his nails on the blood-drained flesh. We were afraid of him, and when he turned around to the rest of us and laughed at the rising tears of our classmate, we laughed as well, disloyal and cowardly as we were.

Blackie was not satisfied with the regulation 'leather' issued to the rest of the Brothers, he had one made to his own specifications by a cobbler. It had a criss-cross design indented into the leather, which resulted in raised surfaces and left a curious pattern on our palms after he belted us. Sometimes he would stand in front of the class and practice how quickly he could draw the leather from his tunic, like a gunslinger of the Wild West. At other times he would swish and swathe it through the air like a Samurai with his sword. There was always order in Blackie's class, but he was not much of a teacher. All my memories of him are negative.

Brother Gannon, who had charge of the fifth and sixth classes, was another man for beating it into us. He used a cylindrical piece of solid wood, about the same length but double the thickness of a drumstick. Making a fist of his hand, but with the second joint of his middle finger sticking out, he would crack people on the back of the skull with the hinged bone. It was excruciatingly painful. Luckily I managed to avoid coming under his scrutiny and, in general, escaped his worst excesses. Gannon was different from Blackie, however, in that he did have a wider and more progressive view of education and he did make a genuine attempt to broaden our horizons. He maintained a class library of 'Boys' Classics' books, which held me spellbound. It was there I read *White Fang, The Swiss Family Robinson* and *Coral Island*. I never wanted them to come to an end and would have liked each to be another thousand pages long.

※　　※　　※

From the time I first learned to make out the words on a printed page, books held a fascination for me. In my grandmother's house there was an old ragged book entitled *Strange as it Seems*. It was full of remarkable facts and strange trivia, some of which continue to take up space in my memory bank. For instance, do you know the one and only word in the English language with three consecutive sets of double letters? Well, I do! My grandmother also had an old – a *very* old – Pears Encyclopaedia, which was well used by several generations. It was A5 in size, with the most compressed print imaginable, and illustrated mostly by line drawings. One showed Watts' steam engine in exploded detail. The few photographs included a distant shot of the Pyramids. It entirely captured my imagination.

The first real storybook that I bought, read and that was mine alone was *Black Beauty*. It was a hardback, with a beautiful beige dust cover, decorated with a drawing of a horse. I treasured that book. Beauty, Merrylegs, Ginger and the rest galloped through its 208 pages, the same number as the medium wave frequency of Radio Luxembourg, a coincidence that I discovered when I was a grown-up ten-year-old.

By the time I was eight years old my godmother, Aunty Phyl, had had enough of being bossed around by her mother, Bridgy Fitz. When the family thought she was in Dublin, spending a few days with her sister, Ita, she had actually decamped to London, from where she sent them a letter, telling them of the *fait accompli* and that she would be staying there. Phyl's only other trip abroad had been on a pilgrimage to Lourdes the previous year.

'Didn't I tell you, Bridge,' said Seán the Grove, 'there'd be no stop to her gallop after you sent her to that Lourdy place last year.'

Phyl put her years of training behind the counter in Dingle to good effect by picking up a job in Harrods. That year, 1955, she sent me a letter to say that she had posted my Christmas present, but that it was a surprise so she wouldn't spoil it by telling me what it was. I had never received a letter addressed to me before, and the notion of receiving a present in the post was almost too much. Every day I went to meet the postman, without any luck. 'Maybe tomorrow,' he'd say reassuringly. But tomorrow came and went. Christmas was getting closer. Then it was Christmas Eve and my parcel had still not arrived. Myko tried to console me.

'Christmas is the busiest time in the Post Office. Everyone is sending cards, letters and presents, Aunty Phyl's present probably got caught up in all of that. It will arrive after Christmas. Don't be too disappointed.'

But I was. By that time the present had taken on an importance even greater than Santa Claus himself. A few days after Christmas, Mr Kevane, the postman, delivered the package to my grandmother's for me. With all the packaging and wrapping, it seemed huge. It was as big as his letterbag and it was heavy. I tore off the paper, fought my way through the cardboard and finally pulled out … a book. My grandmother was dismissive, and delighted to be able to have a go at Aunty Phyl who had, as she saw it, treacherously deserted her for London.

'Is that all she sent, after all the talk?'

I barely heard her. *Odhams's Children's Encyclopaedia* had all of my attention. It was the nicest book I had ever seen. Inside, on the flyleaf, there was an inscription: *Christmas 1955, To Joseph from Aunty Phyl.* The illustrations, the photographs, the colour – it was breathtaking. I started turning the pages, discovering sections on Nature, Discoverers, Inventors, Space, History and much more. I don't think I took my head out of that book for a year. At least. It was there I saw flying foxes, met Alexander Fleming, found out how far away Pluto really was and learned of the fate of the wives of Henry the Eighth. The breadth of information in that one-volume encyclopaedia is probably the basis for an insatiable lifelong interest in everything around me.

To his credit also, Brother Gannon gave me my first introduction to classical music. In an unprecedented initiative, he set aside three-quarters of an hour every Friday afternoon in winter to let us hear the great composers. It required dragging the overly large and old-fashioned music centre from the monastery out to the classroom. There it was lifted on to a table top so we could hear the sound. The first classical piece I can remember Gannon explaining and introducing was Beethoven's *Moonlight Sonata*. He painted pictures from the music.

'Close your eyes and let the music in,' he instructed. 'Can you see a bright moonlit night? Listen to the sounds of the night.'

Those lessons were oases of calm in what was normally a frenzied theatre of terror. I have thought about it a lot since then, and cannot reconcile how a man could be so sensitive in matters of music and literature while at the same time being so sadistic in his dealings with his pupils.

Though I could never come to terms with, nor forgive, the violence he perpetrated on the class, I do have one other very tender recollection of Gannon. Jimmy Rua was the son of a well-known family in the town. He was, in local parlance, 'not the full shilling'. Jimmy was harmless and lovable and had a fixation with the local fife-and-drum bands. Learning to play the fife was clearly beyond his capacity, but he was forever plaguing people to give him a fife and to teach him. The townspeople looked out for him and minded him most admirably, but were generally impatient with him. One day he came and knocked on the classroom window, and knowing that Gannon was in charge of the school band, he asked him for a fife. We fully expected our irascible teacher to run Jimmy, but Gannon melted. To our amazement, he spoke to him for a while and then went into the monastery, returning with a most ornate, silver-coloured concert flute, which he gave to Jimmy. Despite Gannon's best efforts, Jimmy never did learn to play the instrument. But on that day, as he walked out of the monastery and down the Mall, he was a king. It was, to my mind, Gannon's finest hour.

As for Jimmy Rua, he died while in his thirties. He was always safe in the town, and it is a tribute to the people that he was accepted and integrated so well. Some time later, a play called *Them* was written by a man who had taught in Dingle, and some alleged that it was based on the character of Jimmy. The play was an exploration of the perception of the community in a small town through the eyes of a person of below-average intelligence and capability. It caused a certain upset to his family, though I thought it was written both sensitively and sympathetically. Not so long ago, I read a biopic of Van Morrison in the rock critic's column of a national newspaper, in which he was quoted as saying that he chose the name of his first great band, Them, from the title of a play that he had seen and that had moved him. No doubt the outsider theme would have attracted Van, but I doubt if he would ever have known of the tenuous connection with a silver concert flute.

While Brother Gannon was unnecessarily hard and violent, he was definitely committed to our education. But he could also be rude and insensitive. During my last year in primary school, Gannon met my mother, and when the conversation turned to me, no doubt she was unrestrained in her view of my potential. Gannon would not have liked that. He became, according to her, 'quite nasty'.

'How was that?' I asked her when she told me about it, more than a year later.

'Well, he said that I needn't expect that you would be receiving the gold fountain pen that he awarded each year to the top pupil in the Primary Certificate class.'

The net effect of Teresa's discussion with Gannon was that I, innocent of the reason behind it, was pressurised and chaperoned through my studies until I sat the Primary Certificate examination. I did better than I could ever have expected. Teresa had made her point and, yes, Gannon did have to present me with that fountain pen. It was then I found out that it was simply the nib, and not the whole pen, that was gold. Teresa was vindicated, but in fairness, Gannon was probably right; I was never going to do well the way I had been approaching my work. Maybe Gannon was smart enough to know that his comment to Teresa would be the catalyst.

But, when all was said and done, I was glad to finish primary level and looked forward to going upstairs to secondary school.

At the beginning of my own teaching career, corporal punishment was still the norm and I used it. We were actually shown how to administer it in a safe and, at that time, acceptable manner. In hindsight, it was unnecessary. No matter how humanely it was administered, it must have had the effect of dehumanising and perhaps brutalising children. More sinisterly, it also taught children that violence was the way to correct unacceptable behaviour. No doubt I held the view, as a young teacher, that I was better than the Blackies or Gannons because in my case corporal punishment was only ever used as a last resort. That is no more than a Jesuitical distinction. It was wrong. I was wrong. Violence breeds violence, and it is certainly something that I regret. By the time I had spent a number of years teaching, I had heard too often the protestations of older teachers who maintained that the past pupils who had received most corporal punishment were the ones quickest to buy them a drink in later life. It did not make sense. It could even be argued that in those cases buying a jar for the former teacher was a conditioned response, hearkening back to the classroom days when the pupil was required to curry favour from some brutes.

'Beat them up when they're young and they'll buy you drink when they're old.' Somehow I don't think that would be the formula of the good teacher!

Between Blackie and Gannon in third and fourth classes we had Brother Spollins. It may be hard to believe, but I was a teacher, with responsibility for a class of my own, before I realised that this man had been abusing pupils for years. Ignorance is no protection for innocence against the wiles of a child abuser in a position of authority. My sense of anger in recalling this man's abuse was overpowering and frustrating. Eventually, I made enquiries to establish if he was still teaching. I traced him to a school in the midlands and found that he was about to retire. I rang a teacher in the school, who had been in college at the same time as myself, and told him the story. On the basis that Spollins was about to retire, we left it at that. Maybe we were wrong.

From the 1850s the Christian Brothers had been educating the children of West Kerry and they gave generations an opportunity that they would otherwise never have had. Their outstanding work has too often been unfairly eclipsed by the terrible behaviour of a tiny number of their Order. It should never be used to diminish the immense contribution made by the rest of them to the development of modern Ireland. In Dingle there were many families whose children would never have been educated without the Brothers. Their legacy is one of pride, even if it has been tainted by those who abused their positions. Part of the problem, I believe, was that the whole system of recruitment and training of the Brothers was highly questionable. Taking young people, some only eleven years of a, away from their homes and into a novitiate to become members of a religious Order, before they ever had the experience of growing up and maturing, was unnatural. It was bound to have consequences for their personal development.

❖   ❖   ❖

After they and I had left Dingle, I never met Blackie or Spollins again. Brother Gannon I came across twice. In the year when I graduated from teacher training college, he was principal of a large primary school in a Leinster town. He had a number of vacancies in his school and called personally to the college to look up some potential candidates from among his most favoured past pupils. I received no call from him; as far as I know, he met all the others and quickly offered jobs to three of them. Whether it was that he did not think me good enough, did not remember me, or just considered me to be a potential dissident in his school, I will never know. It would have afforded me considerable satisfaction to have had the opportunity to refuse him; maybe he had figured that out.

A decade and a half later, I was in Dingle with my own children; we had rented a house on the Mall for a few weeks. Joan answered a knock on the door while I was out. It was Brother Gannon, who was himself on holidays and had heard we were in the locality. He would come back to see me. By the time he came back, I was well prepared.

'*Dia's Muire dhuit, Joe. Conas tá 'ann tú?*'

But I was having none of his friendliness, and had no intention of inviting him inside the house. '*Táim-se* fine, thank you,' I said politely but unsmilingly. 'What do you want?'

He got the message and we had parted in seconds.

I suppose it would have been easier to welcome him in and to indulge in a nostalgic pretence of the good old days. It is true that I was much less ill-used than most of the others. My memories are mainly of what I saw rather than what I personally endured. I also recognise that, as a pupil, I could be awkward and irritating, and I have some sympathy for any teacher put in charge of me. However, I am firmly of the view that in his application of corporal punishment – to which I did not have a principled objection at the time – Gannon had clearly crossed the line between use and abuse. In those days we expected teachers to use the stick; it wasn't its use *per se* that caused the resentment, but the unfairness and the cruelty with which it was administered. Physical punishment of pupils for their inability to learn was unconscionable, and those images from my schooldays of nice guys being hammered by Gannon rose up and made me angry all over again. I felt that a welcome from me would have been a betrayal of my former classmates and that it might reinforce and give retrospective approval to his cruelty. Perhaps my actions were inhospitable and cruel in themselves, but there was nothing else I could comfortably and honestly do.

'You look a bit better, Uncle John. Did the doctor say anything about your improving?'

This was a lie, and it was also a stupid question to put to someone as acquainted with dying and as experienced in undertaking as my uncle Foxy. Wasn't he the one who had shown me how to line and prepare a coffin? How many funerals did we attend together? Hadn't Pádraig Lynch, the sacristan, let us into the church mortuary in the dead of night to replace a broken coffin handle so that it wouldn't break under the strain of the ropes lowering it into the grave the next day. Lying there on the bed in the front room, above the shop on Main Street, big man though he was, Foxy John looked shrunken and worn out. The disease was winning, and he knew it. There was no point any more in asking about the latest blood count.

He turned towards me with his wry smile and his trademark grimacing squint, born out of short-sightedness.

'Boyeen, I've discharged all my responsibilities. My accoutrements are packed and I'm ready to go.'

My best attempt at a response was a pretty inane remark about how the Moriartys tended to make a bit of a drama about dying. He gave a tired chuckle. We said very little more after that. We shook hands.

'I'll be fine,' he said.

I couldn't face going in to Hanora. As I went out, I saw Foxy's nephew, Donal, in the bar pulling a pint. I just shook my head at him.

Going down Main Street to the christening party of Seán, the child of my cousin Fergus Flaherty and his wife, Angela, there were tears in my eyes. Inevitably, my mind was filled with all the familiar clichés around births and deaths. One coming and one going. The Lord giveth and the Lord taketh away, and all the rest.

How to say goodbye to Uncle John without mentioning death,

though we both knew he was near the end, had occupied my mind throughout the journey down to Dingle on what was certain to be the last time I would see him alive. Softie that he was, despite his reputation as a hard-nosed businessman, he had made it easy on me.

Foxy John died a short time after that. It's a strange thing about the Moriartys, they never mind too much about dying, but they hate growing old. My mother, Teresa, takes the concealment of her age to extraordinary lengths. I have never known her to celebrate her birthday and she quite simply refuses to discuss her age, so much so that none of us knows either her age or the date of her birth.

Foxy's was the type of business to be found in most Irish towns of the period. To the left, inside the door, was the public bar, with a hardware counter to the right. His sister-in-law, Betty, was in charge here and highly efficient she was. But the real action was behind in the yard. Here, there was a long store for furniture, mainly beds and wardrobes, but also some dressing tables and chairs. Wallpaper and paints were housed in another area, along with a selection of lamps and lampshades. The coffins were kept above the furniture store, in a suitably dark and quiet area that would give you the shivers every time you walked into it. Across the yard was the holding area for the bicycles and mopeds, and down at the very end a workshop where Florrie carried out repairs and Paddy made the gates. It was a thriving business, strategically situated with its front entrance on Main Street and the back gate on Green Street. It was not huge in area, but every square foot paid its way. It is impossible to categorise Foxy's business – whatever people needed, he sold.

So, in addition to the above, he also sold ropes to the fishermen and seed and plants to the farmers. He had a genuine liking for and interest in his customers, and was very loyal to them in his way.

Foxy John had shown me the tricks of the trade; had taught me about money and business and how to deal with people. There were constant words of advice: 'Always mind the customers and value their custom. Remember who's putting the clothes on your back.'

From him I learned the importance of a hickory handle on a hatchet or hammer, the difference between a poor quality mattress and the Quality Odearest product that he stocked, and why his cabbage plants and seed were so superior to all others in West Kerry that you'd have to wonder about anyone who purchased anywhere else! He showed me how to pull a perfect pint, taught me to tap a barrel, and let me in on the finer points of the undertaker's trade. And he had a gentle way of communicating his disappointment when I made a mistake. It was a marvellous technique of correcting without blaming so that your confidence remained intact.

I remember a woman coming in to buy an electric kettle. At the time we didn't sell electric kettles in Foxy's and I was about to send her further afield when he intervened.

'We're just out of them at the moment, Ma'am. I heard there's new ones on the market and we are changing brands so we can have the most up to date. Only the best. Could you call in on Saturday? I'll have one for you then.'

This was said in his most sharing, confidential voice – a real Sergeant Bilko job. The woman had hardly pulled the door of the shop behind her before he was on the phone to Kelleher's, ordering a dozen of the newest and best electric kettles. Not only did the satisfied customer have her kettle on Saturday, but she was able to tell her neighbours that she had one of the latest models, purchased in Foxy's.

'Never send a customer to another shop. They might get in the habit of going there. If we don't have it, order it, or say we're out of them, but don't send them to the opposition.'

Above: My grandparents, Sean the Grove and Bridgy Fitz, on their wedding day.

Left: Aunty Phyl, Uncle Foxy
John and Aunty Ita on the
beach in Jersey, 1959.
Below: Uncle Foxy John behind
the hardware counter.

(Photo courtesy of Aodán Ó Conchúir, Baile
an Fheirtéaraigh.)

Above: The remains of the house built by my
great-great-great grandfather, John O'Toole,
on Eanach Mheáin, in South Connemara.
Right: Grandfather Joe O'Toole.

Above: The pub in Galway which was run by my O'Toole grandparents in 1907. It was the birthplace of Pádraig Ó Conaire.

Below: Three of the Moriarty sisters – Teresa, Ita and Phyl; Molly is not pictured.

Above: The wedding of my parents, Myko O'Toole and Teresa Moriarty, Dublin, 1946.

Left: Early days.

Right: My First Communion, 1954, with my sister, Mary Sabrina.

Above: Sullen me at Doonshean with Teresa, Aunty Phyl and Aunty Ita.

Below: With my sister, Mary Sabrina, outside the Mall house in Dingle *c.* 1954.

Above: Granduncle Jim, myself and Uncle Benny, with 'Little Nell'.
Left: Margaret Sullivan and Phyl Moriarty dressed up as Princess Elizabeth and Prince Philip for the 'Wran'.

Foxy was full of devilment too, and every day there was a bit of fun. Toos's mother was wanting a pickaxe handle for her husband. Foxy had only the one left and it had a bit of a bend in it. It was unusable really, but he couldn't resist a sale and didn't want her going to Latchford's for it.

'These are the brand new hickory handles from America.'

'But there's a bend in that one, Foxy.'

'Yes, they have a curve in them for extra strength,' said he, making a virtue of necessity and knowing well that Toos's father would be raging as soon as he saw it. And Foxy would get a lecture on being a typical townie who had never swung a pickaxe in his life. Had he any idea of the impossibility of using one without a straight handle? Did he know one end of it from the other?

And that was exactly what happened a few days later. Foxy listened benignly and started pulling a pint. As the complainant was running out of steam, Foxy landed a fine creamy pint in front of him. He had figured out that once the woman had taken the bent handle the sale was made, and by the time they came to return it he would have new ones in stock and would simply present a perfect replacement. No harm done and a sale kept.

'Why don't you drink that and not be giving out? I suppose I'll have to give you one of the new ones just in, even though they are more costly. That's no bad deal for you: a free pint, a new handle – I won't ask for the other one back – and not a shilling in it for me.'

End of argument. You couldn't fight with him, and the customers knew it.

Of all the aspects of Foxy's business, buying and selling wool was the trickiest and most challenging. It was commodities broking at a time when that expression would have meant nothing to any of us.

Sheep were important to the local farmers. Most of them had very small holdings, but they had commonage rights on the hills and that was where the sheep were kept. They would be brought down regularly during the course of the year for dipping, lambing and then, a bit later on, for shearing. The wool money was vital to the family finances; they depended on it. The farmers kept an eye on fluctuations in wool prices and, naturally enough, they tried to time the shearing and selling to get the best possible price. Foxy would purchase the wool from the farmers and store it over a period of a few months, until his wool-store was full. This required a sizeable outlay of money for the purchase, and no return until it was sold. Market fluctuations made it a very high-risk business and you had to suffer abuse from small farmers who complained if they heard that we were giving a higher price this week than we had given them the previous month.

'Jack Tomás told me you're paying one and six a pound for wool. One and four pence was all you gave me!'

Jack Tomás was a great friend of Foxy's, but a great man to stir it up as well.

'It's just that the market price has gone up,' explained Foxy.

'Market price, my arse. I'll go to Joe Curran's the next time.'

'Away with you, boy, if you can do any better.'

Foxy would hate saying that, but he would never give them the satisfaction of thinking that he was depending on them. Anyway, he had a full year to win them back. Eventually he settled on a strategy. No money would be paid out until Foxy had reached an agreement with the buyers at the woollen mills on the price at which he could sell it on. So, no matter when the wool was bought, no cash changed hands until the end of the season – although there might be a bit of an advance for valued customers. Everyone was happy with this arrangement. They each got the same. True communism! More importantly, Foxy's margin was secured against the market.

All of this high finance stuff made very little difference to me; I was at the dirty end of the wool operation. My job was to check the wool from the seller before we bought it. Goods Inwards, that was me. Now, let me advise you here to immediately forget all those images of nice, fluffy wool that you may have acquired from various advertisements. Ditto with sparkling white little lambs gambolling about in their pristine fleeces. Wool is filthy. It is smelly and oily. As well as 'ordinary dirt', it is full of sheepshit, briars, thorns and the dreaded bloodsucking *sciortáins* (ticks). Every time you drove a hand into the wool you could expect a briar around the arm, a thorn under your fingernail, or the squish of the soft marbles of sheep shit. Nor would it be uncommon to find a few small stones in the middle of things.

'Jesus, how would they get in there?' you might ask innocently.

The seller would shake his head at the mystery of it all and mutter, 'It must be that young fellow helping me. He's useless. I'll kick his arse when I go home.'

By pointing out the attempted deceit without an accusation, you had won a small victory. You were in control.

So after a day of it – dragging, searching, feeling and sorting the wool – you ended up oily, dirty, scratched and with a few *sciortáins* sucking blood from the most private and sensitive parts of the anatomy. You couldn't even ask your mother to help pick them off! By the time I was in my mid-teens I hated the sight of wool.

Another tricky part of my job was to explain to farmers why the wool had to be sorted into fleece and loose scraps, telling them that the loose stuff made a lower price. The fleece had to be free from tears and nips that reduced its value. It had to be a complete and unbroken piece. Of course, they knew this very well, but every year they argued. It was psychological warfare and you lived or died by your gut. The biggest danger was the farmer in a hurry.

'I have no time, boyeen. Just throw that up on the scales and see what I'm owed.'

If you fell for this one you would be no relation of Foxy John's. The greater the hurry of the seller, the more you could be sure that there would be a problem. So, no matter what the professed hurry, you had to open up the bags to sort it and check it.

Then came the weighing. Counterweights on the balance were slid across until the arm of the scale balanced precisely. Too much counterweight and the arm banged against the bottom of the gauge; too little and it rattled the top. The weigh platform of the scales had been extended to take the large wool packs, so there was a big area to watch. While you were trying to get a precise reading, you had to make sure that the seller was not casually resting a knee against the scale.

If you suspected trickery, the drill was to say something like, 'We'll just stand back from it a minute, to make sure it is steady on the scales and that we are not doing you out of money.'

Storing the wool was also critical. The air had to circulate through it; otherwise it would begin to overheat dangerously.

The big day came when the buyer arrived and we started packing the wool into sacking that was then stitched up into huge, slightly rounded cubes, before loading onto his truck. Need I say that we employed every trick we had learned from the sheep-farmers to put loose stuff in with the fleece and to conceal any small tears. It was an object lesson in pulling the wool over people's eyes, and no doubt the origin of the saying.

Working with Foxy was non-stop learning; there was some new lesson every day, either from him or from Paddy Sullivan or Florrie

Donoghue. He was an entrepreneur long before the word became familiar to us; he was progressive and forward-thinking, always looking for opportunities and ready to try things. He never stopped testing the market, constantly on the lookout for a gap that he could profitably fill. He installed a welding plant when they were extremely rare in our part of the world. In no time that business was paying for itself through the production and sale of field and garden gates. Paddy Sullivan, from up beside the Holy Stone, was the welder, and he was a genius at his craft. You would hear Paddy before you saw him, because he always sang or whistled while he worked.

'Come, Mister Tallyman, tally me banana. Daylight come an' me wanna go home.'

He was perpetually good-humoured.

'Do you know the happiest time of the week?' he asked me once, and then provided the answer. 'Five minutes to six on a Saturday evening.' This was the era of the six-day working week.

Paddy was dapper and outgoing, and his Saturday night ritual was sacred. A pint or two after work, home for a bite to eat, a quick bath and then out again for the night. Eventually he emigrated to the US, where he married a West Kerry woman. But some years later he returned and set up his own welding business.

Welding was the one thing I was not allowed do. It was considered too dangerous, and I firmly believed that if you looked directly at the welding flash you could permanently damage your eyes. But it was a great spectacle to watch from a safe distance. The drone of the welder, the crack of the contact and the hot blue flash created a real *son et lumière*, which filled the yard on a dark winter's evening.

As people became wealthier and grew tired of the humble bicycle, Foxy negotiated the agency for NSU Quickly mopeds and small motorcycles. They became very popular and were a significant source of income. Conversely, as the tourism industry began to develop, Foxy's became the first bike-hire depot in West Kerry. His slogan, 'Foxy John's for the best Raleigh hire bikes in Dingle', might not win any marketing awards for creativity, but it seemed to make its impact, one way or another, on every tourist who came into the town. Right through the season, from Whit to September, there was a constant demand for his bikes. He loved making money and was good at it, but I got the impression that starting new lines of business and moving into new services was what really gave him the mighty buzz.

◈　◈　◈

When I was in my early teens, Foxy showed me his account books. It was a defining experience. The huge ledgers with their heavy leather covers and the thumbnail indented letters of the alphabet were neatly kept, with debtors listed in alphabetical order. There was line after line of handwritten information: the year, the month, the date, the item and the price: 1957, June 22, to one pair shears £1 7s 6d.

What left a lifelong impression on me was the amount of money outstanding to Uncle John. Here was a man who had the reputation of being the hardest-nosed businessman in the town and his books showed that he was owed money by half the hopeless cases in Dingle. Truly thousands of pounds of debt, much of it dating back many years. Even to my inexperienced eyes, a significant portion of it was undoubtedly irrecoverable. I asked him for an explanation.

'They're good and honest people,' he said. 'None of them are crooks. Some of them have fallen on bad times. They'll pay when they can. Some might never be able to pay, but sure that won't break us!'

A few would come in after the fair day. 'I'll pay a few pounds off what I owe you, John.' They would, but they would never quite catch up.

'Sometimes I charge a bit extra to people who can afford it,' he said. This was true. All of the stock in Foxy's shop was marked in a code of his own devising, rather than with a regular price tag. The code gave him two pieces of information: the amount he had paid the wholesaler for the item and the price he required to make a profit. The fact that no customer knew or understood the code gave him great leeway. The wealthier you were – and he would know – the more you were charged. Some customers were hagglers who always insisted on getting something off the asking price. No problem. Foxy would simply add on a few pence or shillings to the asking price in order to be able to do the decent thing and satisfy the customer by seeming to reduce the price, while at the same time maintaining his profit margin.

Less well-off people tended to do best. It was a sort of benevolent, patronising capitalism and it seemed to work. He might occasionally be cornered and challenged about a price, but he was never caught. He thrived on these situations. A knowing nod or wink, plus the comment, 'Well, to tell you nothing but the truth and between ourselves, the one you got was better quality. There were a few seconds left, if you know what I mean.' Or, 'To tell you the truth, the new ones just arrived in this morning, Jack got the last one at the old price.'

While he would argue over a halfpenny in the shop, Foxy John was a great man to spend when he went out. He loved to travel and over the years availed of any opportunity to go abroad. Jersey, Rome and Greece were some of his destinations. A few bets on the horses appealed to him, but he would have to face a bit of bantering from his wife, Hanora, when he lost money through gambling.

'He thinks he's smarter than the bookies, you know. Sure they are only laughing at him, my eejit, they love to see him coming,' she would say.

When Foxy wanted to place a bet he would wait until Hanora was out the back with a customer before ringing the bookie in Tralee. Sometimes he would forget to check the post and if the bill arrived from the bookie he would have to endure further good-natured scolding from his wife. On the plus side, Hanora was a tremendous cook and served up the most spectacular of foods. Bacon and scallops was a Hanora breakfast special. Foxy loved his food, and cute hoor that he was, always praised her cooking to the skies so that she would be continually encouraged to surpass herself. Hanora was no fool though, she knew well what was going on, but she humoured him.

One day, when he had gone racing to Killarney and I was in charge of the business, he arranged for me to be taught a little lesson. I was behind the hardware counter when Mikeen Long from Ventry came in to buy some rope. Mikeen was a character and I knew he should be watched carefully. He started measuring out the rope from its coil and counting it by the yard along the brass measure screwed along the edge of the counter. He was giving plenty of slack between each measure and was delighted with himself.

'Nine yards of reins,' he said. 'At two shillings a yard, that's eighteen shillings altogether.'

Nice try, Micheál, I was thinking to myself.

'No, we sell it by the weight, not the length,' says I, throwing it on the scales and fierce proud of myself at the thought that I was going to best him. 'That'll be one pound three and six.'

'Oh no, boyeen, Foxy always sells it to me by the yard. It's only to the fishermen he sells it by the weight. Look here, I have a receipt from the last time.'

The crowd in the shop was beginning to enjoy the duel. The lads across at the bar counter were quietly taking it all in. Embarrassed and bamboozled, I conceded. Mikeen paid me immediately. I knew by the glint in his eye that he had taken me. O'Toole was the loser and there was no chance of keeping it quiet. Foxy had it before he arrived into the kitchen.

'And I thought you were too clever to be caught by the likes of Mikeen Long. You've a bit to learn yet.'

He never let me forget that lost 5/6d and would wonder aloud if the youngsters of the day would ever survive in the world. It was the kind of mistake that I would not make too often. But the great Foxy himself was put in his place by a most delightful occurrence the following year. By that time the bike-hire business was booming. A great tourist attraction was to hire a bike for a day's cycle around Slea Head, through Ventry and Dunquin. On the way, the cyclists would pass Mikeen Long's pony-hire business at Ventry strand. Some of them stopped off there for a few hours and took a pony for a ride along mile after mile of the silver semicircle of sandy beach.

Mikeen felt it was a bit of a sin to have Foxy's bikes lying around idle while the tourists were out on the ponies, so he took to hiring them out for the couple of hours. He made a nice few shillings for many months before Foxy heard about it. At least it gave me ammunition against him. It gave me great pleasure to hit Foxy with one of Seán the Grove's lines when two hard men clashed: 'Diamond cut diamond and he's a rough diamond.'

As for Mikeen, he was not the least bit embarrassed and used to boast to Foxy about his ingenuity.

Tapping a barrel of Guinness was a challenging undertaking. The single, solid smack of the mallet, hammering home the silver tap through the bung of the wooden Guinness keg, reflected both expertise and experience. It was an art in itself, as I knew to my cost from my early botched efforts behind the bar of Foxy John's pub.

Strike too hard and the tap went in so far that it did not operate; strike too gently and porter spouted all over the shop with the pressure of a fire hose. The task was not made any easier by the fact that there was always an eagerly expectant audience when the young fellow was in sole charge of the shop.

In those days, a drinker kept the same glass all evening, handing it back to be refilled as required. Oh, the terror of being handed an almost empty pint glass and being asked to put a 'meejum' (medium) into it!! The medium was a measure half way between a half pint and a pint. It has not stood the test of time, though in Dingle it is still used as a colloquialism for a half pint. Drinking mediums was not what 'real men' did in those days. In fact it would very quickly lead to a nick-name such as 'Matt the meejum' if one got the reputation of drinking them.

So, on the odd occasion when hardened drinkers wanted to drink a meejum, they would hand me their almost empty glass, fully expecting to receive a full pint in return, even though they were only asking for and paying for the equivalent of about three-quarters of a pint.

It was psychological warfare as the glaring, challenging eyes of the customer watched the glass being filled, willing it to the brim. If the glass was not filled to the brim, you were the worst in the world with the customer. If it was filled, you were sure of a lecture from Foxy about being fooled and giving away the profit. Eventually, the compromise would be a not quite full glass of Guinness, with a much larger than usual collar or head on it. *An té nach bhfuil láidir ní folair dó bheith glic.*

We grew up under the influence of these characters, the 'rough diamonds' of Seán the Grove's description. Every street and village had them. Crystallised into reality by the cultural weight of countless generations and cut and shaped by all the facets of the daily grind. They made us what we were.

＊　＊　＊

Foxy's legacy remains. Work hard but leave space for enjoyment. Be as hard as nails doing business but be generous with people. Have pride in yourself but don't be proud. Make money but don't be tight. Like Foxy, the traders and business people in Dingle at that time were motivated as much by the challenge of survival and success as they were by the desire to make a profit. But they also understood the importance of social capital and were prepared to give something back to the community. So they would give time to the Race Committee or the Regatta and other voluntary groups. It is a tradition that is dying fast nowadays.

＊　＊　＊

Foxy John prided himself on having friends among both rich and poor and never differentiating between them. Once I heard him say, '*Beidh gach prionnsa agus bacach I gCorca Dhuibhne ag' mo shochraid.*' (Every prince and beggar in West Kerry will be at my funeral.) And they were.

On the day of his funeral, six of us nephews – three on each side, in pairs – shouldered the coffin into Milltown cemetery, about a mile west of Dingle. We were muttering to each other the usual banalities of pall-bearers: 'Just because I'm the tallest I shouldn't have to carry most of the weight.' 'If your shoulder is too low for the coffin take some of the weight with the heel of your hand.' 'Jesus, Foxy! there's still some weight in you, boy.' 'Link your partner around his waist rather than his shoulder or the coffin will leave your shoulder blade black and blue.'

Ahead of us I could see one person standing alone at the open grave. As we got nearer I recognised the silver hair and slouched figure of that colossus of Kerry football, Paddy Bawn Brosnan. The

Bawn used to visit Foxy every single day. He usually brought a bit of the very best fish – crab claws, scallops or lobster. They talked about everything, especially horses and fishing, but only very rarely about football. When Paddy was having a drink it was always in the kitchen with the family, never in the bar. They were the best of friends. At the graveside Paddy was in tears. We shared a loss. A chapter of my life had ended.

SUMMERS IN
GALWAY

Because we lived in Dingle among the Moriartys, it was only natural that the Moriarty side of the family had a greater influence on our rearing than the O'Toole side. Myko, however, took pains to ensure that the Galway roots and relations were an integral part of my life.

During my growing years I spent weeks every summer in my Granny's in Lettermore. It was something to look forward to with pleasure and excitement. Heading off with Myko, just the two of us in the Ford Anglia, with me in the front seat, was a great adventure. Two hundred miles was a long journey. Early to bed the night before; up before seven o'clock the following morning; a big bowl of steaming porridge waiting for me on the table, cases in the car. Myko would be looking at the watch.

'We should be on the road before the half-seven bus.'

Teresa saw us off with her customary caution: 'Drive carefully, Myko.'

'We'll cut the corners and skim the hedges keeping into our own side.'

Myko always gave that advice to anyone taking the Dingle–Tralee road.

Then it was off out the main road while most of Dingle was asleep, except for Benny Malone waiting for the bus, or Babs Flaherty heading from Cooleen down towards the pier.

'I hope you filled yourself up, because there will be no stopping now until we reach Galway,' Myko would say. But there were two Galways. There was Lettermore and then there was the rest of the county.

In through Tralee we progressed, with a beep of the horn and a wave to any garda leaving the station or on the beat, and a running commentary about any of the citizens Myko might see.

'There's Joe Mulchinoch on his way in to open up McCowen's shop.'

Usually there was a quick stop at Pádraig Kennelly's in Ashe Street to drop in some returned Confirmation photographs. Pádraig was a professional photographer. In fact, his qualification was as a pharmacist, but he got bored with that and started into photography with great success. As well as Press shots, he also did the bread-and-butter work of Confirmations and dress dances and First Communions. He had tremendous energy and he travelled the county. When Mossie Moore, the murder victim whose story was the basis for *The Field*, was missing and the gardaí were looking for a photograph to display, it was Pádraig who found one in his archives. It finished up being enlarged on every shop window in North Kerry.

When he covered Dingle functions, he needed a place to have the photographic proofs displayed for those who wished to purchase them. That was how Teresa came to act as agent for Pádraig in Dingle. She would display the photos in the shop and take orders and handle the money. There were always arguments about whether the photo was the one ordered and people were forever ordering without paying and then not collecting. It was real trouble.

But Pádraig, he was a real character. Always with a new idea or a new project.

'Pádraig is talking about starting a newspaper,' says Myko with a chuckle. 'Another one of his notions.'

But Myko might have held his chuckle because some years later Pádraig did eventually publish a thriving and successful local newspaper that went from strength to strength, and today *Kerry's Eye* is an established part of the week in Kerry.

Then we were on the Listowel Road. We reached Tarbert and the mighty Shannon. Myko would point: 'That's County Clare across there.' Then I would listen in amazement as he told me about the flying boats – planes that could actually take off and land on water – which operated out of the harbour in Foynes because it was the most westerly location and the planes could start the Atlantic crossing with a full fuel load from there. Later on, the new airport was built on the Clare side at Rineanna (now Shannon). Then he would add the Hollywood connection: that Maureen O'Hara's husband was one of the chief pilots who landed flying boats at Foynes. Sure I knew very little about Maureen O'Hara except that she was a film star. And for good measure he would draw down the last scene in the film *Casablanca*. While Humphrey Bogart held the gun on the corrupt police chief, his true love, Ingrid Bergman, escaped on the last plane out. On her way to the USA.

'Do you know,' he would say, 'that plane probably refuelled at Rineanna Airport!'

Great story, Myko, but I wonder was the airport even built at that time?

Long before Mungret, the chimneys of the cement factory could be seen against the skyline. Did I know how cement was made, Myko would ask me, and go on to explain the process that turned lime and gypsum and other magical names into the stuff that I saw being mixed with sand and water and becoming the building blocks and walls of new houses and other buildings.

As we drove Limerick's long Dock Road, with its high buildings, he would remark, 'Aunty Sarah lives in Catherine Street, just two streets up and Aunty Han used to live here in Limerick as well ...'

Crossing the Shannon always prompted the story of Patrick Sarsfield and how he surprised the English military when his intelligence discovered that the password that night was his own name, and hence the famous greeting to the unfortunate sentry as Sarsfield and Galloping Hogan launched the attack: 'Sarsfield's the name and Sarsfield's the man.' That kept us busy until Bunratty, and as we passed the road down to Rineanna Airport, Myko would try to work out the difference in the Atlantic crossing-time of an ocean liner and an aeroplane. We wouldn't feel it to Ennis ...

As soon as we saw the sign, 'Welcome to Gort from Glynn's Hotel', Myko would pull in for a cup of tea and a sandwich, and even though we had completed only about two-thirds of our journey, we were already in County Galway. We had bridged between the two cultures. It was pretty grown-up to be having food in a hotel on my own with Daddy. He talked away.

'Ruairí O'Connor's mammy is from here. A place called Peterswell.'

I knew Ruairí's cousins because they came to Dingle sometimes. But their journey was a lot shorter than ours!

At that time there was a swing bridge at Béal a' Daingean, which was the entrance to Lettermore Island and only two miles from Granny's house. As I grew older, the symmetry of leaving An Daingean (Dingle) only to arrive, after travelling all those miles, at Béal a' Daingean (The Mouth of the Fort), struck me. The swing bridge opened many times daily to let the red-sailed Hookers pass up to Camus. For road-users it was the access to what was then the island of Lettermore. For me as a child, it was the high point of the two-hundred-mile journey from Dingle to my Granny's. The very thought of the bridge swinging open and the road moving was magical, and the tantalising expectation of seeing it in operation carried me expectantly for many a long mile.

My cousin, John Michael Jack, owned the pub on the island side of the bridge. It was notable for the fact that, as far as I know, it was the only Fine Gael voting house among my Galway O'Toole cousins at that time. The O'Tooles had always been staunchly Fianna Fáil. Many years later I attempted to find out why they had changed their colours. The story as told to me was no doubt less than objective; certainly from a very young age the concept of political 'spin'

impacted on us and it must also have informed the telling of this tale. It would appear that in the 1930s the then FF household lobbied on behalf of a family connection for appointment as some local functionary. As I recall, it was something to do with a local cemetery. It became a political matter. Dev's new government was in power and expected to deliver. It did not. The 'wrong' person got the job and since then the house had been very openly Fine Gael. But prior to the 'conversion', one of the sons of the house had married a woman in Louisburg, County Mayo, bringing with him his FF beliefs. It is ironic that his son, Martin J O'Toole, became a Fianna Fáil Senator and TD. He was a colleague of mine in Leinster House, where it was that I got to know him well. We calculated that we were third cousins. In our family that is close.

Those times holidaying with my Myko among his own people were wonderful. Being the oldest of the new generation of O'Tooles in Lettermore and older than any of the cousins – except for Max, but he was in Dublin – was a great passport and it made me the centre of attraction everywhere I went.

My father's brother, Uncle Jack, was a doctor. He had surgeries from Lettermore to Leenane and I got to know a huge slice of Connemara as we travelled to his appointments. Because of the size of the area he was constantly on the road. The car was packed with equipment, medicines and documentation. He acted as dentist as well as doctor so he also had to have all the necessary tackle for that part of the work, too.

Jack was one fast and impatient driver and the first person I ever heard shout, '*Fág an bealach*!' (Get out of the road), at farmers who might be driving cattle or sheep along the road when he was rushing to reach a surgery. On the other hand, it was easy to see that his patients respected and trusted him.

He expected his advice to be followed to the letter, and even though he would listen to a sick patient for as long as it took, and would take plenty of time on examination and diagnosing, he had no tolerance at all for any questioning of his diagnosis or prescription.

'Will you do what I tell you, *agus ná bí ag cur mo chuid ama amú.*'

His impatience was his driving force; he arrived and left everywhere like thunder and lightning. No matter how great the number waiting in the surgery, he would put the head down and get on with it. People with dental problems were lined up on one side, medical cases on the other. At that time the main dental work was extractions and Uncle Jack went at it with a will. As Peter, my first cousin, said, 'Christ! On a good day he'd fill a small galvanised bucket with teeth!' At a half-crown (2/6d) a time, it was a profitable sideline.

Jack was an entertainment. He would fly off the handle and argue passionately, with eyes flashing, but he never took offence for longer than it took him to cool down. And he was generous to a fault, no matter what the company. Even though they were lifelong close friends as well as brothers, there could never be two more different twins than Jack and Myko. When people gave out about Jack, Myko would advise them: 'Sure, don't mind him at all. Aren't you worse to be taking any notice of him?'

Uncle Jack was driven in every aspect of his life. In particular, this applied to politics. He was irreversibly Fianna Fáil and would brook no opposition. This was a real culture shock for me coming from the unwavering and unchallenged Fine Gael Faith of the Dingle Moriartys. Jack would dismiss James Dillon, the leader of Fine Gael, with the same contempt that Seán the Grove reserved for de Valera.

I was smart enough to keep my mouth shut, but it did create some internal turmoil for me in that it was the first time I came face to face with the possibility that maybe the certainties of life were not that certain really.

My father's eldest brother was Patrick, known as Patsy. He worked in the head office of Galway County Council. His wife, Darlie, was a primary schoolteacher from Sligo who taught in Lettermore. They later moved into Galway City and lived in Renmore. Patsy was a soft and gentle person, with a permanent twinkle in his eye and always the beginning of a smile on his face. Later in life he suffered a stroke, which left him with a slight drag on one side of his face. Even though he recovered, he died a relatively young man.

On our summer visits, Patsy, Jack and Myko would take me swimming with them in the evening time in Trawbawn, near Teeranea, across Lettermore bridge. Those were great outings and left me with a lasting love of the sea, which to this day is my main leisure-time focus.

Although Granny was still very much around at the time of my visits, the family home in Lettermore was really run by Aunty Lena. Married to Plunkett, the youngest of the O'Toole brothers, she was a most tolerant and quietly-spoken woman, probably a great asset when you are sharing a house with your mother-in-law. Lena was like a second mother to me in Lettermore; she addressed everyone as 'a ghrá,' (love), and nothing was ever too much trouble. She and Uncle Plunkett ran a general store, which meant that he was rarely able to accompany his brothers and myself on our swimming trips. The time constraints imposed by managing a shop was something that I well understood from home.

Plunkett was the O'Toole most like my Dingle relatives. His general store had to be diverse enough to meet the needs of an extensive but remote local population. It was no wonder that in later years he became very friendly with my uncle Foxy John; they operated similar types of business. It was always interesting to work with Plunkett, he was forever explaining the business and the customers to me. He added to the skills I had already learned from Foxy John, teaching me about petrol-serving and bacon-cutting. He was a busy person, forever impatient to get things done. He tended to have a somewhat expectant frown on his face and usually tried to look cross but had a great sense of humour, always ready to laugh and stretch the dimple on his face.

And it was just as well that he did. At some family gathering or other Foxy from Dingle and Plunkett from Lettermore got together. They had a lot to talk about. In the way things happen, it turned out that Plunkett was selling a hearse and Foxy was looking for a good second-hand estate car. Another couple of drinks, and in the most natural way in the world the deal was done; sight unseen, Foxy agreed to buy Plunkett's vehicle. Plunkett promised to take out the fiddly bits of chrome and the high floor so that it would not look too much like a vehicle employed in the transport of the dearly departed when Foxy was using it for furniture deliveries. Foxy didn't mind a slight resemblance; he would put the word out that things were so bad that he was reduced to buying a second-hand hearse to keep the show on the road. The two lads shook hands on the deal and agreed to meet in Limerick the following Sunday to do the switch. Foxy would have the cash and Plunkett the hearse and the paperwork.

Foxy got a lift to Limerick and brought Florrie with him to drive home. Plunkett and Peter drove down in the recently renovated hearse, with the intention of getting a bus back to Galway City. From there, Uncle Jack would drop them home to Lettermore. They rendez-voused in Cruise's Hotel, as arranged. Foxy went out with Plunkett to look at the estate. He was more than pleased with it. They had a drink to celebrate.

'I suppose I'd better pay you before we go.'

'That'd be a good idea, Foxy. Here, I'll do out a receipt.'

'Oh Christ, there's no need at all for a receipt,' says Foxy, pulling a large, loose wad of single pound notes out of his pocket. 'Here, Florrie, will you bring over the rest of that money for Plunkett.'

Florrie walks across the lobby with two very heavy-looking, bright-coloured cotton bank bags full of silver coin.

'It's all there, Plunkett. Betty counted it out just before we left. You won't be a penny short.'

'Jesus, Foxy, can't you give me a cheque?'

'What cheque, boy? Do you want everyone to know our business? I'm gathering that money for you all week. Take it now and nobody is a blind bit the wiser. Just between ourselves.'

'Well, fuck you, Foxy. I should have known you'd have some trick.'

What could Plunkett do except stuff the notes in his pockets, gather up the two heavy bags of coin and head off to the bus station, looking more like a bank robber than a businessman. He spent the journey trying to mind and hide the bags from greedy hands and prying eyes. His most embarrassing journey.

UPSTAIRS IN THE
MONASTERY

'So, who can tell me which State separates the Gulf of Mexico from the Atlantic Ocean?'

'Well done. Florida is correct.'

'Do you know, young O'Toole, the name of the famous holiday resort in Florida for wealthy people?'

'Is it Palm Beach, sir?'

'It is indeed. And some day you'll be there yourself, lying under the hot sun, eating oranges. And guess who'll be peeling those oranges?'

This last bit was said with a smile, a wink and a wagging finger, and we'd all laugh without knowing the reason why, or what it meant. I think it might have been a line from a film. It didn't matter. Tomo was in high good humour and, as usual, making the geography class live. He was a great man for the memorable phrase.

'The Italian lakes – Como and Garda – beautiful. Now, remember, that's the place for the honeymoon.'

'Cruising on the Rhine through the Black Forest; there's romance.'

We were only twelve years old and not long in secondary school. Romance and honeymoons were not really part of our argot, but we lived the dream and enjoyed it. Tomo was a great teacher and I always enjoyed his classes, but then I found secondary school much more interesting, principally because they were a far livelier bunch of teachers.

In Dingle the primary school was called 'The Monastery' and the secondary school was 'Upstairs in the Monastery'. The doors were right beside each other off the schoolyard. It was a great day when we took the door leading upstairs. As we climbed up, we could see our erstwhile primary school friends filing into their classrooms. We felt so superior to them now.

One of the big changes about secondary school was that we acquired new classmates. After coalescing into little groups of pals throughout primary, we now had to expand our horizons as we were joined by lads from all over the peninsula who would have attended primary in their own local villages, but had to come to Dingle for further education. Kennedy's bus collected pupils from east of Dingle, from Annascaul and Lispole. Brick's bus did the run from the west. In the beginning there were tensions. We envied the newcomers being brought to school by bus while we had to walk. They were more than a little apprehensive about settling into a strange school among the 'townies'. The lads from the west were all native Irish speakers, which added a further dimension to the new situation. For the first week or so we stayed in our established cliques, but the Brothers made sure that we shared desks with new classmates, and within a very short time the differences evaporated and friendships developed; friendships which in many cases still flourish.

After eight years of nuns and Brothers, we finally had some lay teachers. Two of them, Tomo and Ritchie, saw us through the whole period, while others came and went, including, for a short time, a lovely man called Seán Ó Mathúna. Ó Mathúna widened our horizons. He was humorous and a great lover of language and literature, and during the few years he was with us he certainly communicated that love to me. It was he who introduced us to what was later called 'creative writing'. He was very much a free spirit and probably did not relate to the strict regime enforced by the Brothers. Whatever the reason, he left. It was no surprise to me to find that years after he left Dingle his work was published both in English and *as Gaeilge*.

All our teaching was done through Irish. I can never remember speaking English to a teacher outside of the English class, and all our written work was *as Gaeilge*. It created some problems because, in the main, it was impossible to get up-to-date textbooks *as Gaeilge*. Consequently, we found ourselves, for instance, studying Latin through Irish from an English text! Similarly with geography, history and physics. Usually the teacher would give us a list of the core terminology in Irish and off we went. It was a very broad education. We travelled the world in those classrooms. The world was within our grasp and we saw it all courtesy of our imaginations, driven by creative teaching. It was a living, organic education.

◎　　◎　　◎

Compared to the humdrum existence we had at primary school, some unbelievable things happened in secondary. Corporal punishment was part of the regime, but it was rarely overused. And the teachers were now dealing with bigger lads. We were hardly a month in the school before there was this amazing incident where one of the students took a swing at Ritchie. The guy involved was not a delinquent, but just reacted when he believed Ritchie went too far. For us it was a bridge beyond our imagination. We just could not believe it.

The school was quite progressive and argument was very much valued and encouraged; we were always allowed put forward our viewpoints. Debating was part and parcel of school activities. It suited me and I loved the involvement. I made it to first sub. on the school's Irish-language debating team. In the Gael Linn competition, we were drawn against Coláiste Íde, a local Irish-speaking girls' secondary boarding school, and because someone dropped out, I was selected. I was delighted to be on the team, and delighted to get inside the hallowed cloisters of the legendary college. We had no doubt but that Coláiste Íde would be favourites. They took this competition very seriously and would be very well prepared. But our captain, Breandán MacGearailt, was a mighty debater, so we were not without hope. In high spirits, we headed off in Stevie Kelleher's minibus back to Burnham and Coláiste Íde. In fairness, *bhí fáilte mór romhainn* when we arrived. The *realpolitik* was brought home to us very quickly however, when it emerged that the impartial neutral adjudicator, a well-known Cork Gaeilgeoir, had been wined and dined all afternoon by the nuns of the college. No point in crying foul. On with the show.

The motion before the house was: *Gur féidir le náisiúin bheaga tionchar a bheith acu ar chúrsaí domhanda* (That small nations could have an influence in world affairs). We were to oppose the motion. In the main, the audience was composed of pupils of Coláiste Íde; my sister, Mary Sabrina, was one of them. We had no one to cheer us on. Every girl got a thunderous round of applause, while we got a polite ripple. Still, we did fine, we were pleased with ourselves and Breandán played a blinder. Then came the moment of truth. The adjudicator stood up to give his assessment. He told us that we had been brilliant; we had strong points of argument and we had presented them well and convincingly. However, surprise, surprise, we had been edged out of victory on the night by the girls.

All we could do was console ourselves with our belief that it was all a fix. We got a schoolboyish moment of vindication too when Breandán, in graciously accepting defeat and congratulating our opponents, managed very subtly to upstage the adjudicator by pointedly repeating and agreeing with his final sentence, except that Brendán repeated it in the correct, dative case. '*Bhaineamar an-taithneamh as an ndíospóiracht comh maith,*' said Breandán, stressing the 'n' before '*díospóiracht*', which had been omitted by the adjudicator. We loved that, even though nobody but us noticed. Still, it's tough being sixteen and defeated by girls in front of an audience of girls.

There was nothing for it after that but to head straight home. Breandán was furious, and with some justification. He had been superb, and should definitely have been awarded the prize for best individual. Still, it didn't hold him back and he went on to make a name for himself: he became Chair of Kerry Local Authority and published a number of books *as Gaeilge*.

It did us a lot of good on the way back to hear Ritchie offer a stream of abuse about the biased adjudicating and say that in his opinion we were clearly the best. That in itself was a moral victory, and would be some compensation in the discussion in school the following day. Ritchie was the teacher in charge of the debating team and he did not like being beaten either. That was the thing about him; he got passionately involved with the business at hand.

The school principal, Brother Lennon, introduced us to the Patrician Society and we met two nights a month. It was quite unique. The model was one of structured discussion, incorporating debate and argumentation. The themes were religious and we had to take sides on the issue of the evening. The five proofs of the existence of God kept us going for a month and I remember that the logic appealed to me enormously.

'Look at this watch. Imagine the complexities of making it. Could you ever believe that something so complicated just happened to fall into place together? That nobody made it? That all the bits and pieces fell into place by accident?'

'Of course not. It couldn't happen.'

'Remember then that the universe is many times more complex than a watch. There is no logic to thinking it just came into being by accident. There had to be a God to create it.'

'That's all very logical, but mustn't we also ask the question: who started God? Who made God?'

On it went. It's mere speculation as to whether or not it deepened the religious fervour of those of us who participated. I think not, but it certainly did sharpen our approach to argumentation and articulation.

I carried my taste for argument into the classroom. More than once I got carried away and got into trouble with teachers who, quite naturally, were tired of me and wanted to get on with the curriculum. Unfortunately, I didn't bring the same enthusiasm to homework and study, which I found a real drag. I enjoyed all subjects, although I did have extraordinary difficulty in coming to terms with geometry – not the theorems, but the applied questions that related to the theorems. As I would be sitting my Intermediate Certificate examinations the following year, Myko and Teresa felt that a few grinds now might be a good idea, to get me up to speed. Teresa employed the services of Miss Healy, a teacher in Coláiste Íde, who lived in the Spa Road. I was most unenthusiastic, but under pressure I agreed to go for a few grinds. I sneaked over to Miss Healy's, hoping that Pat Neligan would not see me. Grinds were an admission of failure, and very bad for the image. Thankfully, none of my classmates found out.

Miss Healy was a highly organised, no-nonsense, delightful woman. I liked her immediately. She took me for about six geometry lessons. By the end of lesson one, she had drawn me completely into it. I could see where I was going now, and by the end of lesson two she had cracked it for me. I found myself looking forward to our third session. By the end of my time with her she had me convinced that geometry was the most interesting subject on the syllabus, a view I held for the rest of my schooldays. It would be no exaggeration to state that in two hours Miss Healy impacted on my whole life. It is a truth about all great teachers that their influence on their pupils continues long after they have parted.

The monastery was a dominant building in the town. Made of red sandstone, it was surrounded by immaculately kept grounds. From the entrance gate on the Mall, the path stepped upwards along cascading lawns to the school. Madge Donoghue, the housekeeper, was a great favourite with both pupils and townspeople. She was a customer of ours and I regularly delivered groceries to her. There was an old-fashioned bell pull at the door, but it had not been in working order for years. One day I managed to repair it by connecting a length of wire from the bell to the pull. It was basic stuff, but Madge was forever grateful.

At the rear of the monastery was a tiny but beautiful churchyard, the final resting place of Brothers over many generations. It was a quiet spot, shaded by a number of yew trees, and the graves of the deceased were marked by rows of neat black crosses, with the names printed in white lettering. My grandmother, Bridgy Fitz, maintained proudly that she had two granduncles buried there and that they had worked with Edmund Ignatius Rice, the founder of the Christian Brothers. As far as I can recall, one was a Fitzgerald and the other a Donoghue.

One summer, Brother Lennon was trying to give a bit of holiday work to a few of the pupils and he asked Tommy to tidy up the little graveyard and to paint the crosses and names. Tommy was diligent and enthusiastic. The names were cut into the wood so it was a simple matter of painting the whole cross black and then carefully overpainting the indented lettering in white. For greater accuracy and to ensure that the white did not run into the black, Tommy decided to take up the crosses and do the job in the workshop.

'*An-mhaith, Tomás,*' said Brother Lennon when he saw what he was doing. 'Nicely done. I suppose you kept a diagram of where each cross goes in the graveyard?'

Well, no, actually. Tommy hadn't thought of that.

To give him his due, Lennon did not make a big issue of it. He claimed he knew the proper location for each cross, and I'm sure he must have known a few.

Of course, we will never be certain of the truth of it, but is it any great harm if the prayer for the repose of the soul of Brother Donoghue is said over the grave of Brother Fitzgerald?

Brother Lennon had his own way of doing things. There was a time when two of the younger teachers found it difficult to get to school on time after late nights. They might be only five minutes late, but it happened fairly regularly and Lennon was sick of it. Rather than address the issue directly with the teachers involved, he subjected the student body and the rest of the teaching staff to long lectures on the importance of punctuality. He hoped that the offending teachers would get the message; they did not. Lennon raised the heat by threatening to lock out any student who was not inside the door punctually for the morning start. The teachers still missed the point.

One morning, he locked all the doors on the dot of nine thirty. Two minutes later our two heroes arrived. Finding the door locked, they used their wits and came in the primary school door, then climbed over the bannisters into the secondary area. They were at the top of the stairs almost as soon as Lennon. No words were exchanged, but they were never late again.

So far, I had spent my whole school life with Pat Neligan and Thomas Lyne and Ronan Bourke, but after I did the Inter. Cert. things changed. Teresa and Myko had been talking to a few people about the importance of being mature at third level, and at the rate I was going I would still be a few months short of my seventeenth birthday when I was sitting my Leaving Cert. Teresa pointed out that Pat was a good nine months older than me. Would I mind staying back a year? I wasn't too fussed; I had not found the year too difficult and the idea of a doss year appealed to me. When the exam results came out, Pat and myself had done quite well and he didn't want me to stay back, but the arrangements had been made. So after the Inter. Cert., Pat and the others went on and I ended up with a whole new group of friends again.

FAIR DAY IN
DINGLE

The biggest day of the month in Dingle was Fair Day, held on the last Saturday of every month. The town was a maelstrom, animals everywhere – dogs barking, cattle milling, sheep flocking, pigs squealing. And far and away the busiest were the July and August fairs, which were the two big sheep fairs of the year.

For me, the fair began on the previous evening, when Uncle Benny and myself would bring in the sheep. We would head up to the Grove, taking the short cut between the Temperance Hall and Dineens', through Moriartys' farm, then past the Holy Garden to the top of Cruach a' Chairn.

'Lord have mercy on the dead,' Uncle Benny would say as we reached the Paupers' Graveyard, and he would remind me of all the poor souls buried there from Famine times, and how, during the Second World War, the German airmen whose plane crashed into Mount Brandon were also buried there. Further up Cruach a' Chairn, as we walked along the New Line – an unfinished road built during the Famine times as a public works project – the whole town and harbour came into view.

All the sheep had particular marks to identify ownership; Uncle Benny's were the ones with the green-painted horns. One of his dogs, Toby or Sailor, would be despatched to round up the sheep. Then we would herd them down the hill, to be lodged safely overnight in the Holy Garden, an area that was reputed to have been the location for secret Masses during Penal times, when the celebration of Mass was illegal.

'Go to bed early, and be here at seven o'clock sharp in the morning,' Uncle Benny would instruct.

Shortly after seven on the following morning we'd be on our way down Chapel Lane and into Goat Street. 'We should get a good stand inside the gate at this hour.'

The fair was held in 'the brewery', a field on the Spa Road near the creamery, on the edge of the town. 'Tom the Boy' and 'Minnie the Brewery' lived in a little house in the middle of the field, and Tom directed affairs at the gate on the day of the fair. At the really big fairs in July and August the flocks spilled right back along the Spa Road, halfway up Main Street and John Street and down the Mall. Each flock would be guarded by a farmer, with his young son and an alert sheepdog. Every square yard of footpath would be utilised. The man, boy and dog would have been on the road from 'sparafairt', before the first crack of dawn, sent off with a blessing from the woman of the house and a bottle of cold tea with a crust of buttered bread. After the long spring of lambing came the early summer shearing. They would shortly get the wool money, *buíochas le Dia*. All week there was only one topic of conversation – the price lamb was making. Discouraging rumours of low prices circulated from fairs in Annascaul and Castlemaine. '*H'anam an diabhal*, but those jobbers are robbers.' Still, they remained optimistic, and the previous night the household would have shared hopes of selling at a good price. It was important to get to Dingle early, as prime selling positions would be staked out well before dawn. There were no fixed divisions in the open fair field. Each little flock of animals was carefully herded by the owner who was constantly keeping them in order, settling them down and separating them out from those of the next farmer. As we waited for the buyers to appear, neighbours talked with neighbours, everyone feeling the tension.

The jobbers, as the buyers were always known, strode imperiously through the fair in their cavalry twill trousers, tan boots and soft tweed hats. These weren't locals, but dealers from up the country. Mainly they were loud, rude and boorish, conscious of the power they wielded. The small farmers would be apprehensive and perhaps even fearful. There was an awful lot hanging on doing a good deal at the fair: their winter livelihoods, the cost of Christmas, and much else. They were never greedy or grasping. A fair return for their labour and product was all they sought. But fairness did not enter into it, this was the free market, naked. If they had to face back the long road home with their animals unsold, it meant a hard winter, or maybe having to sell even cheaper next month. The buyer would poke contemptuously at the animals, muttering unflattering comments.

'What are you asking for them?'

'One pound, two and six each for the ewes is my price, sir.'

Whatever price was named, his inevitable follow-up was: 'You'll be lucky to get the half of it,' as he walked off. It was a game calculated to soften and break the seller. First the query that showed interest and raised hopes, then the response that dashed them again. But the ritual had started. The seller had been here before, too; he knew there was interest and that the buyer would return. He did. An offer was made and rejected. The various stages were played out: outrage at the offer, astonishment at the response, establishing the gap, narrowing it and the penultimate scene of stand-off. The jobber would leave again in high dudgeon and loudly carry on business with another farmer, complaining about the unreasonableness of all around him. Then came the intervention of a third party, a deal-maker, usually a friend of the farmer's. 'What's between ye? Ye're not going to fall out for the sake of a ten-shilling note!'

Shortly after the buyer had raised his offer by five shillings a head, the mediator would intervene again, cajoling. 'Would you not do the decent thing, split the difference and offer him seven and six?'

'*H'anam an diabhal*, take the seven and six, Mícheál. Sure you don't want to take them home again for the sake of half a crown.'

On it went. The jobber, under no pressure to buy, held all the trump cards and played the farmer like a fish on a hook. It was always a buyers' market. It was always an unequal match. The overbearing buyer, loud, well-fed and paunchy, and the needy seller, hungry and spare.

Now the offer was tempting: too low to accept and too high to refuse. It would pay the bills and the young lad's Confirmation. If it could just be edged up another bit ...

No deal was complete without the 'luck penny', a token amount per beast, which the seller gave back to the buyer for luck. There was an unspoken rule governing the importance and sensitivity of negotiating the 'luck penny' without actually asking for it. It was all done by nods and hints. Then came the final scene, the big gesture. The buyer would spit in his hand, hold it up at the ready, and offer a final shilling of movement. 'Put out your hand. 'Tis my last offer.'

Slowly, reluctantly almost, the farmer stretches out his hand, palm upwards. The jobber claps his bespittled hand hard down on the farmer's. A done deal and honour satisfied. Nothing written, nothing signed. Their word was their bond. Those were different times.

In the early 1950s farmers were lucky to get a pound note for a sheep. It was poor reward for hardship.

As well as the buying and selling, which was the main business of the fair, there were numerous hangers-on and diversions: hucksters, stall-holders, spongers and the inevitable fights that broke out when drink was taken and old scores were resurrected. I'd be looking for any excuse to leave Uncle Benny and wander around the stalls that displayed wares from all over the world. There were sets of cheap Japanese screwdrivers that fit snugly into each other, bicycle pumps, hammers and an ingenious, multi-size German spanner, which, it was claimed, would fit every nut on a bicycle. The clothes stall was festooned with woollen drawers, trousers and rolls of material. And, inevitably, there was the loud guy shouting and roaring at people to buy 'the best delph at give away prices'. I was always wary of getting too close to him.

In those days Dingle was not equipped to meet the needs of tourism or travellers. There were no restaurants or cafés, not even a sandwich for sale. There was, of course, Benners' Hotel, but that was strictly the preserve of commercial travellers, visiting dignatries and wealthy foreign tourists, and definitely off-limits to ordinary folk. Country people in town for the day's shopping had to rely on the welcome of relatives or the hospitality of shopkeepers to get a mug of tea or a bite to eat. But there was one exception: Fair Day. On that one day in the month, McKenna's in the Dykegate Lane sold tea and sandwiches, and Griffin's Pie Shop on Main Street opened for the sale of Dingle pies. A Dingle pie had the look of a steak-and-kidney pie about it except that it was filled with mutton, and served in a large soup dish swimming in mutton broth. The hot, steaming plates of Dingle pies were a huge attraction on Fair Day. As they say, there was "atin' and drinkin" in them. No wonder there was a queue of customers out the door and down the street by the time the shop opened in the late morning of a fair day.

On the afternoon of Fair Day, my grandmother was at her busiest and I was under instructions to be available to her as soon as I had finished with Uncle Benny – to run messages to the tailor's, to help customers with their shopping, or to search the pubs for their errant husbands. Like my mother, Bridgy Fitz went by her maiden name; their married titles were only ever used by polite strangers or 'blow-ins'. Bridgy Fitz's tiny shop would be teeming with customers. Suits of clothes ordered, wellington boots sold, caps and hats being fitted, Confirmation and First Communion outfits being readied. It was non-stop. Men were involved only when it was an item of attire that required them to be present and even then they were reluctant and reticent participants. Rolls of cloth were laid out on the counter –

navy, brown, dark grey with a bit of a line running through it, but nothing flashy. The women felt, squeezed and studied.

'Stand there, Jim, and let me hold this against you.' A roll of suiting material would be draped from his shoulder. 'What do you think of it, Bridgy?' Other customers would join in, uninvited, and offer their tuppence worth.

'The grey suits him, doesn't it, Mary?'

'I'd like to see that brown one on him.'

The whole process would start over again, with the entire shop now focused on choosing the cloth. Everyone is canvassed except the poor man himself. At this stage he would settle for a shroud just to get away. No chance. At least he's in off the street, where the pals can't see him being made a fool of.

'Step outside the door there, Jim, and we'll have a look at it in the light.'

Mortification multiplied. The decision finally made, he bolts for the pub next door with no clue in the world as to which suit length he finally agreed upon.

When the husband was out of the way I would be privy to the exchanges between Grandma and the wife. For all that she was criticised for being bossy and imperious, Bridgy Fitz was generous and charitable to a fault. She was always genuinely interested and concerned, and regarded her customers in that small but thriving shop as an extension of her family. She passed on to them the same sort of advice that she would hand out to us.

'How is Maura getting on in Springfield? Did she call to my brother John? What kind of work is she doing? A lot of the Kerry crowd are going to night schools over there. Would she think of it at all, sure she was very bright.'

And Bridgy provided other services, too. The small farmers who had concluded the sale of their animals were now burdened with the responsibility of carrying in their pockets the most money they would handle for the entire year. These hardy but gently dignified men would edge into my grandmother's and stand there until she asked: 'Did you sell? Did you get a good price?'

Having established the situation, she would enquire, 'Are you carrying all that money around in your pockets, and I suppose you'll go drinking now?'

A sheepish nod.

'Here, give me the money until Máirín comes in on Tuesday.'

The wad of money from the sale of the beasts would be handed over without a whimper. It would be held securely in my grandmother's big safe until the wives came into town shopping or to Mass the following week. As a child I thought those grown men looked so bashful when handing over the money, but when I was older and wiser I realised that the only reason they came into her in the first place was to rid themselves of the burden of carrying the money, so that they could drink in peace and to excess for the rest of the day. A pleasurable, immoderate, intoxicated end to the biggest day out in the month and a break from the constant battle to survive on a couple of acres of farmland and mountain commonage.

By the end of the day, as the light disappeared westward behind Mount Eagle, the town was a sorry sight, the morning smell of wet wool replaced by the pungent odour of sheep dirt, footpaths and shopfronts spattered with the evidence of the fair. Business people engaged in the dirty work of hosing and brushing clean their patches of pavement. They did it gladly before counting their takings. In Dingle, as elsewhere, 'where there's muck, there's money'. Luckless, downhearted small farmers driving out their unsold animals, facing home without the wherewithal for the winter. *Siopa na bPíonna* on Main Street long since sold out of Dingle mutton pies. Patient horses harnessed to traps tethered outside pubs. Younger, more skittish ponies at the end of long reins, which trailed their way through a dark doorway to a strong farmer, pint in one hand, reins in the other. Loyal sheepdogs awaiting their masters, their slumbering heads resting on front paws. A noisy and constant intermingling of man and animal. In my memory all the conversations and banter *as Gaelainn*, the soft, expressive Irish dialect of West Kerry, the language of *An t-Oileánach*, *Fiche Bliain ag Fás* and *Peig*.

And above the talk, the whinnying and the barking, from every pub door came the wail of *sean-nós* singing. It would be unheard of for the day's drinking to conclude without a few *sean nós* songs. Among the favourites was *An Ciarraíoch Mallaithe* (The Cursed Kerryman):

'Má leanfaim go dian tú siar go Cairbreach
Caillfead mo chiall mura dtriallfair abhaile liom'
(If I follow you all the way west to Cairbreach
I'll go out of my mind if you don't return home with me)

In West Kerry it was the custom for the singer to ask another man to hold his hand as he sang. This example of male bonding is something I have never seen elsewhere.

Finally, last stories exchanged and last drinks having been called again and again and again, each would venture out onto the street and head back against the prevailing wind, relying on the pony to find the way home.

BURIED TALENTS

'You're going to learn the piano,' Teresa said brightly. I wasn't so sure. As far as I can recall, I had shown no particular 'bent' for the piano, but music has always been highly valued in Dingle and Teresa obviously saw me going all the way to concert performances. Kathleen Griffin, an elderly, solitary woman who lived in the Holyground, was the organist for the church choir in Dingle. She had a good reputation, which apparently was well deserved. So I was sent to Kathleen for piano lessons. I would have been around eight at the time.

It wasn't so much that the understanding of lines and spaces, quavers and semi-quavers was all that difficult, it was just deadly boring and irrelevant. Oh, I got to know that E-G-B-D-F are the lines (remembered by the mnemonic, Every Good Boy Deserves Favour), and F-A-C-E are the spaces. Or is it the other way round? But I was not engaged. I wanted out and I told Kathleen that I was giving up the classes. Teresa would not agree, so I had to go back. The lessons took place in Kathleen's front room, a dark place, littered with sheet music and the bits and pieces that go with the whole business. There was a smell that I didn't like. The piano was situated along the side wall, and everything and everyone passing the window caught my eye.

Seán Cleary, turning into the archway, going around the back of his garage; Garda Cremins coming out the side gate of the station, and heading away home; Begley taking his greyhounds for a walk around Cooleen; Johnson pulling in Ashe's small lorry to deliver porter to Hanora. Anything was more interesting than what I was doing.

I sat on the piano stool beside Kathleen. She did her best for me and gave me every encouragement, but with scant success. We both knew that I was there under duress. Things got so desperate that eventually Kathleen was holding my hands and quite literally manipulating my fingers to play the piano keys with them. It was a strange tableau indeed: me looking out the window, Kathleen concentrating on knocking a tune into me, my fingers doing the playing and music emanating. And whereas she could play a very good tune with my fingers on her piano, it was hardly appropriate preparation for my future concert performances. By the time my mother accepted that the piano was not my forte and released me from my torture, I had become reasonably proficient at 'Three Blind Mice' and the first few bars of 'Hail Glorious Saint Patrick'. But that was the beginning and end of it. To this day there has been no improvement.

Put bluntly, this first venture seemed to indicate that the eldest of the O'Tooles did not have musical talent. My mother's humour was hardly improved by seeing the prodigious adeptness of my incredibly talented first cousin, Etna O'Flaherty. Etna was a year or two younger than me, but she could paint, sing, dance and play with the ability of a professional. In fact, all the musical talent of our generation of the family went to the O'Flahertys, any one of whom could knock music out of a stone and could master any instrument in a matter of minutes. Of course the genes make their own pathways and both parents of the O'Flahertys were highly talented. Aunty Molly was an accomplished musician, and her husband, Paguine, was a genius at the bodhrán. Meanwhile, to rub further salt in the wound, my closest friend, Pat Neligan, was playing jigs, reels and miscellaneous airs with unrestricted ease on his piano accordion, to rounds of applause from all and sundry. I would watch Pat's extraordinary coordination in stunned amazement, his arms constantly pulling and squeezing the huge instrument, while the fingers of one hand played the tune on the black and white ivory keys and the other kept the rhythm on the buttons. And all on a brute of an instrument that was almost too heavy to lift in the first place. Impossible!

The signs were that I was never going to be a virtuoso, but because I have a very poor memory of my shortcomings, didn't I try again with the school marching band. Clearly I saw this as a great opportunity to awaken my latent musical talent. Nobody pushed me into it. It was all my own idea, though I cannot for the life of me think why. Pat and myself went to Brother Hannon, who was in charge of the band. There was no audition or anything like that.

'*Maith go leor, lads,*' he said. '*Tosnóimís leis an bhfeadóg.*'

So we began our lessons on the tin whistle. Well, more correctly, I began, because by the time I was wondering how to play the High Doh, Hannon was already suggesting to Pat that he should try the fife. I tried it too, but I couldn't even get a note out of it so I had to go back to the whistle. Meanwhile, Pat moved on and went straight into the band, leaving me behind, still doing scales on the whistle. I can claim that I became quite impressive at 'Happy Birthday to You' and a short blast of 'Fáinne Geal an Lae' – the tune later immortalised as 'Raglan Road' – on the tin whistle, but that was it.

The general consensus was that my musical talent would not be any great addition to the band. But they let me down gently, and all was not lost because I got the important job of carrying the red-and-white flag of Dingle. I marched on the left of the front row, behind the band leader. Cynics will have their say, but there was a certain amount of skill required. It involved seating the pole firmly into the leather sheath that hung around my neck, placing my hands at the appropriate height and at the right side to allow for the wind. Talented types give you no credit at all for working out these intricacies! On the first day that we rounded the town with me in my new role, I was so proud of myself that if pride could play a tune I could have knocked a concerto out of that flagpole, no bother at all.

Once or twice I was promoted to the right-hand side of the band and this meant carrying the green, white and gold of the tricolour.

Wow! There was one glorious outing when they were seriously stuck for bodies. The guy who carried the big drum was missing. What would we do? We had to have a big drum. Who would do it? I began to dream. Hannon called me. Was this it?

'Billy Dillon will take the big drum.'

I was devastated!

'Can I trust you with the triangle?'

Yes!

'Of course, sir. I know what to do, sir. I'll strike it in time with the big drum.'

I was doing fine at the beginning, striding along in step behind someone's younger brother who was my replacement on the flag. I struck, tingled, beat, or whatever is the appropriate verb for playing the triangle. I was full of myself. I had been promoted into the percussion section; sure it was only a matter of time before I got a run at the cymbals. I'd love that. My day-dreaming interfered with my concentration on the job in hand. Jimmy Flannery, who was at the back playing the side drum, brought me back to harsh reality. Jimmy was one of the main guys.

'Toolie, for Jaysus' sake, would you strike the triangle in time to the drum, not to your step, or else put the fucking thing down altogether.'

After that, I became so intent on the drumbeat that I found myself completely out of step.

So, as things turned out, that day with the triangle was the pinnacle of my musical career.

Pat Neligan went from strength to strength, and years later when he returned to settle in Dingle he took charge of the band as bandmaster. He never asked me to coach the guy with the flag.

As in every other part of Kerry, Gaelic football was *the* sport in Dingle. The football team also played a very significant role in school life. It was the ambition of every boy, including myself, to be on the team. A seven-a-side tournament was held in school in order to give everyone a chance to impress the selectors. The seven captains were appointed more or less by popular acclaim and the teams were then picked according to merit and by lottery. The names of the captains were put in a hat and when his name came out, that captain chose one boy for the team, until all places were filled.

We all sat around the room, nervous with excitement and anticipation. I had got my first new pair of football boots. I was going to make a name for myself. None of the captains picked me as their first choice, but then again we were younger than some of the lads selected; we could wait. The second round of choices came and went. No joy there either. Neligan was picked in the third round. He didn't even say goodbye to me as he tore across to his new team-mates. I consoled myself by thinking that it was their loss – they could have had *me*!

But nobody else saw it that way, and I was still standing there like a wallflower when even younger guys, like John Martin and Tommy Dowd, were selected. Then, kindly Tom Shea from Ventry called my name. He's my hero forever. I was the seventh and last person chosen for my team. Football, along with playing the piano, was apparently not my forte.

Tom chose *Fanairí Fionntrá*, the Ventry Rovers, as our team name. Tom Shea was soft-spoken and easygoing. Everyone liked him. The day he picked me, he made me, because I can claim to my grave to have played on the same team as the Sheas from Ard a' Bhóthar. That's a story that doesn't lose in the telling, and if you didn't listen closely I could easily leave you with the impression that my footballing skills were so well remembered and regarded that even

Páidí Ó Sé as Kerry team manager might have felt it necessary to seek my advice the odd time on team tactics and the like. After all, wasn't I a mainstay of his brother Tom's team years ago? Of course I wasn't, but the Sheas are far too nice and decent a family to let me down by telling the world the truth about me – that I couldn't kick a ball out of my way.

Tom protected me right through the school competition. He tried me everywhere on the field: as a forward, a back and finally in goal with big Muiris Scanlan from Burnham guarding me as full-back. Poor old Muiris had to be both full-back and goalkeeper. To say that I failed to impress would be a euphemism. I was an utter disaster and the principal reason why our team failed to take the honours. To his eternal credit, Tom never complained. He was seventeen and the only boy who drove a car to school. It was so American to see Tom drive up in the Ford Prefect. I'll never forget it; the registration number was BIN 77. Tom was also the only boy who smoked reasonably openly. They had given up trying to stop him; he only smiled when they gave out to him. Tom went on to represent Kerry as a minor, as did his brother, Micheál. They were all noted footballers and their little brother, Páidí, became a Kerry footballing legend. To think that I patted him on the head when he was a baby and none of it rubbed off on me!

I was still keen to be a sportsman. I tried the golf as well; there was the old nine-hole course in Doonshean, just about a mile beyond Beenbawn. Even women could play golf. Aunty Phyl and Aunty Sheila played, so I reckoned it would be no problem to me. Unfortunately, even though we played a good few times, my skill levels remained static. Put it this way, I was not the best at driving or chipping, but I learned a lot about divots and sods. I just could not get excited about the game. From where we played, there were wonderful views of the Short Strand, Dingle Bay and Carraig an

Mhionnáin, and I found the scenery much more attractive than what was happening on the greens and the fairways. One day, going up the hill of the long par 5, I lost my ball again. While I was poking about the bushes and having no luck locating it, the light finally dawned. This was a total waste of time. There and then I decided to give it up. I picked up the golf bag and headed home, leaving Pat Neligan, Eoin Kane and Thomas Lyne to finish by themselves. I was sixteen. I haven't played golf since.

It became clear to me that a career in sport was unlikely to be successful, so it was around this time that I took up snooker. Snooker was different. There was a cost per game, but you only had to pay if you lost. This created a completely different motivation; it required me to be cautious and careful. Soon my proficiency improved. The lads who hung around the snooker hall might not have been the preferred role models of most parents, but they were decent and likeable, even if a little roguish. They certainly taught me the importance of the rules, particularly where they were of use in gamesmanship; lulling opponents into a fatal error, despite their much better ability. Controlling the ball was the test. To be effective and successful you had to put a spin on it. I quickly learned the value of putting the correct and most effective spin on the ball. Now there was a transferable skill – controlling the spin.

I did manage to acquire a few medals over the years at school. I could run pretty fast and I put a lot of effort into the high jump. High jumping was a lot different in those days, none of your fancy foam rubber or cushion-soft landings. There was a sandpit that Mikey Houlihan, who worked for the Brothers, would dig up and fill with fresh sand at the start of the summer term. Then it was up to ourselves to make sure it was forked and raked each day so it was mounded three or four inches above the surrounding ground level. There was no question, however, of landing on your back unless you wanted to be crippled for the rest of your natural. You had to land on your feet. Only then, after the fall was broken, was it okay to collapse over into the sand. In other words, there were two skills required in our version of the high jump – to get over the bar and to land safely. Nowadays, athletes only have to clear the bar and it doesn't matter a whit how they land. In fact, the comfort zone of three feet of cushion to land on must be a psychological boost. Like jumping on to a bed.

We had a choice of three jumping styles. The traditional way was to run from your favoured side and try to clear the bar sideways. Olympic athletes at the time were all using a technique called the Western Roll. After the run up, the trick was to lift the foot furthest out from the jump first and then, just like it sounds, the idea was to roll over the bar. Another emerging fashion involved running straight at the right-hand upright, then just before the final step, swerving to the left while at the same time swinging up the right foot. The theory was that the impetus of the swerve and swing gave you greater lift over the bar. It was called the Eastern Cut-Off. We had great fun experimenting. Of course this was before Dick Fosbury won gold in the Mexico Olympics by going over backwards, thus creating the revolutionary technique known as the Fosbury Flop, used by virtually all high jumpers nowadays. We didn't think of that one.

My lack of prowess in the sporting arena was brought home to me again during the first week of lectures at teacher training college when I met Commandant Joe O'Keefe, who was in charge of Physical Education. He was nicknamed 'The Jeweller'. As far as I know, this arose from his habit of cautioning the protection of certain male anatomical parts during the course of vaulting or other risky PE activities, by advising us to 'mind your jewellery'. He went around the group, asking each of us what our favourite sport was. He was a loud, garrulous man and macho to boot. He discussed rugby, hurling, football, boxing and other manly sports with my classmates. When I named snooker as my favourite sport, it did appear to silence him briefly. But he recovered quickly and delivered the predictable lecture on a misspent youth. My argument – that the experiences and surroundings of snooker constituted a most appropriate preparation for life – caught him off-guard, but left him more than a little unconvinced. The rest of the group sniggered, but it raised my stock significantly because they took the view that I was poking fun at him. That is, until they discovered that I was useless at everything. There was no snooker table or club in the teacher training college.

'Joseph, mind the shop!'

The shop was the centre and the bane of my life. It was impossible to escape it. Never a chance of sneaking out to play without the risk of being collared to do duty behind the counter. In many ways I grew up behind that counter.

Our shop was a mixture of grocery, fruit, confectionery, stationery, sweets and tobacco. Teresa took great pride in it and the goods were always attractively arranged; the place was a credit to her. She kept it spotlessly clean and would don a fresh white chemist's coat every morning before starting work.

For a small shop, it was very well stocked. Teresa was quality- and brand-conscious and would only stock what she considered the best. Once or twice a week a large, grey, canvas container, padded and strapped, was delivered to the shop from the CIÉ bus. It seems extraordinary in this era of seemingly inevitable transport delays and glitches, but in fact this was HB ice cream arriving – still frozen – by public transport from Dublin. In those days, timetables and schedules were sacrosanct and fresh produce could be entrusted with confidence to CIÉ. The Tralee bus would stop outside the door and Billimite (Bill Dillon, the conductor), would land the goods on to the footpath. There would be a rush to open the container to check that the ice cream was still frozen and to stack it immediately in the shop fridge.

'Not so fast!' Teresa would caution. 'First take out all the old ice cream in the fridge and put the fresh blocks in at the bottom so that it is rotated and we sell the older stuff first.'

The ice cream already in the fridge would be rock hard and the icy packaging would stick to your fingers. The stuff off the bus would be softish, and if you stacked too many of the older ones on top of them, you risked squashing them. There was also another level of sorting: Vanilla on the left, Raspberry Ripple in the middle and

Banana flavour on the right. There was a right way to do everything. Around St Patrick's Day we would also get a delivery of patriotic green, white and orange ice cream. I have no idea what went into it to make these colours, but it was very popular on the feast day, particularly if Patrick's Day fell during Lent, when there was a sort of twenty-four hour amnesty for kids who might be 'off' sweets and ice cream for the duration.

Cutting and selling wafers of ice cream may not seem overly complex or challenging, but Teresa had perfected it into an art and her instructions had to be followed to the letter. Hands spotless, open the block on the tiny ice cream counter; fold back all the sections and sides of the carton; carefully place the marker on the ice cream, making sure that the edge is firmly against the side of it before pressing down to divide out the eight threepenny portions. Now, with your right hand take the knife from its jug of water, while at the same time placing a wafer against the left side of the block. With great care and accuracy cut through the ice cream exactly on the mark. Watch it there! Remember that if you go beyond the mark then the next customer will get a smaller portion, or, worse again, we will be left with an unsaleable bit at the end. Use the flat blade of the knife to press the ice cream against the wafer and onto your hand. Put away the knife. With your right hand take another wafer and place it on top of the ice cream and hand it to the customer with a smile. That will be three pence please.

Hard-earned coppers.

And even when you thought you had done it perfectly, there would always be something more you could have done to make the transaction better.

'You should talk more to the customers when you're getting the ice cream.'

It always came down to people in the end. No matter what the advice or direction, the end focus would be about treating the person on the other side of the counter properly. There was a constant and unremitting programme of moulding and leavening to refine my approach, demeanour and attitude. Teresa never factored in any lower level of expectation simply because I was young. I seem to have been doing things of a responsible nature from a very young age. You were told and shown how to do it; the importance of getting it right was explained; then you just got on and did it.

In the ice cream department we also stocked Choc Ices and Golly Bars, but no ice lollies. My mother would not sell what she considered to be inferior products, and she felt that they were a cheap waste of money.

Another weekly delivery from Dublin was Fuller's cakes. They were a favourite of ours, especially the chocolate ones with the little button sweets on the icing. The square-shaped Battenburg with its pink-and-yellow chequerboard insides and the almondy marzipan icing was not our favourite. Mind you, Teresa was very proud of the Battenburg and would remind us that this was the *real* Battenburg, not like the chocolate-covered version produced by another supplier.

The shop was a Moriarty endeavour, owned and run by my mother. The big gable-end of the house that faced down the Mall carried the name 'Moriarty's Shop'. In West Kerry most married women retained their maiden names after marriage. My mother, her mother and my father's mother in Lettermore were businesswomen – strong, dominant and independent. They each married men who were tolerant, good-humoured, good company and very clear and determined in their views. Regrettably, my grandfather on Myko's side was long dead before my birth, but it can be said with absolute truth about my father and my maternal grandfather, Seán the Grove, that they never criticised their wives, found fault with them in any way, or gave out to them. Their wives always seemed ready to defer to them, but somehow never really had to. Neither couple would ever argue in front of the family. When I was growing up I had the impression that all the decisions in our house and in my grandparents' house were taken by the women. As I got older a slightly different picture emerged as I began to recognise the more nuanced comments of the men and realised that the final decisions generally coincided with their opinions. Rather than say outright, 'That's a bad idea', the male folk would be more inclined to adopt a tone of agreement, while pointing out the possible negative consequences. This would eventually lead to a reconsideration and a different outcome, with honour satisfied on all sides. Very sophisticated stuff really.

My mother had never been very robust looking, and during her schooldays was a regular absentee through indifferent health. Eventually, this led to her quitting school altogether and her parents set her up with the shop in the Mall. Though she was young, she was nonetheless fully responsible for the shop and the house that went with it. The Moriartys believed strongly in the discipline of responsibility. One of her brothers or sisters would stay in the house at night with her. She was an independent woman with a small but successful business when she met my father. Her life changed very little after marriage.

The whole daily life of the house centred around the shop. It dominated our lives and controlled our time. Someone always had to be on call. My mother, with the full support of my father, was firmly of the view that the discipline of shopkeeping and having to contribute to the family business was good for us. But did we appreciate that as youngsters? Of course we didn't.

Now I recognise that doing deals with suppliers and customers all day long was a great training for life – and for some of the positions in which I later found myself. It was a constant exercise of judgement. Even relatively simple things, like whether it was safe to leave the shop for a moment to check something while there was just one customer in it. Generally, it was pretty easy to spot if something was pilfered or a few sweets missing, but the real pain was knowing that you had made an error of judgement and having to suffer Teresa's censure: 'You should have known you couldn't trust him!' There was an unbreakable rule that all such matters were confidential to the family. It left us in the rather uncomfortable position of knowing, in a small town such as Dingle, those who could be trusted and those who could not, but not being allowed share that knowledge with others, even when it might be to their benefit.

Teresa was wise to all the tricks of the trade. 'Make sure that no customer puts a finger on the scales.' This was a favourite scam of a small number of people, leaning across the counter on the pretext of checking the items on the scale while surreptitiously placing a casual finger under the tray of the scales and pressurising it ever so slightly upwards, thereby gaining an extra half-ounce in the quarter-pound of sweets.

Others took a different tack. As you were going to the scales to weigh the filled bag they would say, casually, 'Sure, give me one of those, Joseph, while I'm waiting.' Taking a sweet out of the bag before it was weighed raised their hope that it would not be allowed for in the weighing. No chance!

We were never allowed to challenge a customer over an attempted fraud, but we did our level best to make sure that they didn't get away with it. In fairness, the vast majority of customers were as honest as the day was long, but obviously it was the others who made the most impact. So, although you had to be trained to look out for and expect the trickster, in truth they were few and far between. So sizing up a customer across the counter had to become second nature. Is he straight or is he crooked? Decide now.

I have often wondered since how many such judgements of mine were flawed and how often was it a mental detraction of a good honest character. Undoubtedly it was across that counter that I learned about human behaviour. It is easy to see that now. Then, it was a bore, an intrusion and a millstone that held us back from the true enjoyment of life. To this day I am still governed by that early training and tend to make very early judgements on people and to go with that judgement until I find I was wrong. This has proven to be not a bad thing, because even though it may not be possible to 'read the mind's construction in the face', it certainly is the case that demeanour, expression and manner can be great clues. Tight people have mannerisms; the way they have money twisted into a tight bundle in their pockets; the way they almost have to tear away a note from the bundle; the way they hold the money in their hands below the counter level so that you cannot see it; the way they hand over every coin and note, one at a time; the way they scrutinise the change, checking each coin to ensure that it isn't a dud. And the way they press their lips together into a thin line, giving them crows' feet at the corners. You don't believe me? Exaggeration, you say? Well, maybe, but the point is that, for me, even if they never did those things in exactly that way, they were somehow giving off an aura which left me with the impression that they were.

Of course that is very unfair and of course I have been wrong. But there are positive aspects. I learned that it was important to make judgements about people and I still believe that to be crucial to positive interaction and engagement at all levels, whether it be social, personal, or business. Secondly, because so many people are reticent and guarded with new acquaintances, when someone appears to trust them, they pick up positive vibes and they open up. Anyway, it is more fun to make a judgement call about people and to go with it. That kind of open engagement usually impacts on the other person in a most positive way and creates a warm and trusting environment. Things go wrong when people consciously try to make an impression. Attempting to portray oneself as being something different just stores up problems down the road. A 'Take me or leave me' attitude may be difficult to deal with in the beginning, but is easier all round in the end. Most people today are threatened by openness and feel challenged by it, even at a very elemental level. Try walking down a city street today and merely making full eye contact with other citizens, and see the unease it will create.

So much to have learned from the school of human learning that was our small shop!

Teresa had very good taste. She was particularly good at window-dressing, and her Christmas window of boxes of chocolate was the highlight of the year. She would spend days planning and preparing for it. In the style of the time, the boxes would be arranged on different levels. Some sat on columns, while others lay on flat surfaces which were draped in satin. Many of the presentation boxes tended to be overly ornate for the Christmas market, so Teresa would always balance her display by ensuring that a much more restrained box of quality chocolates, such as Terry's, was given pride of place as the centrepiece.

She particularly liked the large, chest-shaped Black Magic box, unadorned except for tassle and ribbon; this always got a prominent position. Then the inevitable Christmas clichés, with snow scenes, cute cats, overblown flowers and the rest were displayed to best effect. We were of the view that the people who bought the classically simple caskets were those with the best taste, but each to his own, and I'm sure the chocolates tasted the same, whatever the picture.

When Teresa was satisfied with her arrangement and had made the few final, critical adjustments, the blind was raised and she waited for the compliments of customers.

'The window is just beautiful this year, Teresa. Will you give me that box of Milk Tray with the little girl on it. It's for my godchild.'

'That's great, Sheila, but if you don't mind I won't take it out of the window yet. I'll put your name on it and keep it for you. Is that all right?'

◼ ◼ ◼

Getting to know the suppliers and getting them to understand your needs was crucial. Teresa had a strict rule for all suppliers, but especially for the fruit suppliers.

'If you expect me to buy from you, you'd better call to me before any other shop in town.'

If they hit town and visited another premises before hers, Teresa would simply refuse to do business with them and send them packing. She wanted first pick and she wanted to be first with fresh fruit. And, boy, could she remind them of the fact that she was their best customer!

She was an expert at buying fruit. It was surprising how much there was to learn – the best time for tomatoes; the difference between the Irish, Dutch and Canary Island types; making sure that there was still a little green on them when we bought, so that by the time the 12lb chip was nearly sold, they would still not be overripe. 'Don't get stuck with too many of those Spanish ones today,' she would advise, 'because the new season Irish will be available by the end of the week.'

Oranges were difficult to judge. The sense of smell was all-important here. By sticking my nose into a box of oranges, I came to be able to tell whether or not there was a rotten one in it, or if they were about to go off. Teresa would never buy a box of oranges without submitting it to that test. Those were the days before global politics, and the Jaffa orange from Israel and the Outspan from South Africa were the big sellers. At that time I had no knowledge of the Palestinian question and made no connection between apartheid and the Cape oranges. Simpler times, yes, but infuriating now to think that we were facilitating and supporting injustice in other places.

The shapes of the fruit containers varied considerably. The bananas – green and underripe in their long, rectangular, coffin-like boxes – were, appropriately enough, left to ripen in the darkest corner to be found. Sometimes we would cover them with brown paper to hasten the ripening process. The oranges came in divided wooden boxes; we put the riper ones all together on one side, to be sold first, with the harder ones finishing their ripening on the other side. Spanish tomatoes arrived in shallow wooden trays, whereas the Dutch and Irish were in rectangular basket-like containers woven from light flexible wood, with a carrying handle made out of tin. Strawberries were bought and sold in the familiar 1lb punnets. I was amazed to see the name 'Jesus' printed along the side of many of the Spanish boxes and couldn't believe that anyone, other than the Lord himself, was actually called Jesus. It would have caused a riot at an Irish christening font, and I cannot imagine it on a GAA match programme!

The grape barrels were my favourite. They were beautifully constructed from perfectly-fitting laths and strengthened by encircling hoops of wood. The barrels were packed to the brim with cork chippings. These chippings had the consistency of gravel but were wonderfully smooth and warm. It was with an air of expectancy that I would carefully delve down through the cork, searching for the first grapes and fish out a large, intact and perfectly shaped bunch. I would gently shake off the cork and hang the bunch by a small meathook from the metal bar along the fruit section of the shop. There was an almost sensuous feeling to searching around the bottom of the barrel, with the cork up to the elbow of my bare arm, as I felt around for the final bunch.

Throughout the year the ever-changing permutations of colour, smell, shape and texture created new vistas in the fruit section, as the seasonal produce was displayed to best advantage. The top layer of apples had to be polished to a shine. Oranges were a devil. They usually came individually wrapped in tissue paper with the producer's brand on it. We would have to unwrap the tissue paper, smooth it out, fold it diagonally from corner to corner into a triangular shape, wrap the long edge of the triangle around the circumference of the orange and then knot the ends before placing it carefully on the display shelf. A lot of work when you think that this had to be done for every single orange in the box.

The arrival of the Granny Smith apple turned the world on its head. Up to then, every child had learned from nursery rhymes or old wives' tales that red apples were sweet and green apples were sour. Didn't witches always poison the red side of the apple, knowing that unsuspecting children would bite that side? But now we had the Granny Smith, a fully ripe eating apple that looked like, and was, as green as a cooking apple. Well, it was the talk of the town for months.

Every shopkeeper has to be conscious of their margins: how much to pay for produce? What selling price will the market bear? Dealing in fruit, there were so many factors which could bring disaster in some form. How much do you pay the supplier for a box of oranges? If they could be sold for sixpence, then they had to be bought for less, that much was clear enough, but for how much less? Allow for a few to be overripe, a few to be wizened, a few to be left unsold by the time a fresh box arrived. It was always a gamble, and if the original estimate of the sale price was wrong, then the rest collapsed like a house of cards.

One of the embarrassing aspects of the job was counting the number of pieces of fruit in the box and then challenging the supplier if there was an error. Part of the reason we did it was to ensure that we were not at a loss, but the real reason was to let the supplier see that everything was checked and counted. That way he was always more likely to try and unload the box with the few rotten ones at the bottom on another shop; this was our insurance. My mother impressed on me that it was more important to know and understand the person selling than it was to know his product. Since that early training, it has always been an attraction for me to do business with someone with whom I feel comfortable, even if another seller's product might appear more attractive. It builds trust and it leads to the situation of being happier spending money where the seller appreciates receiving it.

'Minding the shop' meant that we handled money at a very young age. Teresa worked on the basis of us getting used to being surrounded by temptation. I did not have permission to take a sweet without asking, even if I had been working in the shop for hours. There was very little difficulty in getting that permission, but the discipline was that it had to be sought. She would also caution about new people being in the shop. Nobody was ever allowed behind the counter.

'You are used to dealing with amounts of money and will not be tempted. Most people have never been responsible for, or handled other people's money. It's not fair to put them in a situation where they might be on their own in a room, with a bundle of money sitting there. You shouldn't do it to them.'

I knew that my mother was being realistic, and, when you think of it, doing no more than obeying the wish expressed in the Lord's Prayer: lead us not into temptation.

Some of our customers were very poorly off – people from families that relied on the few shillings to be earned from casual labouring work by the father and maybe from a couple of hours of housework by the mother. They really did live from hand to mouth, and putting bread on the table was a daily worry. Even though the shop was run on a strictly 'no tick' basis, there were a few trusted customers who had a credit arrangement. For these customers we kept a 'tick book'. When one of them bought a pound of butter or a tin of beans, details of the purchase were entered into the book there and then, in their presence. This had to be done no matter how busy the shop, so that there would be no doubt or dispute when it came to settling the bill. The bills would be paid in full, weekly or fortnightly, usually at a quiet time of the week. The 'settling up' was a pageant all to itself. In those times, before copiers or calculators, the cash book was opened on the counter and Teresa would go through the individual items with the customer. In order that they could both see the page and neither had to read upside down, the book was placed so that each looked at it from their own side of the counter. Customer and shopkeeper would be bent over the book, checking it, line by line and *tête-à-tête*. Teresa disliked the process and as soon as I had the confidence and authority to carry it off, the task was delegated to me.

Needless to say, the responsibility came surrounded by a multitude of instructions and cautions: Check each item and confirm the price. If there is a query, remember what you have been told – 'Be polite but firm.' Usually, my explanation would be accepted with good grace by the customers and just the odd time a purchase had to be deleted when a customer was certain it was entered in error, even though we knew for a fact that it was correct. This was a concession to an honest mistake rather than an attempt to defraud. How we came to that judgement I can't explain, but I suppose it arose from knowing the customers very well and from the fact that any customer with a tick book was considered to be above suspicion in the first place.

Totting up the bill was generally done *as Gaeilge.* Nobody in Dingle had ever learned arithmetic through English. The addition had to be done aloud so that the customer could hear and check. Those long tots were a test in themselves, with the customer listening to every word and mentally making their own calculation.

'*Cúig agus a h-ocht sin a trí déag, agus a seacht sin a fiche ... sin naochadh-sé pingin ar fad, sin ocht scilling; cur síos an náid agus tóg an h-ocht.*'

And so carry on to the next page. Sometimes the customer would correct an error I had made when perhaps distracted by the arrival of another customer.

'I think you added that "*seacht*" twice.'

'Oh sorry, you're right.' No harm done.

Now and again, if it appeared someone was a bit embarrassed about correcting me for the sake of a few pence, I might deliberately skip a figure in the next tot so the customer could say, 'Oh, Joseph, you're doing yourself there; you never added the six. Teresa will sack you.'

Sometimes I might do it just to see if he would point out the error, and if he didn't, well, there was a lot to be learned from that too. And it was very easy to appear to lose track towards the end of the page, and with a sigh start again, ensuring the pick-up of the dropped figure this time. No loss recorded but much intelligence gained.

Sometimes a helpful customer might make the offer: 'Here, I'll add it up for you.' I might have been happy to let them at it, but I had been warned: 'Always do the tot yourself.'

Why? Because otherwise you are going to have to correct the customer when he makes a mistake, and that is not good. There was always a reason. That was the way it was in the shop. Always checking, always balancing.

Teresa kept the books with scrupulous honesty. Charge for everything, but no customer should be charged even a halfpenny too much. Now and again the system would fail. You could nearly see it coming. A quiet nod of greeting from the woman as she comes into the shop. She is looking at various things while you are dealing with customers. But when it comes to her turn, she defers to a customer who has arrived after her. Finally, when the shop is empty, she makes her request.

'A quarter of tea please, Joseph.'

And you get it and you put it on the counter and she puts her hand on it. Then she looks uncomfortable and says matter-of-factly but with a slight quiver in her voice, 'Will that be all right until Saturday? Tommy is out and I have no change with me.'

Now, you saw Tommy go in home ten minutes ago and you know that Teresa has warned you 'no tick', but you know the woman is as honest as the day is long and you know that she has nothing and that a refusal will hurt and embarrass her interminably. You know she knows this, and you see she is desperate enough to risk it. You say, 'Don't forget on Saturday.'

'God bless you, boyeen.'

When you tell Teresa she just nods. The woman returns on Saturday.

In my memory, people's poverty never made them dishonest. The association of crime and dishonesty with poor people and what would now be called 'disadvantaged areas' was never a factor growing up in Dingle. It is a lesson I have never forgotten, that poverty and criminality are not two sides of the same coin and neither are wealth and honesty. I also learned that some of the most intelligent people I met were people who had dropped out of formal education at a young age. Intelligence and education are not joined at the hip, and usually, in your dealings with someone, if you are more aware of their qualification or position than their ability, then you can probably put a question-mark over their level of intelligence. Maybe that judgement is a bit hard, but I don't think it is too wide of the mark.

Mind you, we were often put to the test by our own. Uncle Jonty, handsome, gruff and wild-eyed, was full of devilment. He would come into the shop when Teresa was missing.

'Is Teresa in?'

'She's upstairs, Uncle Jonty.'

'That's all right. Look, just give me ten Players Medium and I'll pay you tonight.'

'Sorry, Uncle Jonty, I can't do that.'

His eyes would flame with anger. Then, just as I was about to wilt, he would laugh and throw the half-crown on the counter.

'You'll do fine, boyeen. Give me twenty altogether, so. Will you come down below the hill to look after the butcher's shop for me for a few weeks in the summer?'

Looking at Uncle Jonty, who was one of the hardest and toughest and hot-tempered men around, it was difficult to reconcile that image with the fact that, by rights, he should not have been alive at all. Always the wild one of the family and never looking after himself, he developed rheumatic fever as a young lad. That passed and no more thought was given to it. He regularly suffered from septic throats afterwards but not much notice was taken of them. As Aunty Phyl said, 'Sure he was always in some *achrann* anyway.'

It all returned to haunt him at the beginning of the 1950s, when he was in his twenties, and his heart valves became less and less efficient. Local doctors and county physicians were brought into the case, but his health deteriorated rapidly. The prognosis was bad. Seán the Grove and Bridgy Fitz were told that their son would die. The family were devastated. Was there any point in going to Dublin or London? Money was no problem. But no, there was nothing to be done. The family started praying. Someone suggested that they make a novena to an Italian nun who was about to be canonised in Rome.

Bridgy Fitz decided to bring Jonty to Dublin anyway. The physician they met was a young man called Risteard Mulcahy; he was up-to-date with the most modern of techniques. In his view, a new type of operation, called open-heart surgery, might help Jonty. The problem was that the surgery was in its infancy and was not yet available in Ireland nor was there much experience of it anywhere else. He was urged to do his best, and following consultation with the surgeons, he concluded that the operation could be effective. He could not be certain that Jonty would survive, even though, apart from the heart condition, he was physically very strong. If it were done, it would be the first time the surgery had been undertaken in Ireland. For the family, watching Jonty deteriorate by the week, there was no choice really. They opted for the operation.

Meanwhile half of Dingle was praying and making novenas to the new Italian saint. When the operation was a total success, some put it down to modern medicine, others to the power of prayer.

On the first visit to the recovering Jonty, he was shown a

photograph of the saintly nun. Religion had never been high on Jonty's agenda. His eyes widened. 'Show me that again,' he demanded and they gave him a better look at the saint.

'That's the woman I saw in my mad dreams during the anaesthetic. Who is she?'

Well, she was Saint Mary Mazzarello, canonised on 24 June 1951, and after that she got full credit for the miracle of Jonty's recovery. Two babies were born into the extended family the next month, and in thanksgiving they were called after the saint. So we got Mazzarella O'Flaherty (I assume they changed the 'o' to 'a' as it would have been a bit of a mouthful coming ahead of O'Flaherty) and Norella Moriarty – the latter being a combination of Nora and Mazzarella to avoid the confusion of having two Mazzarellas and also to recognise Norella's grandmother, Nora McCarthy. That's how my two first cousins, Mazzarella and Norella, two lovely women and well-known in their own right, came to be named.

Despite the many times my siblings and myself roundly cursed the shop and the hours of captivity we endured when we would have given anything to be outside with our pals, in retrospect it was a very valuable training for life and for many of the situations I later found myself confronted with. And, of course, it was another income. The shop was the difference between us being financially all right and financially comfortable. Myko's garda salary would have provided for us, but the shop gave us the wherewithal for a bit of luxury. Over the years, we had a few Ford Anglias and a few Morris Minors. Myko and Teresa could afford the odd holiday abroad, we wore good clothes and there was always meat and bread on the table.

All in all, there was a lot to be said for it.

THREE CHEERS

FOR OUR LADY

OF FATIMA

'Three cheers for Our Lady of Fatima,' he shouted. A diligent Knight of Columbanus seeking to curry favour and ingratiate. It was the day of the inaugural blessing of the new shrine to Our Lady of Fatima in Green Street. The procession was huge, the enthusiasm great, but unfortunately the liturgy was somewhat dull. The knight had been seeking to rehabilitate himself following some ill-considered amorous adventure, details of which had leaked widely. What better way than to take a stand with the Mother of God?

The procession had followed the traditional route around the town. Setting out from the church, it wound its way to Canon's Corner and then proceeded down Main Street to the small bridge. It was longer than the Mall and the leaders had crossed Hudson's bridge on to Holyground when the tail end was still only leaving the small bridge. At the root of the pier, where a number of gardaí had the traffic from the west halted for the duration, the procession swung right around, back towards Green Street and up to the church again. Every man, woman and child participated. As the Blessed Sacrament passed them, the gardaí came to rigid attention on the orders of the Superintendent and saluted. It was just like Corpus Christi. The walkers in the procession were segregated into groups: the grey-suited men of the men's sodality, the black-shawled heads of the older women and then the dark mantillas of the women's sodality. Muted blocks of serrated dullness were suddenly lifted by the bright blue cloaks of the Children of Mary. Then came that year's First Communicants, dressed in immaculate white except for the splashes of red from the boys' ties and the pastel colours of the girls' sashes and ribbons. Each spotless child carried a basket of rose petals, which fluttered, one petal at a time, from their innocent fingers to scent and purify the ground.

Immediately behind them the honour guard of Knights of Columbanus attended the large statue of Our Lady of Fatima that was being conveyed in an open carriage and for which the rose-petalled path had been laid down. The knights also had the privilege of holding a canopy over the priest, who carried the sacred host in a golden sunburst monstrance.

Buntings stretched across the streets. Every second house displayed a window shrine with a little statue of the Virgin Mary flanked by two lighted candles and decorated with flowers in ornate vases and crêpe paper. Many flew yellow-and-white papal flags, bearing the Vatican insignia of crossed keys, from their upstairs windows.

The procession brought the town to a silent standstill, capitalist commerce and compliant citizenry each ensnared by an ecclesiastical show of strength. It was a surreal sight; the roadways thronged by the muted mass of diligent faithful, line after line in military formation, marshalled by officious church-steward types, but framed by empty pavements. Hundreds of people, yet no talk or chat, the unnatural quiet relieved occasionally by the murmur of a decade of the rosary led by the Legion of Mary.

'Hail Mary, full of grace … '

The crowd would fall silent again and then the church choir would strike up one of the well-worn hymns:

'O Sacrament Most Holy,

O Sacrament Divine …'

Everyone knew the words and joined in with full voice, reaching a satisfying crescendo on the last two lines:

'All praise and all thanksgiving

Be every moment thine.'

The new shrine was built in a neo-Gothic style beside the church. When the procession finally reached it, the great statue was solemnly lifted from the carriage by the knights, brought carefully up the steps and set into its final resting place in the shrine. The crowd stretched to see the action. The canon spoke to them. He worried them with hints about what might be in the Third Secret of Fatima, which was reputed to be so ghastly that the visionaries had confided it to no one but the Pope. Its content, he said, was now held securely in a locked and sealed vault in the Vatican.

Then there was the solemn blessing. And suddenly it was all over. The event that had been talked about for weeks was at an end. There was a palpable sense of anti-climax. The crowd was reluctant to disperse, hoping for something – anything – to prolong the moment. Then into the lacuna jumped our hero, the disgraced Knight of Columbanus. With an athletic leap he bounded to the top of the steps and called for 'Three cheers for Our Lady of Fatima'. The crowd responded with enthusiasm. It made the day and made *his* day. He was back.

A lot could be learned about the people of Dingle by looking at the way the congregation seated themselves at Sunday Mass. How far up the centre aisle someone chose to go was a fair indication of their view of themselves, status-wise, in the community. The back of the church, particularly the space between the outside door and the internal glass ones, was always the most popular. There was no class division down there. It invariably contained a most eclectic bunch, bonded together by a total lack of religious fervour and ready for a quick exit during Communion. Spiritually, they were too lethargic to be atheistic; indolent 'census Catholics', not assertive enough to stay at home. It was easier to go to Mass than to draw attention by not attending. Those who stopped going became targets for evangelising visiting priests during the annual Mission. It was not an enviable experience. One Passionist father, with a thundering voice and a fire-and-brimstone approach to catechetics, was given the task of convincing one recalcitrant, who was considered an atheist, to return to the fold. He met the lost soul and set about convincing him of the error of his ways. In fact, he got very little satisfaction, but never one to admit defeat, he tried again. Eventually he gave a report to the parish priest, reassuring him tha,t 'Donaleen is no atheist, he's just too damn lazy to get out of bed for Mass on a Sunday morning.'

The parish priest of the time was Canon Lyne. He was an important man and made sure everyone knew it. He came from a well-off family in East Kerry and his people were very involved in Kerry footballing circles. Without doubt he ruled the roost in Dingle. He commanded respect and not a little fear; he had scant tolerance for opposition or dissension. It was only the odd brave citizen who squared up to him. Before he came to Dingle he was parish priest in Annascaul, approximately ten miles east on the Tralee road. The parish had some property and land at Inch and the PP had a little market garden there, of which he was very proud. One day he discovered his garden produce eaten, trampled and ruined; he was inconsolable. He was also angry and frustrated because, though he could not prove the identity of the culprit animals or their owner, he had the strongest suspicions. He restarted operations and, the time of year being right, he put down cabbage plants. They came on well in the sandy soil of Inch. He minded and watered them in his spare time. Round about the time when he was planning to cut the fine heads, he arrived one morning to find the garden full of marauding goats who had satiated themselves on the juicy young cabbages. Overcome with rage, he strode into the nearby farmhouse of Pat Foley, the unfortunate owner of the goats. Correctly including the earlier episode in the list of transgressions, he laced into Pat, and as he was at it, he threatened him with bills, the law and the loss of his immortal soul. He left poor Pat shivering, cowering and grovelling. As for the PP, by the time he had reached home his anger had cooled and after a few days Pat had mended the fencing and the garden was replanted with some help from Pat and his family.

A month later, when the plants were healthily above ground and thriving, didn't Pat come out one morning to find the goats once more gorging themselves on the fresh greens. There was nothing to do except wait for the inevitable. An hour later, he spied the red-faced PP, accompanied by his newly arrived and impressionable young curate, approaching the house. Pat ordered his entire family on their knees and began the rosary, a gesture of religious fervour which he surely believed would cushion the impact. He miscalculated. The fury of the priest exploded into a rant from the moment he reached the threshold. As well as giving vent to his righteous anger, he was, no doubt, intent on giving the young curate a lesson on how to deal with an offending parishioner. But he had miscalculated, too. His thundering interruption of the family at prayer was, in Pat's eyes, sacrilegious. It also diminished Pat as master of his own house. He felt fearful, guilty and ill-used all at the same time. When the priest threatened, 'I'll turn yourself into one of those goats,' it was too much for Pat. 'Well, and if you do, by Christ 'tis I will sink my horns into the hasp of your arse,' he exploded, his normally soft features wild and black with fury. There was a sharp intake of breath from the curate, and nervous sniggers from the younger family members, followed by a shocked, silent retreat by the parish priest.

The Foleys of Inch were always a solid crowd, fair play to them!

A short time later, Father Lyne was transferred to Dingle and promoted to the rank of canon.

Being an altar boy was a notable progression in our stages of development. The first test was to be able to recite the Latin responses to the Mass: *Introibo ad altare Dei – Ad Deum qui latificat juventutem meam,* (I will go to the altar of God – To God who gives joy to my youth). The beautiful sound of the Latin mantra merged with the ceremonies and pageantry of the Church. We sang it out with gusto. The significance of office and the authority of those inside the sanctuary became apparent to every altar boy as soon as he pulled the starched white surplice over the long black soutane with its million buttons. People looked at us somewhat differently. The Church was where the power resided; we were part of it and we felt important.

And even among the altar servers there was a clear hierarchy. Four was a full complement for serving Mass. The number one boy served 'right', that is to say he knelt immediately on the priest's right-hand side. He was responsible for all the important aspects of the server's role, including the moving of the Mass book across the altar from the Epistle to the Gospel side, and, most importantly of all, the striking of the bell or gong with the drumstick. The second altar boy was his sidekick for the bringing up of the wine and water and also at the symbolic washing of the priest's hands. Altar boy number four had an inactive, non-starring role. But altar boy number three got to meet the people. He accompanied the priest during the distribution of communion, holding the shiny gold plate under the chin of communicants as they humbly closed their eyes and opened their mouths wide for the reception of the host. It gave an extraordinary perspective on the condition of people's mouths and throats and certainly dampened any enthusiasm for a career in dentistry. Not that that sort of thing crossed our minds as we sought to ensure that any minuscule piece of host which might drop from the priest's fingers would be saved by the plate, because if even the tiniest bit fell to the floor and was trodden on, it would be as if Jesus himself were trampled underfoot. And we watched that no piece of host touched the recipient's teeth, which, we had been assured, would have the same effect as biting into the body of Christ. We were worriers, we were.

There was always a lot of manoeuvring about getting chosen to serve at weddings and funerals. There was money to be had, in the form of tips, so there was usually an enthusiastic group of volunteers available.

There was one, almost secret ceremony that as an altar boy I always found curiously uncomfortable. It normally took place on a quiet mid-week morning. As soon as the small congregation had left, a lone woman would, by arrangement, silently approach and kneel at the altar rail in front of the side altar, close to the sacristy. One of us, carrying the holy water, would accompany the priest out to the woman. There he would perform some type of elaborate blessing. The woman would never say a word; there would be no eye contact, no warmth of communication. There appeared to be embarrassment on the part of the woman and almost irritation on the part of the priest that his breakfast was being delayed. Certainly I invariably felt relief when it concluded. It was probably the only ceremony that took place in the open church without congregation or celebration. There was something diminishing and demeaning about the whole procedure that defied the articulation abilities of my young mind. Because I knew it was to do with babies being born, I was smart enough to know not to ask. And nobody told me. It was, of course, the ceremony of 'churching' – a cleansing blessing which apparently re-consecrated the bodies of women who had recently been 'defiled' by having given birth to a child. My mother, to her great credit and no doubt at some worry to herself, refused ever to be churched and in later life explained to me how she believed it was a horrible, humiliating and ugly experience for any mother. She was right. It does seem inexplicable that a woman who had carried her child for nine months, given birth and nursed new life, in effect engaging in the most sacred and valued of experiences for the good of all, should then require cleansing and blessing. No doubt the initial sexual catalyst to conception was the church's problem. I always thought that artificial insemination would have been very popular with the priests. 'Churching' does not appear to happen anymore.

May, 'the month of Mary', was a time of special religious observance: May altars in the home, decorated with bluebells and other seasonal flowers, processions at school, and the service of Benediction every evening in the church. This was an impressive production. Truly a *son et lumière,* with light, sound, flame and smoke. It was our job as altar boys to prepare the props. We would light the little disc of charcoal and place it in the thurible, an ornate silver vessel with openings to let the air through. The lower end of the thurible was half a spherical pot and was connected to its high, conical cover by a complicated system of chains, which could be used to open and close it. The altar boy swung the thurible to create a draft and so keep the charcoal burning. The smoke wafted out through the openings and drifted through the church. During the Benediction, the priest added incense to the burning charcoal as part of the ceremony. Then the smoke would billow out and spread through the church, carrying with it the pungent perfume of the incense. The building vibrated as the huge organ bellowed the *Tantum Ergo.* The choir sang wholeheartedly and the priest faced the congregation from the top step of the altar, holding up the monstrance in which was displayed the white, circular host of bread, now the body of Christ. The people bowed their heads in reverence. Even the hard men at the back of the church went down on one knee, some of them using their caps to save their kneecaps from the cold floor.

Within minutes they would have bolted out of the church and across the road, to stand sheltered from the wind – polishing Dick Mac's gable-end – while they commented on the 'talent' emerging from the church.

'Jaysus, I wouldn't mind her. Was anyone there yet?'

'Ne'er a one. There she is, walking around like she owns the place, a fine thing and the bonnet never even lifted on her yet.'

The comfort of being one of the lads, the shelter of the gable and the safety in numbers brought out all the cant phrases. The church was the social centre of the community and the place most certain of seeing someone. For eager adolescents, dying to see and be seen, it was a godsend. The routines were well established. Closeness with the opposite sex, without the risks of having to engage in conversation or the danger of gauche interaction, made it very attractive. When we felt overwhelmed by shyness, it was easily disguised as snootiness. When we felt unable to make or hold eye contact, there was usually the option of an angelic uplifting of gaze, or even entranced absorption in religious fervour. Many first fantasies were lived out while sneaking a look at the current object of boyish and impotent lustful thoughts across the middle aisle between the Consecration and the Last Gospel. In those days we used to have a second gospel at every Mass. It was the Gospel of St John, said at the end of Mass.

The church was central to everything. It charted our lives and provided both a frame and a focus for all our activities. The clergy were there at birth with the water and flame of baptism, they were in at the death with candle, oil and holy water, and they missed very little in between. All the important moments of life centred around the church. First Communion, Confirmation, weddings and funerals – there was no escape from the religious. They completely hijacked all our celebrations as well, making Christmas and Easter their own.

In case they might be forgotten, they would also be there to bless the new house, factory, or football pitch. And just to make doubly sure, there was the constant visitation to the schools, the Men's Confraternity and the Women's Sodality, the annual mission and the procession on the feast of Corpus Christi in June.

The superstitious nature of fishermen was well exploited at the annual Blessing of the Boats on 29 June, the feast day of those biblical fishermen, St Peter and St Paul. The whole fleet, cleaned, decorated and bedecked with bunting, cruised from the pier, loaded with townspeople. We always tried to get on the *Ros Dubh*, Paddy Bawn's boat. The flotilla headed out beyond the harbour's mouth, out near the Crow Rock, where they all formed into a mighty circle. The canon would intone the Rosary from the deck of the flagship boat, the *Elsie Mable*. His words were carried across the open water by the ships' two-way radios, all tuned in to the same channel and turned up full volume. As the boats rolled in the swell, the occupants dropped to their knees and dutifully answered the five decades. In Dingle, the priests made certain that we knew that God was everywhere.

The missioners were great men for the parables. They had a clear understanding of the strength of stories to sell the message. The stories were impactful and often unforgettable. Many of them were variations of the maxim of 'do unto others as you would they would do unto you'. With the experience of life, it is now clear that many of the guiding principles of Christianity as expounded by these men of the 'one, true Church' were echoed in other religions. The Buddhist view, that 'what comes around goes around', is not that different.

There was a mission priest from the Passionist Order who made a great and fiery impression. One day at the children's mission, when it had been well signalled that the homily would be about sex, or at least impure thoughts and actions, he started into a story about three soldiers trying to find their way back from the battlefront in Northern France towards the end of the war. They were in high spirits, happy to be away from bombs, bullets and death. They had taken drink. It was unlikely that they would ever have to return to fighting. Everything was fine. As they were walking along, arguing their relative merits as marksmen, they saw a grotto of Calvary away in the distance. Christ on the crucifix was clearly visible. The corporal claimed that he could shoot the statue through the heart, though it was a long distance away. We in the body of Dingle church were taken aback that such a thing could be suggested, even in a story. We shifted uncomfortably. Back on the green fields of France the argument progressed to the point where the corporal became determined to prove his prowess. He unhitched his rifle and, despite the objections of the young private, took aim and fired. The breastbone of the statue shattered. The second soldier felt obliged to do as well, but not being quite so accurate, managed to hit Christ on the leg. The young private, lacking the moral courage to say 'no', took careful aim at Christ's hand and hit the little finger.

Honour satisfied, the corporal led his little group onwards with swaggering bravado. He had barely travelled a quarter of a mile when he trod on a landmine. He was killed instantly and his shattered and broken body blown to a million pieces. The second soldier, following immediately behind, had been sheltered from most of the force of the blast. He was thrown to the ground, alive, but with his leg missing from the knee down. The young private escaped the blast, but was hit in the hand by a piece of flying debris, which took off the top of his little finger. The preacher could not resist a self-satisfied, triumphant smile as he let the moral of the story sink in. He needed no further emphasis. We were appalled. Statues would be safe from us. We understood now the power of God; it was better to be on his side.

❈   ❈   ❈

There were very few Protestants in Dingle. Those that there were tended to have more novelty value than anything else. Certainly no animosity was expressed towards them and generally they were popular among the community. Teresa, in fairness to her, always felt the need to remark about any Protestants mentioned in conversation, 'They're a lovely family.' Nonetheless, they were clearly different from us. After all, as the Christian Brothers never tired of reminding us, they were not part of the 'One, True, Catholic and Apostolic Church' and of course we knew that the Blessed Virgin Mary should never be mentioned in their hearing, because Protestants did not acknowledge her. In point of fact, it was a serious error to ever raise or argue matters of Catholic faith or dogma with non-Catholics in case our beliefs would be threatened, particularly before we became effective Soldiers of Christ through the sacrament of Confirmation. We also believed it was a sin even to enter a Protestant church.

One visiting missionary warned us to be very careful if we ever found ourselves sitting alone on a train and some friendly stranger sat down beside us and started talking about religion. We were to leave immediately. For months afterwards I had this image of armies of stalking proselytisers, stealthily creeping up on unsuspecting young people, while criss-crossing the country on the trains of Ireland, and trying to trick them into talking about religion. It was a foolproof system. Once we knew that every stranger who raised a point of belief was the enemy, and that under no circumstances should we discuss beliefs or religion with strangers, then we were locked in. Proofed against proselytisation. Total consolidation.

JIMMY TERRY'S
STALLION

Ah yes, the sex bit.

The Christian Brothers made valiant but restrained attempts to make us aware of the more basic elements of procreation. Such information was, by well-established precedent, greeted with embarrassed sniggers. There was very little new in what we heard, though I do recall sharing the amazement and surprise of others at the notion that the baby emerged from the front, rather than from the back, of the mother.

'I mean, how would it fit?'

They also gave us the amazing piece of information that sometimes the energy of blossoming manhood burst loose during sleep and that we should not worry about finding its damp presence when we awoke. It was only a sin if we gave it a helping hand. My mother gave various bits of information which, when pieced together and collated with the fact that I saw her go through four pregnancies, increased my store of knowledge on the subject.

Books were also used. The Brothers gave us a booklet called *Courtesy for Boys and Girls*; it was mighty in the way it explained about holding doors open for the 'weaker sex' and the order in which one used the cutlery on a fully laid table. It dealt with vexed questions, such as whether or not a young gentleman should remove his white gloves when handing a female partner on to the dance floor, but it never really addressed the hormonal issues.

Right through primary school there were the lewd, crude and vulgar jokes, which always received a great guffaw of laughter and knowing approval, even from those of us who did not quite get the joke. And were we quick on the uptake? Well, judge for yourselves. We were in our early teens when we found out, through reliable sources, that syphilis and gonorrhoea could be contracted from dirty toilet seats. We were a fair bit older before we discovered this to be untrue.

My uncle Thomas, who was a Christian Brother himself, gave me, with Teresa's approval, a copy of Neville Shute's *A Town like Alice*. This was a significant development in that the main protagonists, Joe Harman and Jean Paget, got their clothes off and had sweaty body contact under the hot Australian sun. It contained daring words like 'breast', and although there was no graphic language, there was plenty of descriptive stuff and enough pointers. It was a great story too, and well told. There was the first meeting, then the meeting of minds and the growing closer, the inevitable separation, the realisation of love; the anxious search around the world for each other, the climactic meeting and the consummation.

This was sex in the context of love: natural, healthy and heroic. Here was a presentation of sex well beyond the schoolboy vulgarity. A catalyst to thought. The learning process continued.

But we still chased girls up the barrack height and didn't know quite what to do when they let us catch up with them. Oh yes, and we played 'You show me yours' over in the Grove.

The fact of living so close to farms and farm animals, however, was probably the most instructive of all. While there was never a 'birds and bees' lecture, there were many who had a bit part in putting together a picture for our sex education. It was all age-appropriate too, because in many cases the information was prompted by our own childish questions.

'Why are all those dogs trying to get into Spillanes?'

'Because Mrs Spillane's bitch is in heat. The dogs are chasing her.'

Adequate, perfectly accurate, and reasonable to the young mind. Next time the query would be taken a stage further: 'What puts the bitch in heat?'

And so it would go on, a layering of information that built up to a broader understanding.

It allowed us to recognise similar behaviour in other animals. No need now to ask why the frustrated old bullock was jumping up on the young heifers.

A lesson I could probably have done without was the one delivered by Pat Neligan's father in the shed beside the creamery, where he showed us how to castrate a young ram. And at least I was only a spectator; poor Pat had to hold the lamb while his father did the deed. While Pat kept the unfortunate victim still, Mr Neligan took hold of its penis and slapped some horrible, green gungy stuff on it. It was called Friar's Balsam and it had a sweetish pungency about it. Then, just above the testicles, he clamped the penis with two small, flat-sided cipíns of wood, which had been bound together at one end. For some reason, the wood had to be cut from the Sally tree. Now, with the penis clamped, he looped twine around the open ends of the two pieces of wood and began to squeeze and tighten them together. The poor lamb let out a squeak of pain as the knot was finally tied with a last, firm tug. Another dollop of the Friar's Balsam was lashed on, and then Pat let the lamb away before turning his attention to the next patient.

'What happens next, Mr Neligan?'

'Well, we'll come back in a week to check that they have all dropped off.'

'What!!?'

'You see, we have stopped the flow of blood with the clamps, so the flesh without the blood will simply rot away and fall off.'

Seeing the pain that both Pat and myself were feeling, he went on, 'Some fellows in the old days would just bite it off, and spit it out as soon as it was clamped!'

We were both dumbfounded, and for my part feeling more than a little bit sick as we headed home some time later, with clenched scrotums, both of us surreptitiously checking that all our genitalia were intact.

※　※　※

On the last Saturday of every month, while the fair was in progress, Jimmy Terry would arrive from Annascaul with his stallion. The stallion stood and serviced mares in a little garden off the laneway connecting John Street with the Brewery field, where the fair was held. Farmers brought their mares to the garden by appointment. We could be there legitimately, agog at the jaw-dropping activities that ensued.

'Jesus! He's washing the mare's arse with sudsy water.'

It was a functional rather than a cosmetic exercise. The black stallion would nose up to the mare as she was being paraded before him. When he showed a bit of interest after smelling the mare's sexual readiness, the farmer and Jimmy would tease them for a bit, separating them and then bringing them back together, to get the stallion excited. This part of the exercise we knew was called prick teasing, a term which, indeed, a few short years later we would use contemptuously and, as I now know unfairly, about young women who led us so far and then stopped without granting us full sexual satisfaction.

All the time the stallion's manhood was stiffening and strengthening for all to see. He showed all the signs of wanting to mount the mare, and would be bouncing on his hind legs trying to get his forelegs up on her. Jimmy made him wait, holding him back until the crucial moment, then he allowed the stallion to get his forelegs on the mare's back while he personally took hold of the stallion's giant penis and guided it into the receptive mare, before letting them get on with it. It was mighty stuff and apparently the little stallion had a great record and became something of a legend. The crowd always gave him a bit of a cheer when he dismounted.

'Well poled!'

The introduction of Artificial Insemination Officers, or the AI men, as they were called, created great confusion. Their precise job was never fully explained to the farming community, and because of the sheer embarrassment that a discussion on the technical aspects of sex might create between a married couple, many farmers' wives were left in the dark. This led to the, no doubt apocryphal, story of Steve White, an AI man, arriving at a farm where there was a cow to be bulled. The farmer being absent, he was met by the lady of the house who brought him across to the cowshed, showed him the cow and said as she departed, 'Sure I'll leave her to you, Steve, and there's a nail there on the back of the door, if you want to hang your trousers on it.'

As we grew older the jokes about Jimmy's stallion became more relevant. There would be regular references to him outside the church, at the back of the dance hall, on the bridge, or wherever sexual prowess was being hailed, described or boasted. It could also be used to put down the guy who was talking up a mighty conquest.

'Don't mind all that bullshit, just tell us did you leave it in her?'

'Well, I nearly did; next time for certain.'

The riposte was deflating and deadly: 'Ask Jimmy Terry's stallion. "Nearly" never bulled the mare, but "Barely" always made it.' Crude but effective.

There was one well-known auld fellow around the town who was always boasting as to what he had done and what a mighty man for the women he was in his day. The received wisdom was that he had never been 'within a mile' of a woman. He was very low-sized and butty, and the lads would always be rising him about big, attractive women, 'You'd hardly have the equipment for that class of a woman', or 'Who'd put you up to it, Murt?' He had a tried and trusted repertoire of answers ready for all such taunts.

'Long and thin goes too far in and does not suit the lady,

Short and thick will do the trick and surely bring a baby.'

These exchanges, crude and graphic as they were, hinted at experience, but it was often the case that they were rooted in ignorance or innocence. The main contributors were rarely the Casanovas of the town. They were generally those whose race was run and who were dried to cynicism. Their audience usually comprised young bucks for whom it had not happened yet, and 'over the hills' for whom it would never happen again. No doubt it started the youngsters off with a questionable and irresponsible attitude, and probably contributed to later insensitive approaches to women. The matter of feelings and affection, not to mind love, never entered into consideration. On the other hand, those same men who could express such vulgarity in male company, would display restraint and respect towards women when they were in their presence.

As for myself, although I was taken by surprise by the arrival of my sister, Phyllis, I had reached a stage where the 'cabbage plant' tales were wasted on me. I knew where babies really came from, even if I didn't know the full details. By the time Teresa was pregnant with my youngest sister, Grace, I was in secondary school and wise to the ways of the world, so I was well aware of the impending arrival of another baby. There was not a lot more to learn in that area.

I was uncomfortable with the attitudes expressed by the gatherings on the bridge. Being raised with four sisters, and very much influenced by two strong and independent grandmothers, and a mother of similar type, I never saw women as easy. The genuine respect and deference of my father and grandfather towards women, as well as the equality of roles in their households, all combined to suppress my nascent machismo. It never recovered.

Sad to relate, my own sexual development was slow and my experiences in that area hard won. The very many 'Nearly' occasions have confusingly fused with a vivid imagination, so that my subconscious refuses to yield any recollection as to when, precisely, my virginity lapsed. It might be more correct to say that it was erased rather than lost. In fact, maybe I never really lost it.

A TAILOR ON
EVERY STREET

'Go down to Tailor Lynch and collect the suit for John Sheehy.'

'Run up to Tailor Ferriter with that suit length, and while you're there ask him if he has the makings, or will I send him up some.'

Tailors are central to my memory of Dingle. There seemed to be a tailor on every street in the town. My grandmother had been doing business with them for years. Teresa recalled how, as a child, she looked forward to being sent to Tailor Lynch, because even though it was almost the last cottage back towards Milltown Bridge, Ellie Nora, the tailor's wife, would always give her a sixpenny piece. Extraordinarily generous for the times.

The tailors' workshops were surreal. You had the impression of being surrounded by semi-dressed people. Suits in various stages of completion hung all around, some sleeveless or legless, others turned inside out, with the lining and paddings on view. The wide, low work table would be covered in material, on which the tailor chalked out the design and the customer's individual measurements. A good tailor would mark out the pieces and cut them in such a way as to leave very little waste material. The tailor's shop was always quiet and never had the bustle of other businesses. The tailor himself often worked cross-legged, stitching and finishing so that there would be no puckers or pulls in the completed garment. In the Corca Dhuibhne dialect, *táilliúir*, the Irish word for tailor, was sometimes used to describe people who might have had a short leg or a club foot. The reason may be that any such defect was not an impediment in tailoring, and those people could earn a good living in that trade, whereas other jobs would not be open to them.

With the advantage of hindsight, and even though its graph of commerce was firmly heading downwards, Dingle of the early 1950s was a model of self-sufficiency and entrepreneurship. The water supply came from a reservoir on Cnoc a' Chairn and was totally reliable. I can never remember a water shortage or serious difficulty.

There was a waste and rubbish collection every week, even though everyone was also expected to have a dump area in their back garden where some waste was burnt or rotted. All the shops would accept dollars as legal tender across the counter. For as long as I lived in Dingle the dollar was worth 7/6d, seven shillings and sixpence, and there were always dollars in circulation. Everyone seemed busy. Every second house in the town was either producing or servicing.

There were the pubs, of course. I remember as a youngster counting all fifty-six of them. Then there were the busy shops, mainly owned and run by generations of the same local families, but there was also Latchford's and Atkins' – the largest shops in the town – owned by some of Cork's merchant princes.

As well as the tailors, there were numerous harness-makers, carpenters and shoemakers. Billy Neill, the cobbler, lived across the road from us in the Mall. When studying in my bedroom I had a clear view of him inside his big shop window, working away. On calm days during the summer term I would be distracted by the distinct sound of Billy's hammer, tapping in tacks, or smacking on the leather. Although we called all cobblers 'shoemakers', they didn't all make shoes. In fact, only a few of them did and they were hobnail boots rather than shoes. As kids we hated those boots, but they were a great favourite with parents because they were so serviceable and lasted forever. In many ways, getting the pair of hobnails was a mark of growing up; they would normally be worn from late primary school age. They were so stiff and unbending that for the six months it took to break them in, the hard leather would be blistering your heels and grazing your ankles. But there was one compensation. When a pair of hobnail boots was sent to the cobbler for new half-soles, they also came back with a new set of pristine hobnails. Well, we had some fun then, walking the town and knocking sparks out of our hobnails against the flagstoned footpaths.

The cobbler's new leather hung from the ceiling behind the row of lasts. Even though it was thick, stiff, light-coloured leather when it arrived, it still retained the outline and size of the cowhide. When he set about half-soling a shoe, the cobbler would cut off a rectangular section of leather, slightly larger than the area of the sole. As time went on and more and more was cut from the large piece, it began to look less like a cowhide and more like a gigantic jigsaw piece. Billy, sitting in his leather apron on his little workbench, tacks in his mouth, would arrange the rectangle of leather against the sole of the shoe. Then he would nail it on to the shoe, taking each tack from his mouth and using his hammer to strike home the nails in a rapid action which was a combination of strike and stroke. There was a recognisable and unfailing rhythm: Tap, Tap, Tap, Smaaack. Four beats of the hammer, rising to a crescendo, and finally the fourth long hammer blow, driving the tack deep into the leather. Only when firmly attached would the corners and sides of the rectangle be rounded, shaped and skimmed to the shape of the shoe.

Billy Neill's was a place of exotic smells: new leather hides, the wax through which he pulled the thread in order to strengthen it before stitching the upper to the leather sole, the dye he used on the cut ends of the leather and the smell of the polish with which he finished the job. We loved those smells.

Billy claimed to have saved my life. One warm sunny day he was working away on his bench, facing out the window, when he saw Teresa putting the infant me in the pram outside the door. She then went back indoors, leaving me to take the fresh air. Billy and Hannah had no children of their own and they always took a great interest in us. By the path beside our house there was an open area that sloped down into the Mall River, which flowed under the house. Didn't Billy notice the pram beginning to roll towards the water. He bolted across the road and reached the pram just as it turned over into the water, whereupon he fished me and the pram out.

Now, it is not for me to say whether or not he did the world a favour. But I owe him.

There was fairly serious competition between the shoemakers, and for a family to change loyalties from one to another would be a matter of local comment. Not that tey did not try to woo business.

'*Saor, Slachtmhar, Tapaidh*' (Cheap, Tidy, Quick) read the sign on one shoemaker's shop in the Holyground.

'Three damn lies,' agreed all the others.

There were three bakeries and four forges in Dingle. For anyone who grew up near the sound of a forge there is a resonance to the clang of a lump hammer on hot metal which never dies. As a magnet for children, passersby and layabouts there was nothing to match a working forge. The wheeze of the bellows, the heat and flame of the fire, the music of metal on metal, the whinny of nervous horses awaiting shoes, it was all orchestrated by the leather-aproned blacksmith as he tapped nails into hooves held firmly between his legs.

Tommy Barry's forge in the Holyground was irresistible. Apart from being a busy place of work, it was also the repository of all the news, rumour and gossip of the town. From the forge there was a clear and unhindered view out the Mail Road, and the schedule of the town was marked with definitive accuracy.

'Dinneens should have the papers by now. The bus came in ten minutes ago.'

'Run down to Paguine and tell him the funeral is just at the football field, so he can close the pub door while it's passing.'

'Did anyone see the mail van? Is it late again today?'

In Barry's they could tell you exactly how many carts of coal had gone from the quay up to Atkins'. But it was not Tommy who was the purveyor of news and gossip; he was always too busy. There were a few who could be found at the forge door most days of the week, accumulating the news and passing it on to all and sundry, with a word and a question to every passerby, so that they got a new piece of information for every bit that they gave out.

'What was the fishing like today, Babs?'

'We filled a few boxes of plaice and dabs, but the mackerel is finished.'

'How was the fair?'

'Hopeless! There wasn't a buyer in the brewery today. There's more sheep gone home than came in, by all accounts.'

On it went, and all the information would be filtered, edited and regurgitated across the tables, across the counters, over pints of porter and at corners during the next few hours. From a social point of view this was the way people learnt about each other. Information flowed and was traded wherever there was interaction. It also led to a caring and supportive community. The tailor making a wedding suit for a man who was known to be going through a slow patch in his boat or on his farm would not be rushing out the bill. When partial payment was made, with the request: 'Will that be enough until after the September fair?' it was accepted respectfully and with dignity.

It also gave everyone an interest in the September fair of course, and if that was a disaster then everyone felt it and adjustments had to be made. It may not have had the modern vocabulary or jargon, but debt restructuring and contract renegotiation were part and parcel of daily life. '*Ar scáth a chéile a mhaireann na daoine.*'

Youngsters hanging around the forge were in the middle of commercial activity and saw labour being exchanged for wages.

They learnt about people and they learnt how to react to people's difficulties. They learnt to differentiate between wit and insult and they also shared the imparted wisdom of highly intellectual, but barely educated seniors of the community.

'It was our university,' said Ciarán Cleary.

How about Barry's Forge University College? Not bad. I can see it now: BFUC.

❖ ❖ ❖

Uncle Patty, like all the butchers in the town, slaughtered his own meat and it was usually from his own farm. He took great pride in having the best quality cuts. Sometimes I would wander back the yard to watch the slaughtering. There were different slaughtering days for the different animals. Tadhg Lynch worked with Uncle Patty at that time and it would be Tadhg that I would watch in total fascination as he went about his work in the slaughterhouse.

'Ah young Joseph, do you want to learn how it's done?'

The sheep were slaughtered by a knife incision through the neck, cutting the main artery from which the sheep's lifeblood would spurt, to be collected in a container underneath. This would later be the basis for Aunty Sheila's delicious black pudding. Sheep were docile creatures, veritable lambs to the slaughter. Each one was lifted on to a sort of wooden cradle where it was held on its side, feet fettered. Tadhg handed me the knife and showed me where we would stick it in the sheep's neck to make it quick and easy. Then, taking my hands in his, he plunged the knife and withdrew it immediately. The sheep moaned.

'Now, hold the sheep's neck down so that the blood won't splash all over the place.'

Holding the dying sheep while its warm blood gurgled over my fingers seemed like a very natural and matter-of-fact thing to do. I

Above: Teresa with her first cousin, Hilda O'Malley, and Hilda's son, Caragh.

Right: With my pal, Pat Neligan (*right*).

Above: I was never musical, but I was in the school band.
Left: My Confirmation.
Clockwise from left: myself, Teresa, Myko, Mary Sabrina and Anita.

Right: My sisters Grace and Phyllis in the Mall, Dingle.
Below: Phyllis, centre with headdress, on the day of her First Communion. Anita is third from right, wearing the woollen bonnet and facing front.

Above: The Mall, Dingle, with the gable-end of our shop, Moriarty's, clearly visible on the left.

Below: Playing handball against the wall of the courthouse, opposite our house.

Right: A group of boyhood friends in Dingle. *Back row, left to right:* Mattie Maloney, James Shea, Bob Sullivan, Joe O'Toole, Thomas Lyne; *front row, left to right:* the name of the first boy is lost to my memory, James Walsh, Peter Leary, Pat Neligan.

Below: Teresa, Brother Thomas and Fergus O'Flaherty at the Dingle races.

Left: The family at home. *Back row, left to right:* Joe, Myko, Phyllis; *front row, left to right:* Mary Sabrina, Anita, Grace, Teresa.
Below: Granny O'Toole with (*left to right*) Mary Sabrina, my cousins, Geraldine, Clare and Oliver, and myself at Kylemore Abbey.

Right: Private O'Toole, with .303 rifle, in 'C' Company, 15th Battalion, FCA, Dingle, 1963.

Below: Dingle CBS Inter. Cert. class of 1962. *Back row, left to right:* Tom Shea, Micheál Ó Dúda, Pat Sullivan, Sean O'Connor, Paddy Leahy, Seán Prendiville; *centre row, left to right:* Michael McNamara, Seámus Griffin, Sean O'Leary, Joe O'Toole, Pat Neligan, Sean O'Shea, Seámus Moriarty; *front row, left to right:* Ronan Burke, Paddy O'Connor, Tadhg Barret.

Above: Celebrations for the Golden Wedding Anniversary of Sean the Grove and Bridgy Fitz (together at head of table). Paguine is second on right.

Right: Fifty years later and Sr Rose's rocking horse in Dingle convent is still going strong.

(Photo: Tom Fox.)

had the feeling that I was helping rather than killing. As soon as the sheep was dead, it would be hung by its hind legs, head downward and with its front legs sticking out for skinning. It required considerable skill to take the skin cleanly from the carcass without cutting the flesh. Tadhg would gently cut the skin in a straight line along the underbelly and ease it away from the flesh. Once he had made a start, he would alternately use the blade and the knife handle to separate the skin by cutting, pummelling and pulling. When the sheepskin was taken off, the carcass would be slashed open along the same line as was used to cut the skin. Out in a gush of green, white and red would spew the steaming organs and innards of the sheep. The edible and saleable organs, such as the heart, liver and kidneys, were carefully cut and separated. Then every speck of the sheep's insides was cleaned out. The final act was to rub some blood on to the gleaming, hot sides of the white carcass. This gave it a healthy redness. A few nicks made on the stretched outer layer of reddened skin caused them to open, revealing the perfect white of the underlayer.

Thursday was pig day. They were a lot more difficult than the sheep, and squealed and struggled when they were being slaughtered. Pigs were not skinned, instead the rough hair on their hide was burnt away with a blowlamp. The smell of singed hair and hide was horrible, but you got used to it.

Slaughtering cattle became much easier with the arrival of the humane killer. This was a specially developed gun which was held to the bullock's forehead. The crack of the shot was followed immediately by the crash of the dying animal on to the floor of the slaughterhouse.

In hindsight, the whole scene was sickeningly gory, but I must confess that I was usually so engaged with the process that ethical conflicts never arose in my young mind. There was an ordinariness about it all. I could like lambs, but I could still eat lamb. The fact that it was killing never impacted. It is the type of experience that should, at the very least, drive a child to vegetarianism. It did not, and it was not too many years before Uncle Patty was explaining and teaching me the intricacies of slaughtering, a training which stood me in good stead many years later when I got a summer job in Walls' meat-processing plant in Hayes, outside London.

The butchers took a real pride in their product. Of course, they had a vested interest in making sure their meat was of a consistently high quality in order to keep their customers. Dingle customers were demanding and would generally be good judges of meat. From the customer's point of view there was no need to worry about additives or disease; good butchers would neither buy nor kill any animal considered to be in any way defective. The law that made it impossible for small butchers to continue slaughtering their own meat was a mistake. It has led to huge difficulties of traceability. Nowadays not even the butcher knows for certain where the meat originated.

▨　▨　▨

Carpenters were always busy; there was a constant demand for their skills – making coffins, spokes and wheels for carts, etc. They started in a clean workshop in the morning, but by evening they were surrounded by discarded pieces of timber, wood shavings and sawdust. Mind you, the cast-offs and shavings were very useful for starting a fire in those pre-firelighter days. It was not unusual to see people leaving the carpenter's with a sack of bits for the fire.

The fire was built up by a strictly regulated method. First a layer of crumpled newspapers was laid, then a layer of wood shavings, on top of that went a few bits of wood and finally the coal. A match was put to the paper and away it went. As soon as the coal was glowing, more was added and then, to ensure that the expensive coal did not burn away too quickly, a few shovelfuls of wet slack were slapped on top. The slack was really just coal dust and it formed a crust on the fire, giving it a few extra hours' burning time.

The shavings from the carpenter and the coal dust were just part of a thriftiness of approach that was essential in those times. Very often one person's waste was another person's lifeline. Butchers would always give bones to people who asked: 'And a few bones for the dog?'

Everybody knew if the bones were for the dog or for the family soup, but nobody said. The butcher would throw in some dripping as well; this was handy for fried bread if there was nothing else. Bread which was a bit on the stale side for selling would find its way to families in need. Similarly with any fish not sold on the quays.

Dignity and anonymity characterised all such exchanges.

Travellers were plentiful in Dingle, particularly during the summer period. We called them 'tinkers' or 'coffees'. The travellers were well-known and would park their caravans in the same spot, over near the creamery. Their kids attended school with the rest of us while they were in the area. The mothers went begging from house to house while the fathers appeared to do nothing at all. At that stage, the craft of tinkering – mending kettles and pots and pans – which had given them their name, had all but disappeared.

Obviously they had very little money but they nonetheless had to buy bits and pieces. You always had to be on your mettle when dealing with them, as they would argue and bargain forever. They were basically honest people, but were tricksters at heart.

On one occasion one of the traveller clan died and there was great sadness. Plans were made to have him buried somewhere at the other end of the county. But the price of a coffin was a bit of an obstacle and they were certainly not going to pay an undertaker for what they could do themselves. So they went around to every carpenter in the town looking for as cheap a coffin as possible. One of the carpenters in Holyground reluctantly did a deal with them. He was at a loss on the deal, but agreed it just to get rid of them.

They went off to box the body and head out of town. Hardly an hour later they were back to the carpenter.

'We got a cheaper coffin in Fitz's. Will you take this back and give us our money?'

He was only delighted. He could sell it again at its proper price.

'No bother at all. Put the coffin back up there and I'll get the money from the house.'

That was that. But when he was talking to Fitzy a few days later outside Mass, Fitzy denied ever selling them a coffin.

'They never darkened my door.'

The carpenter thought no more of it, but about a week later his wife started complaining about a smell in the workshop. They put it down to rats and he laid some traps. The smell got worse. It remained a mystery for another week until he went to pull down a coffin for a funeral in Ventry. He was struck by the weight of it and had to get help from a neighbour. They lifted it down and opened it up, only to fall back in horror at the stench from the decomposing body of the traveller inside. It was a cheap funeral and no comeback, because when challenged months later, the travellers denied all knowledge and maintained that they had buried their man.

It's a story that I know will cause surprise and maybe disbelief, given that travellers are noted for their funeral rituals, even to burning the caravan of the deceased, but it happened in Dingle. Who knows what circumstances lay behind it.

The Ashes, who lived next door to us, had the Guinness agency. The entire Guinness supply for West Kerry was kept in their store. My abiding memory of the Guinness store was that it had an intriguing device that recorded the ambient temperature. The thermometer was connected to a nib, which then inked the temperature on to graph paper that revolved on a drum. The drum did one revolution every twenty-four hours. The Guinness had to be up to, rather than down to, a particular temperature at the time. Shows how tastes change.

They also had a factory for making soft drinks, or 'minerals' as they were called then. Mr Ashe, who was known as Mikey Joe, took personal charge of the formula for making the minerals. They had a big selection. Apart from the usual orange and lemon flavours, they made Lemon Soda, Red Lemonade, Raspberry, Grapefruit and Cola.

From a food and drinks point of view, the town of Dingle was well served with local produce. Every butcher supplied his own meat from the grass of his own farm, or else bought specially from a neighbouring farmer. Milk was bought at the creamery and churned into butter, which was bought and sold locally. Mrs Quinn from Cam sold a half-stone of homemade butter every Sunday, as did many others. Donal Lynch's family, from Kilfountain, did a twice daily milk round with the horse and cart, delivering in bulk to shops like McKennas in Dykegate Street, but also dropping in pints and quarts of milk to private houses. Lynch's horse knew the stops so well that it didn't matter who was doing the run; the old horse stopped at all the customers' shops and houses without being asked.

Then from the mid 1950s to the early 1960s the town changed rapidly. It was a revolution that crept up on us without warning or anticipation and it resulted in the elimination of almost all the trades and craftspeople and their families in Dingle. Perhaps we had been under the impression that young people didn't want to carry on the family businesses and went on to a different life, exploiting the advantages of their education and seeking their fortunes in other places. But it wasn't that. In fact, all the industrious people in small businesses and trades were the last of their generation because they were hit with the consequences of the second industrial revolution.

From the early 1950s it was cheaper to buy shoes ready-made than to get them from the shoemaker. The carpenter who made carts and and coffins could not compete with the factories who delivered coffins directly to the undertaker. As for carts, they were fast being replaced by cars and tractors. The harness-makers and the blacksmiths went the same way.

The tailors were hit by the fashion for off-the-rail, ready-made clothes, because no matter how well they pursued their craft, they could never achieve a decent rate for the time it took them to produce a first-class garment.

The effect of this on the town was catastrophic. Houses that for generations were centres of a brisk trade and business began to see a sharp and continuous downturn in their incomes. Within a short few years it was clear that there was no future in it for the son of the house and shortly after that the business closed. In their working lives these hardworking and diligent people had had little enough and certainly would not have had the opportunity to invest in pensions or the like. Now they had nothing and were in the main trying to survive on a meagre old age pension. Their homes reflected the change. No craftsman inside the window; no customers. Eventually the name over the door was taken down. The big shop window was curtained and the only people who called were friends and relations. The streetscape changed from commercial to residential, with the incongruously large, gaping shop windows in private houses the only reminder of what once was.

It was a different Dingle.

During the round of the Dingle year there was a series of events that maintained links to generations past and created a cultural bond between the people, streets and groups in the town and its hinterland.

The two biggest traditional occasions in the year were Bonfire Night, 23 June – a pagan celebration as old as history, which the Church had hijacked and renamed as Saint John's vigil – and the Wren's Day, on 26 December, Saint Stephen's Day. We called them 'Bonefire Night' and the 'Wran's Day'. From the first day of June, and sometimes much earlier, we started collecting material for the bonfire. Buggies were constructed to carry the loads, and we would go door to door, asking for wood and any other material suitable for burning, such as turf, coal and cardboard. Used car tyres, which we begged from garages or farmers, were particularly valued. The centrepiece of the fire was the baulk. This was an enormous branch or trunk of wood around which was built the fire. Getting the tree trunk was a huge challenge. Fields and farms were scoured in the search. But finding it was only the beginning. Then you had to drag it secretly into the town and store it in a place where it would be safe from marauding rival gangs who might steal it for their own fires.

Traditionally, there was ferocious competition among the different groups from the various parts of the town: Sráid Eoin, Goat Street, or the Quay. Who would have the biggest blaze? Which fire would still be burning the following day? The Sráid Eoin fire – our fire – was originally on the bridge at the bottom of Main Street. However, in later years, as people became more safety conscious, it was shifted over to the Spa Road. Building the fire would begin in the mid-afternoon. It was no easy job keeping the baulk upright; we jammed smaller logs and branches around its base for stability. Then we surrounded it with the old car tyres. Oil-soaked rags, cardboard, wood shavings and sawdust were pushed into the spaces, and outside of these were placed the additional oddments and fuels. By the time the pyre was built and set it might be twelve feet high. The fire would be lit round about eight o'clock. Torching the fire was a ceremony in itself. A number of tin cans would be affixed to rigid lengths of wire, approximately a yard long. The cans were filled tight with oil-soaked sawdust. Once they were alight they were pushed deep into the pyre to get it lighting from the inside out. The flames from the blazing wood and fuels would leap towards the sky, shortly to be obscured by the thick, black, pungent smoke from the tyres. Eventually, the logs and the baulk itself would take hold and the fire would settle down.

The townspeople went from fire to fire. Then they would bring out chairs and sit around the blaze; how far back they had to set the chairs was another measure of the power of the fire. New potatoes were produced, to be baked in the fire. You had to be fairly hardy to brave the furnace-like heat and get close enough to place the potatoes on the fire and then retrieve them. Only rarely were they properly or fully cooked, but nonetheless everyone remarked on how good they were that year, and what a great night it was.

Then the music would begin. This was music without frontiers: a hornpipe followed by rock 'n' roll, or the twist, or whatever took the fancy. On great town occasions like this, Patrick Cronesberry and his sister Mary Ellen would sometimes perform a wild rock 'n' roll dance. He would throw her over his shoulder, pull her back between his legs, swinging, jiving and lifting her high up in the air, moving more spasmodically than rhythmically, but giving his all to the sound of Bill Haley's ' Rock around the Clock'. The crowd loved it and it probably marked the beginning of my lifelong love affair with rock 'n' roll. Once, when I was watching a Rolling Stones concert, it struck me that Cronesberry was not that different from Jagger!

The Cronesberrys were an interesting family who were originally from England. Patrick's older brother John was the town crier. He would go around the town, ringing his bell and shouting notice of an upcoming important meeting or entertainment. He had a clipped and distinct style of speech and a very loud voice so was well equipped for the job. The sound of his bell and his resonating voice brought people rushing to their doors to hear the news. It would usually be about Duffy's circus or a travelling fit-up show, but I do recall him announcing a meeting to oppose the proposed Turnover Tax, a predecessor of Valued Added Tax (VAT), which caused great grief to retail shopowners, who led a national campaign against it. Amazingly enough, the measure was passed in Dáil Éireann by Seán Lemass's minority government. Fianna Fáil supporters, including my uncle Plunkett in Lettermore, swore that they would never vote for the party again and that it meant the end of the small operator – they did and it wasn't. Lemass was gutsy and he knew that the issue of local shopkeepers having to pay tax more efficiently was not going to bother most ordinary people.

The Turnover Tax protest meeting was of interest only to the shopkeepers and small traders. This lack of interest was of such annoyance to one shopkeeper that he hired a loudspeaker system for the roof of his car and spent an hour touring the town, announcing the meeting, denouncing the Government and pronouncing the end of commerce as we knew it if this appalling tax were to be introduced. He coaxed and persuaded people to attend the meeting. 'Come along and support us. Please be there. This is a very important meeting. Everyone is welcome.' Of course, by the time he had said this for the twentieth time he was in foam of enthusiasm. He got quite carried away with indignation and righteousness, so much so that on his final round-up he announced: 'Everyone must be there, and anyone who isn't can fuck off for themselves!' In those days that kind of language would never be broadcast over a public address system. He was the talk of the town for ages.

Patrick Cronesberry worked in the coal yard at Atkins', one of the biggest general stores in town. In fact, they had shops in a number of locations throughout Munster. His daily grind involved lifting half-hundredweight bags of coal from store to truck and from the truck into people's houses. To save his clothes, he usually wore a jute sack on his head, with the stitched corner sticking up like a monk's habit and the rest stretched down his back. It was hard, dusty and thirsty work, never more so than on the couple of occasions each year when the coal boat would dock at the pier with a cargo of coal. Every available horse and cart in the town would be recruited to move the coal from the pier up to Atkins' yard at the top of the Main Street. A huge bucket crane swung across from the boat and deposited the coal into the carts that were queued up from the quay right down to the head of the pier. As soon as they were filled, the carts trundled their way through the streets of the town to where the workers with their shining coal shovels were waiting to offload and bag the coal. It was non-stop, physical, backbreaking work, with every breath contaminated by the swirling black coal dust. There were no masks or protective clothing, so they undoubtedly inhaled black lung and other respiratory problems.

Patrick Cronesberry would come into Foxy John's bar every evening after work. His order was always the same, 'A flagon of Bulmer's cider and a pint glass, Joe boy.' He was the only person in Dingle to call me Joe. I never told my mother.

'The Wran' was the biggest day of the year in our young lives. No other day came close. Paguine Flaherty's pub was the base for the

Green and Gold Wran from the Holyground. The Green and Gold was always considered the best overall, for music, colour and spectacle. They would have spent weeks in preparation in Paguine's. I used to envy my first cousins, Etna, Mazzarella, Fergus and Kar l– they were right in the middle of the action. Masks, hoods, straws and other costumes were made up; fifes were softened for practice; drums were tightened and banners were painted and sewn. There was absolute secrecy because there was huge competitiveness among the Wrans.

Our local Wran was the Sráid Eoin. The 'Kerryman', a huge, gentle giant of a man, was the driving force, even though young Maurice Rohan was emerging as the leader. It was in Rohan's pub that the Sráid Eoin met for practice and arrangements. Maurice made sure everything was under control. Even when he became a teacher and moved to West Clare, he still returned each year to take charge of the Sráid Eoin Wran. But West Clare also got the benefit of Maurice's organisational skills, as he went on to be one of the founders and main organisers of the Willie Clancy Summer School.

There were other Wrans – from Goat Street, The Quay and Milltown. Some were imaginative in deciding a theme for their group. Others were better at the music. Wrans from outlying areas, especially Lispole and Ventry, came into the town. Each had its own carefully respected traditions. In the Sráid Eoin Wran the hobbyhorse was central. It was made from light, curved, wooden hoops shaped like the torso of a horse. A white sheet covered the main trunk, the tail was stuck on the back, a carved head lead at the front, and the whole thing was carried on the shoulders of one of the Wran members who had a rope stretching back from the horse's mouth, which he could aggressively snap open and shut at passersby or at other Wrans.

All the Wrans did at least two rounds of the town. They each had favourite pub stops where they took a sos. It was the leader's job to make sure that they regrouped after a drink and continued on to the next 'filling station'.

The cry 'Fall In' was the signal to get outside and into band formation. The more stops they made the harder it was to get them restarted. You could hear the leader cursing at the lads in the bar.

'For fuck's sake lads, fall in.'

But he lost a few at each stop, and by early afternoon there was drink flowing in every one of Dingle's fifty-six pubs. Essentially, the Wran was a celebration to mark the passing of the shortest day of the year, and it was as old as mankind. It was the defeat of winter and the optimism of the coming spring, with its lengthening days and benign weather. Nowhere was this more evident than in the defining and defiant cry of the Sráid Eoin Wran: 'We never died a winter yet. Up Sráid Eoin.'

Things would be well heated up by the start of the second round of the town. Drink was taking effect. Even without the alcohol people were intoxicated by the music, the shouting, the dancing and the occasion. Inhibitions were lost. Nobody recognised anybody under the hoods and masks. It was a time when it was okay to grab a woman and feel her in ways that at any other time would have been out of the question. Anonymity gave protection.

If the first circuit of the town was for entertainment, the second was for the collection. The man with the collection box was crucial. People at their windows, usually upstairs to get a better view of proceedings, would throw down their contributions to the collector. Shopkeepers and merchants were watched carefully to ensure they paid up, and the givers were careful to make sure that they gave something extra to their local Wran.

In those days the collection was for the Wran Ball. Well, it was called a Ball, but it was another excuse for a great drinking session.

Towards evening time there was the last round-up. This was where all the Wrans and the various bands came together for one final tour of the town. It was marvellous. The streets streamed with colour and resounded with music, dancing, shouting, singing.

There was no time quite like it. Your blood would be pounding through your veins and the small hairs standing on your neck with sheer excitement and emotion. Dingle that day was like no other place. It was wild, mad, drunk and pagan. Pagan in the symbolism of the straw men and the hobbyhorse. Menacing and theatrical in the masks and disguises. Wild and atavistic in the driving wren tunes and provocative dancing. Add alcohol to that mix and all boundaries, inhibitions and limits collapsed.

Is it any wonder that the Church was less than enthusiastic about it? This pagan day had occasions for drink, sex and a slackening of morals generally, and it diverted collections away from the Church.

Many of my family and friends still make the annual pilgrimage to Dingle to take part in the Wran, leaving their homes before cockcrow on St Stephen's morning. Of course, it has changed and developed over the years. But it still quintessentially 'us'. Of all my friends I am the only one I know not to have gone back for the Wran since leaving Dingle. Why? Well, my memories of the day are so great, that I am afraid that returning would corrupt the magic. Maybe, like Oisín returning from Tír na nÓg and suddenly changing into a feeble, old and babbling man, confronting the reality of four decades of change in the Wran would steal my youth, too. But the memory remains untouchable.

The Dingle peninsula, comprising town, village, country, sea and mountain, is best described by its ancient barony title of Corca Dhuibhne rather than by any of its other names, such as West Kerry, which makes it seem just a portion of a greater integrity.

It is often said of the peninsula – the most westerly point of Europe – that 'the next parish is America'. There is something casually dismissive about that description that I don't like; does it imply that Dingle was 'the arsehole of Ireland', or at the very least a twilight zone between the real Ireland and the vast ocean? We who were born between Blennerville bridge and the Blasket Islands have a different perception. When we stand on Coumenole or Clogher strands, addressing the Atlantic Ocean, and with the land mass of two continents guarding our backs, we truly feel that we are the vanguard of Europe. Slea Head and Dunmore Head, cleaving aggressively into the Atlantic Ocean, give direction to the continent of Europe.

Yet Corca Dhuibhne is more an attitude than a place. Its mark is indelible; there is no leaving it behind. No matter how far we journey, that attitude travels with us and influences and informs what we do throughout our lives. We are unnaturally and irrationally proud of our birthplace

The peninsula is an elemental place, open to the vagaries and moods of Mother Nature. On a bright summer's day, when the sun, sea and scenery are in harmony, it is a perfect heaven. In winter, the sight of fearsome Atlantic waves charging ahead of a southwestern storm and smashing against the fastness of the rocky headlands and cliffs is an awesome and exhilarating experience. Then again, there are few more depressing feelings than being in a sodden and damp Dingle in those airless times when the clouds of oppressive mist that roll in from Greenmount, Conor Pass and Cnoc a' Chairn have hung around the town for four or five consecutive days. You can almost feel the weight of it. On Sunday afternoons, and sometimes on the Thursday half-day, it was not uncommon for people to 'go for a soak', that is, retreat to their beds, away from the depressive surroundings. I remember a former mental health consultant from Killarney making the point that Kerry had a higher than average level of certain types of mental illness and that the weather must have been a significant factor in this. What Dingle people suffered in the reduced daylight of autumn and winter would probably now be diagnosed as SAD (Seasonal Affective Disorder). For us schoolchildren, the shortening days were exacerbated by those teachers who insisted, by way of topical nature study, on drawing our attention to the gathering hordes of swallows getting ready to desert us at the first cool breeze. My schoolboy mind used to wonder whether we couldn't hold back the winter by trapping all the swallows and not letting them migrate – a hope about as futile as that of the other seasider, Canute, plotting against the elements.

The sea was central to life and livelihoods in Dingle, and we were constantly being reminded that it, and not us, was in charge. One day, the arrival of a new fifty-foot trawler, the Ros Mór, was the talk of the town. The boast was that it could handle the roughest of seas. A short time later, a huge storm blew up and the trawler was blown from the pier moorings and lifted over the quay wall, to be deposited, without dignity, as damaged goods on the Milltown Road.

The Blasket Island Sound is a dangerous and treacherous place, which has been the death row of seafarers for centuries. The bones, bodies, relics and wrecks on its seabed are eclectically representative of most of Europe's 'glorious' wars, from the galleons of the Spanish Armada to the U-boats and fighter planes of the twentieth century. The death list also includes ordinary farmers, fishermen and islanders crossing the Sound in naomhógs or trawlers in the mundane pursuit of food and provisions. Old stories hint that sometimes the odds were unfairly stacked against ships that plied these waters. Driven by desperation and the needs of starving families, folk from the coast or the island would lure the vessels towards the treacherous rocks by misplacing navigation lights, in the hope of salvaging survival from the holds and cargo of the wrecks. Who knows whether there was truth in these rumours? Certainly, the most damning insult to any family would be to charge them with robbing the valuables of drowned seafarers who had been washed ashore: 'Didn't your crowd rob dead sailors?' That was considered as low as it was possible to go.

But the sea also brought life and new blood to these shores. Corca Dhuibhne was a trading point from the Continent to Ireland; for centuries, sailors and smugglers, soldiers and swindlers arrived. The stranger and the traveller was part of daily life, and each one brought something of themselves. Some stayed, some loved and left, but either way gave their blood and their genes to add to the glorious mix of what makes Corca Dhuibhne. There is no trace of the dullness of inbreeding. Only those of us with mixed blood are true-blooded Corca Dhuibhne! This is our defining mark and it facilitates openness to change, difference and novelty.

When I was growing up in Dingle in the 1950s and early 1960s fishing was the main source of employment. Fishermen were individually liked and popular, but they worked in dangerous conditions and were poorly rewarded for their labour. At that time, under the rules of the Catholic Church, every Friday was a 'fast' day, which meant that no meat could be eaten, under pain of sin. It seems daft now, but then fish was very much the poor relation to meat, so being 'reduced' to eating fish once a week was seen as a penance. And eating fish by choice on any other day was almost unheard of. It's almost impossible to imagine such a ruling being complied with nowadays. Should we blame the Church or was it a question of our own ignorance and servility? Whatever, it meant that while there was an enormous consumption of fish on Fridays, the other days of the week were not very rewarding for the fishing industry. And, of course, long-term, as everyone now acknowledges, it created a sort of stigma about eating fish that took decades to erode. Can it be any wonder that Irish people were so low in the international league of fish-eaters, when, for generations, eating it was a penance? The negative attitude towards fish resulted in a poor market and low income and consequently a low place in the social order for fishermen and their families. Negativity towards the fishing industry permeated through national policy. Extraordinarily, fishing did not merit a mention in the programmes for economic expansion published in the 1950s. There was no structured investment in the fishing industry and we effectively gave away our fishing grounds in our early European agreements.

'It's not swanky to eat fish,' a woman said to my mother once, and that probably summed up the whole general attitude. It wasn't swanky. There were some exceptions – fish that was expensive, such as salmon or lobster, could be eaten without any loss of face. We would eat scallops, too, and a favourite treat was crab claws, we called them 'thumbs', and cod's roe, which was known as 'payse'. The roe was boiled in its sac and then fried in the pan. It was beautiful. After coming to live in Dublin, I wasted many trips to fish shops asking for 'payse', only to be met by blank incomprehension.

The low esteem in which fish was held is reflected in the saying, 'Making fish of one and flesh of another', the implication being that the latter was getting the preferential treatment. I had a friend whose uncle came over from England for a fortnight every summer. He was a parish priest, therefore an important man, and the family treated him as such. They had the best of food every day. And it was always meat – steak or roasts. The family was reasonably comfortably off, nonetheless the cost of such expensive grub for the few weeks made a dent in the budget. I happened to be there on the occasion of the important guest's departure. We sang and waved our goodbyes. As the GB-registered car moved off, the woman of the house turned for the door, saying, 'That's it now. Fish for a month!'

Because of the nature of their work, the fishermen had many superstitions and pisreogaí that informed the way they went about their business. Redheaded women were considered very bad luck, and a fisherman who met such a lady on his way to the boat was almost certain to turn back. Along with the redheads, feathered fowl and furry animals were never mentioned on board. This had some unusual consequences. My uncle John, who supplied the boats with basic materials such as ropes and the like, was universally known by the nickname 'Foxy John'. But reference to a fox at sea was considered a direct challenge to nature, so the fishermen called him 'Nasty Name' or 'Nasty' for short. Tough on Uncle John, I used to think, but he didn't mind at all.

It is easy with hindsight to laugh at or belittle such notions, but when not just your livelihood but also your life depended on the whims of nature, then it made sense not to take any risks with forces that were beyond your control. The largest boat in the Dingle fleet at that time was fifty feet. Week after week, these boats headed out into the Atlantic Ocean in all seasons. If the weather turned against them, or the forecast was bad, tough decisions had to be made and sometimes they did not work out.

On the day of a storm, the fishermen would be lined up along the shops, bars and houses at the head of the pier, anxiously watching their boats riding the bucking white horses at their moorings a few hundred yards out from the pier. An abiding memory is the tension that would grip the whole town when a boat was caught out at sea in a storm; the anxious wait as wives and friends tried to raise the crew on the radio; the relief when the boat was spotted rounding the harbour mouth between the lighthouse and the Tuairín Bán, heading into the relative safety of Dingle harbour.

There were times, thankfully very rarely, when a boat did not return and lives were lost. This cast a gloom over the peninsula. After comforting the grieving on their loss, finding the bodies became the single-minded concern of all. Our belief was that the bodies of those lost at sea rose to the surface after nine days. This would have been learned from centuries of experience and tradition, but there were, in fact, sound chemical and biological reasons to support the theory. However, bodies did not always come to the surface, to be picked up by the fleet of trawlers, or turn up on the local shoreline. They might have caught in nets, rocks, or debris. They might have been dragged way out to sea by Atlantic currents during the nine days. On such occasions, a religious ceremony was performed by the water's edge, at the point nearest to the drowning site. The priest, in a practice frowned on by many bishops and dismissed by other priests as being pagan, would float a sheaf of oats, bearing a lighted candle, into the water. The belief was that it would drift with the currents to where the body was located and it could then be recovered. Sometimes, whether for scientific, religious or pagan reasons, it did. What was most feared by family and relatives was that the body would rise off the ocean floor and remain suspended somewhere between the surface and the seabed, never to be discovered, a state described by the poet Nuala Ní Dhomhnaill as '*báite idir dhá uisce*', drowned between two waters.

My memory of the pier at Dingle in the evening time, when the fishing catch was being landed, is of hundreds of dogfish floating dead in the water. They are horrible-looking fish, like small shark. Dogfish were considered inedible, and therefore unusable, so they would be dumped overboard when the fish were being sorted into boxes on the pier. The fishermen themselves were left with the unsaleable fish. These would include John Dory, monkfish and the Red Gurnard, which we called gurnet. Many of these fish are sold in the best shops and most expensive restaurants today. They were not eaten and impossible to sell thirty years ago, and dogfish, which even the fishermen baulked at eating, are now fancifully for sale as rock salmon in most supermarkets. Fresh fish was the rarest of commodities in Dingle. All the best stuff was iced and shipped out to the cities immediately. The locals were left with the rest. What a change today when many fishermen can get a ready market in the restaurants, hotels and shops locally.

Dingle at that time was a town living on old money and memories of better days. The population had dropped alarmingly over the previous half-century. Killarney was the major tourist destination in Kerry and Tralee was the county town. Apart from east coast Gaeilgeoirí on their way to the Gaeltacht – not great spenders – there were few enough visitors. The town had no public toilet, one public telephone and the only restaurant was the dining room of Benner's Hotel on the Main Street. In June 1953 the Dingle–Tralee light railway was closed down, which was another blow to the town.

The rural electrification scheme did not reach Dingle until about 1954. I well remember going to school on the day when they started lifting the flagstones in the streets to plant the new electricity poles. Just between the National Bank and Benner's Hotel they had dug a huge hole to receive one of those metal poles that were strategically placed to take the main strain away from the normal wooden ones. A block and tackle mounted on the back of a truck helped hoist the pole upright. It does sound foolish in hindsight, but that pole was the biggest thing I had ever been close to; it dwarfed everything around it. It stretched across the road and its sheer dominance frightened me. I really thought it was the end of the world.

But Dingle had electricity before the arrival of the national grid; a local man called Jimmy Houlihan provided it. Jimmy had his own distribution and generation system, which was mainly intended for lighting purposes, and he was constantly dissuading people against using it for heating. He would dart into my mother's shop and, seeing the single-bar electric heater plugged into the supply, he would go into apoplexy about the drain to the system and threaten to cut her off. Jimmy supplied electricity to the town of Dingle for thirty-three years and it was his proud boast that in all that time there were only two nights when the town was without power. Those two nights were during his final year when he had partially handed over to the new service. Some of my mother's family still refer to electricity as 'the Jimmy Houlihan'. Not a bad legacy by any standards.

The Temperance Hall, no doubt constructed at the height of the temperance movement, was a hive of activity even if by the time I got to know it, its name was the greatest misnomer of all time. In fairness, Mikey Quirke, who was in charge, was certainly a non-drinking Pioneer, and for the short few years when we were probationary Pioneers there were irregular meetings upstairs to confirm our commitment to abstinence. We viewed those meetings more as a legitimate excuse to engage with the opposite sex and a possible occasion to sin than an opportunity to eschew alcohol.

The weekly Whist Drives were also held in the upstairs meeting room. These were a real test of nerve. I think it was Aunty Sheila who talked me into getting involved, although it wouldn't have been difficult, as I loved cards. Whatever, I was one of the youngest players; most of the pals just weren't interested.

Whist was played in tables of four and after each game you moved to the next table. The tension was amazing and to be successful you needed great concentration. The players mostly comprised polite, middle-aged to elderly ladies. They were the ones who attended all the church activities and supported every charitable and Christian cause. In their normal conduct and deportment they were demure; the very models of perfect behaviour and considered by all to be highly respectable. But when they sat at the whist table they became pure monsters. It was not overt. In fact, between deals and during the short breaks there appeared to be great, good-humoured banter going on, with seemingly innocent teasing and a lot of tinkly laughter.

'Well, Sheila, diamonds are for ladies all right the way you won there.'

'Ah, hearts are for lovers, Patsy. Is there something you're not telling us?'

But underneath all that was a war, waged silently and uncompromisingly.

The strictest rule for partner whist is that you are absolutely forbidden to communicate with your partner. The skill lies in being able to read the game and deduce the play. But, by playing a high card at a wrong time you might bury your partner's best card and even though the 'trick' was won, it meant that your partner had now lost the opportunity of taking a separate trick for you both.

Mistakes were scorned, mocked and punished by the other players. So when it was your turn to lead a card you really concentrated. The whole table watched and waited. In your head you counted the number of trumps gone; you tried to remember who had reneged. Even after doing all that you might still have no clue. Your partner waited, stony-faced; staring directly and unblinkingly at you. Then she might suddenly develop a strange and urgent itch under her left boob.

How embarrassing! Stop it. Oh, I get it now! That's where her heart was when she had one. I lead the two of hearts. I got it right. Stonyface lights up; she hammers out the King. We win the trick, but we are cheats.

A new partner might seem friendlier, but make a mistake and those soft, female eyes would turn into daggers. Pointed fiddling with her engagement ring during full eye contact should have prompted me to play a diamond.

Those Whist Drives with the matrons of Dingle were pressure cookers of learning where I acquired a whole new range of tricks and dodges.

⬚ ⬚ ⬚

Downstairs, the Temperance Hall boasted two snooker tables with spotless green baize and the shiny balls reflected the light from the bank of spotlights over each table. The table near the door was where the youngsters played. As your skill and age advanced, you graduated to the newer table to play with the adults. We called this 'the Big Table' even though it was exactly the same size as the other one. The negative opinion that always seems to attach to snooker did not apply in Dingle. It was not a class thing, nor was it seen as a sign of a misspent youth. It cost sixpence a game to play, but only the loser paid, so if you were on a winning streak you could play all day at no cost. I had a bit of an advantage in that there was a full-size billiard table on the top floor of Foxy's shop. It had been left there by the previous owner of the house and was in reasonable condition. I spent many a Sunday evening there, and while I was never going to be a challenge to the Ken Dohertys and 'Hurricane' Higginses of this world, up there in Foxy's attic I did develop some skill at the game of snooker which helped me to survive.

On Sundays after the eleven o'clock Mass there was always a big crowd in the Temperance Hall waiting for the pubs to open. Well, in all fairness I suppose they were always temperate when there was no drink available!

Rather than have the table monopolised by two or four snooker players on the Sunday morning, the custom was to have a game of pool. This allowed for an almost indefinite number of players. Each player paid sixpence and was given an identifiable snooker ball. As well as the normal colours, there was a range of balls of differing shades and markings available. The rules were simple: each ball had three 'lives' so that each time it was potted a life was lost and after the third one the player was out. The order of play was important; the sooner your ball appeared on the table the more likely it was to be potted.

The order was decided by each player cueing off down the table so that it came back off the top cushion and returned towards the baulk cushion. All the balls were left on the table until everyone had cued off. Then the order of play was chalked up on the scoreboard, depending on how close your ball was to the back cushion, with three Xs after each name signifying the three lives.

This was the only time we youngsters got to play with the older, experienced role models and had a legitimate reason to talk to them. Along the wall beside the big table was a long church form. We would sit up on the back of it with our feet on the seat and our backs against the wall. We were above the level of the table, so we had a great view of the play. We would say significant things like, 'I'm playing after you, Tony', or, 'That was a great shot, Liam,' and he might nod affirmatively, 'It wasn't bad, was it?'. On a slack day you might feel encouraged to keep the conversation going with serious adult talk in his area of special interest.

'Spurs did well yesterday, beating Arsenal at home. Blanchflower was man of the match' – even though you were no Spurs fan, had nothing whatever against Arsenal and did not particularly like Danny Blanchflower.

But usually the banter among the personalities and hard men ruled us out of the chat, so we would concentrate on laughing loudly at all the jokes and comments, though we didn't understand half of them.

'You never spotted the "in-off" there, Packy, too much porter in Jack Neddy's yesterday, I suppose.'

'The hole in that pocket too tight for you, Jackie? I'd say you didn't have any trouble finding the hole last night. Jesus, I thought you were going to ride on the floor of the dancehall the way ye were going at it.'

If the guy at the table was lucky enough or good enough to pot the ball of the main smartass, there would be general rejoicing. The crowd particularly loved it if it was rattled into the pocket with a vicious, venomous shot, which was the mark of the expert.

'By Jaysus, but you rattled the brass there, Pluggy. Scratch a life off there, Mikey.'

You had two choices when it came to your turn to play. You could try to pot another player's ball and be sure to get a cheer from the crowd, or else play safe and be ignored.

The game could last for an hour, with the number of players reducing all the time and the tension rising in inverse proportion. Finally there would be only two. Stalking each other and playing cat-and-mouse. Each waiting for the other to make a mistake and finally one of them executing the winning shot. The winner took all, which in those times was not insignificant. If there were twenty playing, then the twenty sixpences made up a very attractive ten shillings for the winner. A day's drinking!

The nuns bought a film projector and showed films a few times a month on winter Sunday afternoons in the convent hall. They were all nunnishly prudish and boring films, but at least they were an attraction and somewhere to go for a few pence. The films were invariably flickering black-and-whites with indistinct dialogue made even worse by the constant whirr and clack of the reel-to-reel projector.

If the on-screen protagonists got too close in any kind of suggestive way, the nuns would protect our innocence with an urgent, loud intervention.

'Look away children and I'll tell you when to look back again.'

They were usually on the ball, but now and again they were caught out. In one film, I think it was *Naughty Marietta*, the nun censor was outwitted by Nelson Eddy, who, in one sudden movement, swept Jeanette McDonald into his arms in a passionate embrace and kiss. The good Sister had not anticipated the action; neither was she the projectionist, so she had no idea how to control the machine.

With a cry of 'Oh my God!' she stuck one hand in front of the lens, blackening out the on-screen image, and with the other she unplugged the projector, which groaned to a halt and threw the hall into darkness and disarray. As far as I can remember, that was the last time Pat Neligan, John Francis and myself attended.

The only place to see real films was in the Phoenix Cinema, which was another brainchild of that enterprising man, Jimmy Houlihan, who had brought us our electricity.

Posters advertising that month's offerings from the Phoenix Cinema were distributed to every shop and pub in the town. We made a mad scramble for the posters, and decided which we would see. Teresa had strict rules. You could go to two films a week during the holidays and one a week otherwise, provided it was suitable.

Excitement built as we queued up at the ticket office to pay our money to Mr Moore. The sight of Mikey Callaghan going up to the projection room was a sign that it was getting near showtime. When the lights went down, Dingle was left far behind. This was another world. The glamorous advertisements enticed us with 'select drinks in luxurious convivial surroundings'. These were usually followed by boring travelogues that just happened to arrive in Jersey or wherever in time for the annual Festival of Flowers. We fidgetted through these prleminaries even though we knew well that they were part of the happy anticipation leading up to the main feature. But first came the short film. It was never listed, so it was always a surprise. We hoped it would be the Three Stooges, or, if not, Woody Woodpecker was a favourite.

Then the main event. Westerns or comedies were the ones we most looked forward to. Big Biblical films, like *The Robe*, were a great draw. Believe it or not, Ben Hur drove that chariot round and round every night for a full week in Dingle. Unprecedented! Elvis and rock-and-roll films were rare but great fun, and we couldn't resist *Dracula* or *Frankenstein*, even though they guaranteed nightmares.

War films were always high on our list of choices. Considering the nationalistic background we all had, and our unquestioning and unwavering commitment to 'Brits out' and the return of the 'Fourth Green Field', it is astonishing that when we were watching a war film in the Phoenix Cinema we were all true Brits. The Tommies were our heroes as they fought valiantly against the dastardly Huns, or the inscrutable Nips. Even into our early teen years, when we should have known better, we could still get totally behind them. They were at their finest in The Guns of Navarone. It was pure magic. For a couple of hours, the only thing of importance in our lives was to blow up the huge guns that were wreaking havoc on the Allied Fleet passing through the strategically crucial Sound at Navarone. There was a mighty roar at the end when the German guns and fortress went up with a bang. We cheered and clapped, and why wouldn't we? Couldn't we claim some local credit? Sure, didn't it take Gregory Peck, one of our own, to blow the shite out of those Germans in Navarone?

I well remember when Gregory Peck visited Dingle. That created a bit of a stir. His grandfather was an Ashe from Kinard, near Dingle, who had emigrated to the States many years ago, but Gregory kept in touch with his roots. Gregory is very much a clan name among the Ashes. By a strange twist of fate, Gregory Peck, freedom-fighter in *The Guns of Navarone*, was a first cousin to Tomás Ashe, the real-life Irish freedom-fighter, poet, officer and teacher who died from forced feeding by the British authorities while on hunger strike, shortly after the 1916 Rising. Tomás, the fearless brigade leader in North Dublin and Meath during the Easter Rising, was a folk hero to us in Dingle. At one time one of the three GAA clubs in the town was named after him, and many of the players, especially the Devanes, were close relatives of his. The football pitch in Dingle is still called Páirc an Asaigh in his honour.

An academic who had met with Gregory Peck told me, many years later, that Gregory was a great admirer of Tomás Ashe, who he invariably referred to as General Ashe. This type of accelerated promotion through the ranks comes naturally to West Kerry folk!

LIGHT MY FIRE

Lyney had a plan.

'We'll join the Fire Brigade.'

Thomas Lyne's ideas were always worth considering. The Fire Brigade in question was the local voluntary fire service. And he had done his homework.

'There's brilliant training trips, payment for any call-outs and it's a great way to impress the women.'

It sounded fine, especially the last bit; status and cachet were desperately needed by two gauche teenagers. No sooner said than done; we joined up. The senior members, who had been there for decades, were delighted with the injection of young blood. There was a great welcome for us. The town could look forward to a safe future.

We duly got the call for fire-fighting drills and practice. Invariably, they took place on Sunday afternoons. The first outing dampened any romantic notions we might have had about tearing through the streets with bells ringing, whistles blowing and sirens resounding. Sad to say, the fire engine was, in fact, a trailer, which had to be hitched on to a small tow-truck. Mind you, it had all the gear. The hoses, ropes, uniforms and equipment were neatly stored and stacked on board. With much bonhomie and good humour we crowded into and onto the truck and trailer and rattled our way west of the town, along by Milltown bridge, past Glens, over the Maam and down into Feochanach, going all out. We stopped on Feochanach bridge; that was the practice site.

The routine was always the same: jump out of the truck, drag the hoses down, uncoil them with speed and sweat. Everything was done 'at the double'. Two of us would connect one end of the first hose to the pump inflow while two more would take the other end with the filter on it and lodge it in a deep part of the river. That was the dangerous bit, because if you weren't careful you could easily get wet. Still, we didn't shirk it. The big, brass end-piece of the second hose was connected to the outflow. Thomas and I would take the other end and charge off down the road towards Feochanach village, dragging the hose behind us, in the direction of the make-believe fire. By pure coincidence, all this frenetic activity of unrolling the hose, connecting extensions and fitting the nozzle brought us just level with the village pub.

At this point our gallant leader would inject calm and control into the drill, shouting, 'Fair play, lads. Ye made great time there. The two new lads know their stuff. Ye deserve a drink, and–'

Paddy Ollie always finished the sentence for him, '…and remember to drink up, 'cos the farmers are paying for it!'

With that, the brigade would adjourn to the pub for more than a few free drinks before casually emerging to roll up the hoses, tidy and store the gear before going home at our ease. A genuine fire alarm at that point might have created more risk for the fire-fighters than the house occupants. Thomas and myself lasted for about four training sessions, but as neither of us had yet begun drinking, we did not get the full potential value of membership.

Unfortunately for us, perhaps fortunately for the local populace, there were no fire call-outs during our stint with the service, so we never got the chance to save the town and it will never be known how we would have coped under fire. But we were treated very well by the team, and not long after that the whole operation went professional.

That voluntary fire service was typical of its time; members of a community supporting each other. You could be sure that however casually and lightheartedly they seemed to take their training exercises, you could depend on them for your life in an emergency.

During my teenage years there were numerous possibilities for involvement in the town's activities. Dingle was a town with a declining population, which posed problems for an infrastructure that had become dependent on a greater number of people. For that reason, the different clubs and organisations in the town were forever headhunting new members.

As well as I can recall, my first involvement was with the newly formed swimming club. Swimming held, and indeed still holds, enormous appeal for me. With the exception of Pat Neligan, all the gang of friends were keen swimmers. As well as the enjoyment of swimming as an activity, it was also a very attractive social event, providing us with legitimate opportunities to spend long periods with girls from the town. Serious swimming was done at Slaudeen, a tiny little beach between the Tower and the Lighthouse. At that time it had separate bathing areas for men and women. It was a private place, unknown to all except locals, until the arrival of Fungi, the Dingle dolphin, which brought hordes descending on the place – but that was many years later. Slaudeen was where I learned to swim. My uncle Thomas, who was a Christian Brother, was the one who taught me.

At that time Christian Brothers would swap monasteries during the summer break, for a bit of variety in their lives, and naturally Uncle Thomas always opted for Dingle. The rest of his family, highly industrious as they were, found it odd that he could be 'swanning around, with nothing to do'. He was the object of much good-natured teasing.

'Thomas, what's the price of a loaf of bread now?'

'When did you last buy a pound of butter?'

He was immune to the slagging. 'The Lord provides for me,' was always his answer.

He went swimming every day of the summer. One glorious

summer, when I was about nine or ten, he took me to Slaudeen day after day. The second little cove in Slaudeen was up against the cliff and when the tide came in it filled up to a depth of five or six feet. We called it The Pool and, enclosed as it was by straight rocks on both sides and the cliff at the rear, it formed a natural rectangular swimming pool until the tide ebbed.

Uncle Thomas was a good and patient swimming instructor: 'Lie out there flat on the water.'

'But I'll sink!'

'No you won't. I'll hold you up. Stretch out there. Let your head back until your ears are just tipping over and under the surface of the water.'

It was a strange sensation, to be looking up at the sky, moving gently with the tide, and not hearing much because my ears were filled with salt water. I could feel his reassuring hands under the small of my back.

'Look,' said Uncle Thomas. 'I have only one hand under you now. The salt in the water keeps you afloat. Did you know that in the Dead Sea there is so much salt that you cannot sink?'

'I wouldn't mind being there.'

Suddenly I could see both his hands; I stiffened in fright.

'You're all right. Don't move. You're floating on your own.'

I was rigid with panic. But I didn't sink. Brilliant. Delirious. Floating on my own under the warm sun. There was no stopping me then. I started with the dog's paddle and graduated to the breaststroke. After that we experimented: sidestroke, backstroke, butterfly and the crawl. Like most of us in Dingle, I swam strongly enough but with an appalling technique. Usually I combined the overhand action of the freestyle with the frog-leg action of the breaststroke. I was a no-style swimmer, but I loved the salt water.

Slaudeen also had what we called a bathing box. It was three-sided concrete structure, with the front open to the sea. There we could sit and change, deposit our clothes and dry off when we were finished swimming for the day. The view from the bathing box, as you gazed out through the mouth of the harbour, with the lighthouse to the east, Tuairín Bán to the west and the restless swell constantly bulging and rupturing in between, is the most evocative of scenes to any Dingle person; a catalyst to memories. Encouraged by the mesmeric effect of the waves, it was so easy to fall into a trance. Even now I can hear again the flocks of screaming gulls diving on the small, unsaleable or inedible fish being thrown out by the fishermen as they sorted their haul into fish boxes on the decks of the modern trawlers, or the smaller, slower nobbies as they swung around into the harbour from the west.

That was nearly the last of the old nobbies, which had been the mainstay of Dingle fishing for about half a century. They were built in Peel in the Isle of Man around 1910, and even though I remember them as having engines, they were in fact originally designed as forty- to forty-five foot traditional sailing craft for the fishing industry. Sadly, their run was almost up. At one time I knew them all by name. *The Angelus Bell* and *St John Anthony* were owned by the Graham families; *The Manx Girl* retained her original name, but *The Leo* and *The Brigid* were rechristened in Dingle. As a child I always looked out for *The Majestic*, the nobby belonging to 'Uncle' Paguine Flaherty, who was married to my mother's sister, Aunty Mollie. Paguine worked *The Majestic* until he injured his leg in a fall on board in the late 1950s. That injury meant an end to his fishing career, and of course there was no insurance to provide compensation.

With no income and a young family to support, he and Aunty Molly had to make a new start. They took over the pub in the Holyground, and being a popular man, soft-humoured and even-tempered, people were drawn to him and to the pub. He gradually built up the business, turning it into Dingle's first music pub. Paguine was also one of Ireland's best bodhrán-makers, and Mollie was an accomplished pianist, which all helped. Although he must have missed the freedom of the sea and the lift of the swell rounding the harbour mouth, he put great enthusiasm into his new venture and made it a wonderful success. The pub became legendary; every Irish traditional and folk musician visited. It is still in the family today, being run by my cousin Fergus. Flaherty's pub in the Holyground has an international reputation and is recommended by every worthwhile guidebook for the area. But the pub will never lose the connection with ships and the sea, because the two striking pillars supporting the beam in the middle of the bar are, in fact, made from the mast of a sailing ship, whose name no one can recall, that went aground outside Dingle harbour in the 1850s.

As one of its first projects, the swimming club fundraised to purchase a raft, which was anchored and moored about fifty yards out from the beach, and fixed a basic diving board off the rocks. We would charge down the narrow concreted pathway to the diving board, bounce off it and belly-flop into the sea, to resurface after a few seconds with an ear-splitting roar provoked by the shock of the cold water. Then we would swim out to the raft, there to lie under the sun for a while before returning to the beach. Sometimes we swam out to the little point under the lighthouse. This was enjoyable until the last ten yards, when the fronds of the long, slimy seaweed growing beside the rocks slithered past your body and threatened to entangle your legs. It was always a relief to reach the solid safety of the rocks.

About a mile further along the coast, and outside the harbour mouth, was Beenbawn strand. This was the social epicentre of

Dingle bathing, where sunbathing in the coves or picnicking on the rocks were every bit as important as the swimming. Because Beenbawn was outside the harbour, the Atlantic breakers rolled unhindered through Dingle Bay and crashed on to its beach. The thrill was to wait in the shallow surf and then to dive into the wall of the wave just as the crest was curling over to break. If you got it wrong and the wave broke on top of you, the agitated surf would toss you around like a cork. If Slaudeen was for the serious swimming, then Beenbawn was for the *craic*.

For us it was the place to meet the girls; to discuss pairing off and plan decidedly lewd activities, none of which, despite our firm resolve, ever happened. The girls would generally have been in our class in the convent until we went our separate ways after First Communion. For the following half-dozen years or so we hadn't even noticed them. Now they were becoming the whole focus of our attention. At the beginning, we would stay on our own side of the beach, then just as the girls were heading down towards the water's edge, we would, curiously enough, feel it was time for another swim. Coincidence that. There were any number of strategies to gain their attention and to guarantee reaction.

Splash! 'How do you like that, Celeste?'

'Jesus, Lyney, if you do that again I'll kill you. And you stop laughing, Kaneen. I'll get you back.'

Alternatively, there was the more polite approach.

'Would you throw the ball back, Geraldine, please?'

Sometimes co-operation worked.

'Come on, girls, we'll throw Ursula into the water.'

This would be followed by false anger and outrage.

'How dare you, Joseph O'Toole!'

It was hardly *From Here To Eternity* and we were no Burt Lancaster and Deborah Kerr, but running for the beach ball, splashing each other, climbing on to a rock to dive off, all led to unplanned but welcome casual touches and brushes of semi-naked bodies. Nobody was fooled as to what was going on, and back on the rocks or grassy areas the older and experienced lads had no difficulty interpreting our actions.

'Ye're starting to smell around, lads.'

Slight embarrassment on our part, but shoulders back a bit, too.

'Ye'll be looking for your iron next!'

Guffaws all round at our puerile attempts sent us scuttling back into our shells ... for another while anyway. But we were finally beginning to understand what the Brothers meant by 'occasions of sin', and we were mad for them.

My first dance, well, it was a disco really, was the Swimming Club Gala Social. It was held in the schoolhouse in the Mall, just a hundred yards down the road from home. It was the only thing we talked about for weeks beforehand, especially at the beach. The lads checked that all the girls were going, and vice versa. Everyone was enthusiastic. Oh, we were manly; what we weren't going to do! On the night, feeling very important but self-conscious, I made my way into the hall, showing the swimming club membership card at the door. Trying to look casual, like I had done this a million times before. Then suddenly I was in the open hall, unprotected and under the full glare of the flashing lights. Panic set in. But all was saved; there were the rest of the lads. I rushed up to greet them as though they were long-lost friends, when I had seen them not three hours before. But there was safety in numbers.

Jimmy Flannery was doing DJ. The music was great but we just stood there, banded into a tight circle.

'Go on, Lyney. You go first.'

'Who'll come with me?'

Nobody moved. Wimps that we were, we didn't have the courage to cross the floor and ask for a dance. The girls waited at the other side of the hall, disgusted at our lack of initiative after all the talk and the planning. Eventually, Jimmy called a Lady's Choice. There was no messing; all the girls crossed the hall in a phalanx and hauled us out on to the floor. God, there was no stopping us after that. Well, until the slow set, when we actually had to hold a girl. I was all thumbs, elbows and feet. Which bit of her did you hold? And how did you avoid touching the interesting bits? Sometimes, people's cheeks even touched. I wished I had paid more attention to Neligan's mother when she was trying to teach me to waltz around her kitchen with a sweeping brush.

But we got through it. By the time we all stood for *Amhrán na bhFiann* at eleven o'clock, the general consensus was that it had been the best night ever. We hung around outside the hall for a while, exaggerating the extent of our interaction with the girls, even though everyone had seen everything. And there was not much to see.

Teresa was waiting up when I got home.

'Who was there? Who did you dance with? ... How can you forget who you danced with?'

But I was giving nothing away.

The swimming club also organised life-saving classes from which I eventually emerged with a life-saving certificate, albeit third class.

Those early swimming lessons from Uncle Thomas, our adventures at Slaudeen and Beenbawn and my activities with the swimming club, gave me an abiding love of the sea. In later life I got involved in sub aqua and skin diving and would defy anyone to challenge the thrill, beauty and ambience of the clear Atlantic, viewed from one hundred feet down in the seabed, along Ireland's west coast on a bright, bright sunny day.

❖   ❖   ❖

Why is it that youngsters are so interested in guns – wanting to own them, fire them, and be expert with them? Maybe it was the sixty-four-page comics, or the war-themed B movies we saw at the local cinema; whatever it was, they represented both danger and power.

The FCA unit based in Dingle was 'C' company, 15th Battalion of the Southern Command. The FCA, or *Forsaí Cosanta Áitiúla*, was the Irish-language name for the Local Defence Forces, or the LDF, as it used to be known. Like all newly created acronyms, it was subject to the usual levels of abuse and ridicule. So, FCA was variously rendered as Fools Carrying Arms or Free Clothing Allowance; there were other, even less complimentary variations. It was a major attraction for us teenagers. The regulations required all members to be seventeen years or over on joining. But those were only rules. Thomas Lyne, Ronan Burke and myself presented ourselves as potential recruits to the quartermaster in the FCA hall in Gray's lane. I was tall, if very skinny; Thomas was burly and mature-looking, but they knew right well that we were not the age. In fact, Thomas was not yet sixteen, and I was only coming up to my fifteenth birthday. Those minor details glossed over, we were accepted. I well remember the sense of shock on being presented with the Bible and having to take the oath of loyalty and allegiance in the dingy back office of the hall in Gray's Lane. It was probably my first really serious adult act.

We learned to march, we learned to drill and we learned how to carry arms. We spent endless hours on parade in the hall responding to the parade corporal's shouted orders. From the basic '*Aire!*' (Atten-shun!), we progressed to the much more complicated '*Taispeáin Airm!*' (Present Arms!). We marched up and down that hall a million times, keeping in step: *Clé, Deas, Clé, Deas.*

Standing to attention became second nature. No easy task that. *'Bolg isteach, ucht amach,* (Stomach in, chest out). We set our shoulders back, arms straight down, our fists closed, but with the index fingers feeling for the seams of the uniform trousers. Knees together, heels together; feet at an angle of forty-five degrees.

The verdict was usually: 'Not bad, we'll do it one more time. *Aire!*'

The salute took some getting used to. Holding your palm flat open, you brought your fingertips to touch the rim of your cap. And you had to remember to bring your arms the longest way up and the shortest way down. This was a vital instruction, because most of us were inclined to mimic the US army salute we had seen in the war movies. This involved bringing the arm the shortest way up. In other words, straight up, and then out from the cap and down.

The drill sergeants, or corporals, tended to be regular, full-time soldiers. In answer to any question, they trotted out the stock army clichés.

'Very simple, sonny, you're a no-star private; salute everything. A free bit of advice to survive in the army: if it moves, salute it. If not, paint it. Okay. Any more questions?'

And then we were introduced to the Enfield .303 rifle and taught to dismantle and clean it. Typical of the army, we were taught to dismantle the gun before we were taught to use it. When the time came to learn how to use the rifle, we lay down on the cold floor of the hall with the rifle held firmly against the shoulder, both elbows on the ground and legs stretched wide apart.

But that was the problem; with my back raised up by my elbows and my legs apart, it meant that I was resting on my testicles. It was excruciating. Every time I tried to relieve the pressure, by shifting my legs closer, the sergeant would roar: 'O'Toole, spread your legs.' I finally found some bearable position.

'Now, aim at the target. Look through the rear sight. Raise the front sight until the top of it is in direct line between the bottom of the Vee of the rear sight and the centre of the target. Now gently feel the pressure on the trigger, and FIRE.'

The concentration was so intense that you imagined you heard the shot and felt the recoil.

'When will we get real ammo, Sergeant?'

'There is real ammunition in your guns.'

'Jesus! You're not serious.'

'Now listen. I'm going to say this just once. *Every* gun is loaded. Even if you have just unloaded it yourself, remember it is *still* loaded. That's the rule. Treat every gun as loaded. It's a court martial offence to point a gun at anyone.'

The functions, specifications and capabilities of the Mills 36 rifle and hand grenade were explained to us in detail. There was something about how the word MILLS was also a mnemonic for remembering its attributes. It has slipped my mind in the intervening period, except for the 'S', which I recall represented 'Susceptible to mud'.

We were given uniforms, and proud of them we were, completely ignoring how grossly uncomfortable the bullswool, as the hard, prickly material was called, felt against the skin. In my case the uniform was also extremely ill-fitting because of the gangly narrowness of my frame.

But most importantly of all, we were allowed to take our rifles home. Without doubt we were bigger men as we carried them down Gray's Lane and over Dykegate Street or up the Mall. Unfortunately, we hardly ever met any girls, so strutted our stuff to little avail. I might have thought I was John Wayne, but Teresa was not impressed. She was less than keen for me to be in the FCA in the first place, but arriving home with a gun was the absolute limit.

'Jesus, Mary and Joseph! What are you doing bringing that thing in here? I am not having it here and that's that.'

Myko intervened, and after a while she stopped arguing, which was the usual signal of a change of attitude. She went out to the shop in a bit of a huff. Myko got the camera and took my photograph. I stood to attention, in full uniform, with the rifle sloped on my shoulder, four fingers taking the weight under the stock and the thumb hooked around the side edge. I showed him how to dismantle the rifle and he was interested in every part of it. He described the guns he had trained with in the Garda Depot as a recruit. This was real man's stuff!

I kept the rifle in the wardrobe of my bedroom and never was any gun maintained with such care and pride. In the stock of the rifle, behind the brass plate in the heel of the gun, was a compartment in which was stored a piece of cotton material, a tiny brass container of Rangoon oil and a rope 'pull through'. A bit of the cotton would be soaked in the oil and then pulled through the barrel of the rifle to oil and clean it. This exercise was repeated a few times, using a clean piece of cotton each time, until all surplus oil was removed and the inside of the barrel was shining. The final inspection was to look up through the barrel and see the light sparkling through the rifling of the barrel. Weren't they the simple times, when the State effectively gave out free rifles?

We couldn't wait to go to the rifle range. I remember the excitement as we climbed on to the green, canvas-covered army truck. But there was no support on the hard wooden benches, and that winding, pot-holed road from Dingle to Tralee was a torture. Whenever we hit a bump or a dip we banged our knees off the bench in front or hopped our arses off our own bench. Every bend and turn meant an elbow or back hammered off the side wall. And, of course, our army driver, Private Kelly, and the NCO, Sergeant Hennessy, were sitting in the upholstered comfort of the front cab, enjoying every moment of our discomfort. Our excitement had been battered out of us by the time we arrived.

'That'll toughen ye up, lads. Dismount and line up.'

We lined up along the firing positions. A few hundred yards away was a row of targets, set in front of the sand dunes. Each target was a huge rectangle on which was painted a full-sized image of the head, shoulders and torso of a man. The enemy!

The adrenalin really got pumping when they distributed the ammunition. Those long, .303 bullets are vicious, evil-looking things.

'You'll get twenty rounds a man. Now, remember your training.'

Okay, I thought. I took careful aim. Although the target seemed miles away in comparison to the one in the drill hall, I was confident enough.

'In your own time. Five rounds. Fire!'

I fixed my sights on the black spot; I squeezed the trigger. BANG! It was angrier, louder, more disconcerting than I had ever expected. Cordite filled my nostrils, pungent, nauseating. And despite all the warning and cautions about the strong recoil, I was completely unprepared for the ferocity of the kickback after firing. My poor shoulder, narrow and unpadded by fat, wasn't able for it at all. Honestly, I thought it was dislocated. I rested the rifle on the ground.

'Your magazine empty already, Private O'Toole?'

'No, Sir.' My voice sounded funny through the ringing in my ears.

'Well, carry on then.'

Make no mistake about it, after that first shot, it became more important to protect my shoulder than to hit the target. Before we started, we were bemoaning the fact that we had only twenty rounds to fire for the whole day. After releasing the first bullet, all I could think of was how would my shoulder stand another nineteen of these? Thomas and myself were black and blue for a fortnight. Ronan Burke was suffering as well, but as his father was one of the senior battalion officers, poor old Burkey had to pretend that all was fine. Our discomfort wasn't helped by the knowing grins of the old hands, who knew what to expect, and who were watching us closely. In our defence it must be said that we might have flinched but we never moaned.

That summer and for the following two summers we attended FCA summer camp. It was an exhilarating prospect: a three-week holiday away from home on our own, and we were to be paid at the end of it. We spent the first two summers in Kilworth camp, which is situated on the main Dublin–Cork road, between Mitchelstown and Fermoy. For us young lads, trying hard to grow up, these sojourns among a very experienced mixed group of Army and FCA personnel were probably rites of passage.

At each camp we were assigned to a special unit where we were given an intense introduction to, and instruction in some aspect of the army. We spent a fortnight on the machine gun – a noisy, frightening, death-dealing weapon capable of firing hundreds of rounds per minute. It literally tore up targets with its ferocity. We also did a course on the Bren gun, a recoiless sub-machine gun that was accurate and user-friendly – well at one end anyway. It became my favourite weapon. We became respectful of the uninhibited Gustav, a short, snub-nosed automatic weapon which sprayed bullets in a manner that would be better described as indiscriminate rather than inaccurate. It was as liable to discharge a round by giving it an involuntary knock as it was by pressing the trigger. In shape it was quite like the Uzi sub-machine gun used by detectives at armed checkpoints today.

We became reasonably expert in the use of the mortar. This discharged bombs that looked like smallish missiles; if memory serves, they weighed about seven pounds each. The mortar resembled a five- or six-inch diameter pipe, extending about four feet at an angle from a small, flat, metal base on the ground. The remarkable thing about this weapon was that it did not have a trigger. The bomb was held at the mouth of the tube and then let slide down inside until it struck the firing pin at the bottom. This exploded the detonator, which fired the bomb back up the tube to its target half a mile away. The team member who drew the short straw got to release the bomb down the tube, but whichever one of us it was, we managed to put extraordinary space between ourselves and the gun before it had slid the four feet to the bottom of the tube. Raw fear is a powerful motivator. Getting out of the way was much more important than getting the correct angle of elevation to hit the target.

One day, after dropping the bomb down the tube, we were waiting with our fingers in our ears for the explosion, which never came. The bomb lay undetonated at the bottom of the tube and nobody was prepared to admit that they could remember the drill for dismantling the gun when it could explode at any moment. We funked it like real men and let one of the regulars deal with it.

But of course it was not for the guns we went to camp; it was for the sex, drink and opportunities. So every night we washed and spruced ourselves up, poured on the Old Spice aftershave and headed out to assert our manhood, or at least find it. Midweek it might be the Glocca Maura or Blue Dragon pubs, which were right beside the camp on the main Cork road. At weekends we would undertake the four-mile walk into the fleshpots of Mitchelstown, or organise a lift for the nine miles to Fermoy. Fermoy was sophisticated; there was even a rumour that there were prostitutes to be seen there.

Undoubtedly we got our opportunities, but to tell the truth, apart from a few poorly directed fumblings, we were less than a threat to the innocence of the local young women. But we learned from seeing others. And we knew what was expected of us; we engaged in conversation with the young Lochinvars, Adonises and playboys of the battalion and ensured acceptance by nodding, laughing and nudging as appropriate. We would know what to do next year. In the meantime we were still young, foolish and game for anything.

THE BEST OF
TIMES,
THE WORST OF
TIMES

'Make sure you tell this in confession and ask forgiveness.'

Canon Lyne was on impurity patrol, and had found an over-zealous young couple in a remote, dark corner.

My teen years coincided with the beginning of the 1960s. All the written evidence now confirms that the early years of that decade were 'the swinging sixties'. Later in the 1960s there was free love; people made love, not war; the hippies helped free the young generation of inhibitions by letting their hair grow and sticking flowers in it. They smoked stuff as well. Except that nobody told Canon Lyne, who refused to go with the flow and continued to use the crook of his walking stick to extract clinging, fumbling couples from dark corners around the town on dance nights. His dire warnings of hellfire and damnation made him a figure to be feared. Singlehandedly he held back the tide of 'corruption' into which we were only dying to jump; we thought we would never get to participate in the 'swinging' bit of the sixties because of him. But his rule only lasted until people got a little more 'cop on' and the couples realised that the whole exercise was far more comfortable in a bed, which had the added advantage of being well out of reach of Canon Lyne's walking stick.

By their nature Dingle people are iconoclastic; clergy were respected for themselves and not simply because they were men of the cloth. They had to measure up, and if they were completely out of line then their writ ran out. Canon Lyne had always been held in high regard and was well liked, but nearing the end of his time in Dingle he became overenthusiastic and therefore ineffective. The world moved on and left him behind.

The 1960s brought a political awareness, especially among the young generation. John F Kennedy's presidency of the USA was an international turning point for Irish self-esteem. He was one of us: 'From the White Cottage to the White House', as the postcards of his family home in Wexford were keen to point out. People travelled from Dingle to Dublin and Limerick to wave at him in that summer of 1963. I was in the shop on a dreary November evening later in the year, tediously polishing Granny Smith apples and displaying Jaffa oranges in the way that Teresa insisted, when Pat Neligan came running in with the news: 'President Kennedy has been shot.' It was incredible and it was devastating. We kept the radio tuned in for any scrap of news and heard of Dallas for the first time in our lives. He was in the hospital. But there was no hope. Then came the confirmed report: President John F Kennedy has died. Teresa cried. Undoubtedly we felt a sense of loss. All Ireland did.

◈　　◈　　◈

During the 1960s, Dingle began to attract a more cosmopolitan clientele; it became more and more touristy and the business community began to respond. In no time at all there was a public toilet.

The next major event occurred when Greaneys opened a chip shop in the Holyground. This was like being on holidays. Soon the bag of chips on the way home was part of every night out, whether you were hungry or not. It was all happening in the Holyground – O'Connor's shop installed a jukebox. Now we were truly international. Joy was unconfined. We would crowd into the shop and sit in a line on a stool that ran along the wall opposite the counter, and soak in the music. It cost sixpence per single. Even if no sound had come out of it at all, it was still a wonder to see, through the glass of the jukebox, the silent mechanism glide along the line of singles, the mechanical arm reach in and extract the precise selection, then rotate it horizontally and transport it back to the centre for placing on the revolving turntable. It was magic!

As for the music – cringe! We thought we were sophisticated, but we had no taste at all.

There was some soft country rock, but as this was just before The Stones and The Beatles had hit the headlines, we were confined mainly to Bill Haley, Elvis Presley and Pat Boone.

Lyney used to throw shapes when Elvis kicked in; Thomas always fancied himself as a bit of a rocker. But that wasn't the worst of it. Painful as it is to confess, it has to be admitted that there would always be strict silence, some closed eyes, a bit of gentle body swaying and full attention for Jim Reeves as he crooned his way through his maudlin standards. Some I can still remember. In fact, how could you forget lyrics such as:

'Put your sweet lips a little closer to the phone,

Let's pretend that we're together all alone …'

Sometimes we might buy an ice cream cone or a mineral. For us, us that was as near as it ever got to American drugstore culture.

As teenagers, the international news that interested us was not the Cuban Crisis or Vietnam, although I still have a vivid recollection of the image of Nikita Khrushchev, the Soviet premier, taking off his shoe and pounding the podium with the heel while addressing the United Nations. What really got our attention, when the Pathe newsreels came on before the 'Big Picture' in the cinema was the footage of Teddy Boys in Liverpool, the Rockers on Brighton beach or the Mods in Carnaby Street.

The Teddy Boys made a major impact on us. Somebody said that they came from an area of Liverpool called Dingle, where Billy Fury was born, and that they were originally called Dingleboys. Whether that is true or not, they were trouble, and they were definitely not the role models that would have been chosen by our parents. Nonetheless, or maybe because of that, they were our spiritual leaders. They established the fashion trends. By then, clothes and hairstyle had become important statements of self. It was important to adopt an identity, but the crucial choice of which look to go with – Mod or Rocker – was difficult to make. I was, as ever, mixed up. I favoured the music of the Rockers but the clothes of the Mods.

The crew-cut hairstyle was all the rage. It began as a tight, shaven look, not unlike the standard American GI crop, but then grew somewhat. The ideal, the Holy Grail of crew-cuts, was to have it growing straight up from your head and be trimmed absolutely and perfectly flat as a plateau on top. Every possible trick was tried to get it right. Somebody even suggested that a light electric shock applied to the hair ends was guaranteed to galvanise recalcitrant hairs into military erectness. That was a thought too far. Personally, I could have made a fair shot at it were it not for a 'cow's lick' of hair, slightly north of my right eyebrow, which stubbornly refused to respond to any encouragement and invariably hung flaccidly and limply to the side when all the rest was at vertical attention. When I mentioned at home that I might get a crew-cut, Teresa was so horrified that I thought better of it.

At the start of that summer, Teresa and Myko took me aside and advised me to make the most of it; the next school term would begin my Inter. Cert. year, and I was warned that after September it would be 'heads down' for serious study for the exams.

It was a great summer. I went to Dublin on my own to stay with Aunty Phyl in her flat in Haddington Road. It was a different world and I was having a ball. Rock 'n' roll was pre-Beatles but was really livening up. Chubby Checker and Sam Cooke had the world 'Twisting the Night Away'; even older people were trying it. Rock films were a new genre. I went to see *Play it Cool* in one of the

O'Connell Street cinemas. It had Billy Fury, Helen Shapiro and Bobby Vee; it was brilliant. We had been talking about it in Beenbawn and I had promised to let them all know about it, so I sent a postcard back to Lyney and a few of the girls with my very first film review. It was that important.

I took the big decision during that holiday. Phyl had taken me to the Metropole to see *State Fair* with Pat Boone playing the lead role. His hit record 'Speedy Gonzalez' was a regular on the jukebox in Dingle, so it was good to see him in the flesh, so to speak.

It seemed that everyone my age in Dublin had a crew-cut. Everyone, that is, except me. So, on the basis that it's better to be dead than out of fashion, I went into a barber's on Baggot Street and asked him for a crew-cut.

'Another one of them,' was all he said.

He cut it tight at the sides and flat as a pancake on the top, and then brushed it back. Despite the confusion around the cow's lick, it wasn't half bad. Aunty Phyl was taken aback.

'What did you do to your hair, Joseph?' There was an unmistakeable edge to the question.

But I was singularly pleased with the outcome and headed home for Dingle feeling fierce proud of myself. I was the bee's knees and the height of fashion. I was soon disabused of my cockiness – Teresa was disgusted. 'It's no style at all,' she said dismissively, one of those rare occasions when she managed to deflate me.

Keeping up with the changing hairstyles was a huge challenge. After the rigidity of the crew-cut came the fashion for longer hair, shaped into that extraordinary style at the back known as a 'duck's arse'. To get the V-shaped DA you first had to rub plenty of Brylcreem into the sides and back of the head. Then you combed the hair from both sides simultaneously, with a comb in each hand, starting above the ears, then backwards and downwards until the combs met precisely and centrally at the back of the poll, thus forming the perfect and greasily gleaming 'duck's arse'.

Narrow-legged trousers were all the rage, 'drainpipes' they were called. Nobody would be seen dead in anything wider than seven inches. It was almost a science; tailors were given strict instructions – 'legs of maximum circumference of fourteen inches' – so that when pressed, the width was the magic seven. Tight black jeans were the real business. The only problem with them was that they could not, under any circumstances, be allowed to look new. In fact, very few items got as much abuse as a new, unworn pair of jeans. They would be washed three or four times before being worn. Some people even took to having hot baths while wearing the new jeans in order to age them, and to achieve the essential skintight shape.

The shoes that were the required accessory to the drainpipes and the hair-do were called 'winklepickers'. They were low-slung and came to a most unnatural point at the toe. According to fishermen, they were so pointed that you could pick the periwinkles out of their shells with them, hence the name.

The auld fellas on the bridge in Dingle were earthier in their suggested use of the new footwear: 'Jesus Christ, you could try a hen with those shoes.' We ignored the comments. We were in fashion and that was what mattered, never mind that no normal foot could ever be comfortable in them. We didn't complain about the budding corns and calluses. The shoes were the nearest thing in torture to Chinese foot-binding, and must in later years have created mighty business for a whole generation of chiropodists. Apart from the pain factor, they were also no good in the wet; kicking ball was impossible with them and, despite the name, they could not pick a periwinkle out of his shell. They were perfectly useless. But we went mad for them – the narrower, the more pointed and uncomfortable, the better. Victims of fashion? You bet we were. And it happens again and again and again, because every generation of teenagers does exactly the same with the fashion fads of the day.

Summer in Dublin was my freedom from jobs, the shop and my parents. The next year I stayed for a while with Myko's first cousin, Max Webster and his wife, Phil; it was the first of a number of holidays there. They made me one of the family. Max and Phil were a married couple in their twenties, with three children under five. They lived in Garda Terrace, just inside the North Circular Road gate to the Phoenix Park. All my memories of my times there are happy ones. There was fun, banter and adventure. The number 10 bus terminus was just outside the gate, and a bus departed every few minutes, so access to the city was simple and convenient.

Garda Terrace was adjacent to the Garda Depot in the Phoenix Park and was occupied by families of gardaí based in the Depot. As in Dingle, everyone knew everyone and they looked out for each other. It was a supportive and co-operative community of people. At that time the Depot was still the training school for gardaí.

Phil was determined to get me fixed up with a girl. That was her project for the summer and she worked hard at it.

'We have just the girl for you here next week, Joseph: Joan O'Brien, the right age, curves in all the right places, and a lovely girl. She's Tim's youngest sister, and sure she's from Kerry as well. You can't go wrong!'

Tim O'Brien was their neighbour and friend. Of course I was interested. Wouldn't any sixteen-year-old? But by the time we finally met, under the microscope of Phil and her friends, the embarrassment was total. Oh, she was definitely a looker, but I cannot remember if we even spoke. Whatever was expected of me I didn't deliver. Not that that stopped Phil with her matchmaking.

'Wouldn't you ask her for a date?'

Max, a real softie like my father – they even looked alike – sensed my mortification and would chuckle, 'Don't mind her, Joseph. Do things your own way.' Thanks, Max.

Max and Tim were members of the Garda Driving Corps and had just been assigned a minister between them. They had the big ministerial car at home every night. What the minister never knew was that on a few occasions Max put it through its paces for me, up around the back of the park near the Ordnance Survey. It was mighty. It could accelerate to sixty miles per hour while still in second gear; you would be jammed into your seat by the G-force. I'll never forget that car – a big, black Mercedes, registration BZI 306.

That year, Max's younger brother, Joe, was home on holidays from England. He had a scooter: a Heinkel, a real Mods job. I couldn't keep my eyes or my hands off it. Joe was great; he explained all the features of the bike to me.

'Do you want to start it?'

Did I what!

It was a great feeling, sitting on that machine and feeling the power quiver through it as I revved the engine. I told Joe of my experience with the Quickly Mopeds in Foxy's, and maybe I talked it up more than a bit! The parking area in Garda Terrace was confined and safe and at the time it was empty.

'Here,' said Joe. 'Drive it across the car park.'

This was heaven itself. I kicked the bike into gear and released the clutch with my left hand. It jumped, stalled and stopped.

'No, no. Release the clutch slowly and gently.'

I did and I was travelling. Joe ran along beside me.

'Squeeze in the clutch again and change her into second gear.'

Never one to leave well enough alone, and with the wide open spaces of the Phoenix Park beckoning, it was only a matter of minutes before Joe suggested I take her on a decent run up the Park. I was doing fine for the first hundred yards, then just at the Depot, I had to make a left turning around by the railings opposite the Zoo. Of course, I leaned over as you would on a bicycle. But scooters are not for banking. The footguard scraped the ground, the scooter spun out of control across the road, and suddenly the side of a truck loomed up in front of me. I was helpless, terror-struck.

By good fortune, I hit the ground towards the rear of the truck, just avoiding the wheels. I remember the truck driver slamming the vehicle to a halt and jumping out. The poor man was white with shock. Joe, who had witnessed the whole thing from the entrance to Garda Terrace, came running over. I was okay, only a few scratches, but felt really embarrassed at my own stupidity. The driver was so relieved to find I was not injured that he made nothing of my dangerous driving and went off about his business.

Poor Joe did not escape so lightly. Max, once he had got over the shock of what nearly happened, tore him apart. Told him he was irresponsible and senseless and more. There was I, witnessing all this and knowing that I was completely responsible, but Max wouldn't even listen to me.

Yes, they were the best of times, a happy household, full of fun. There was always something to do and I was included in everything. But it was less than a year before Max and Phil experienced the very worst of times. It was something that all parents dread. That they would never forget as long as they lived. Max was leaving for work one June morning. He hopped into the ministerial Merc, started up, checked that the way was clear of children playing outside and then reversed. He had not seen, and couldn't have seen, their baby daughter, Bernadette, their pride and joy, because she had crawled behind the car. He thought she was inside, but she was just at that age, sixteen months, when babies are impossible to watch. When he felt the car strike something, he knew the worst. It was too late for help. Nothing could bring her back. Little Bernadette was dead.

My father, Myko, had been transferred to Dublin some months earlier. He was in the Depot a few hundred yards away and he was with Max and Phil within minutes. It was awful. What could you say or do? The wake and funeral were terribly sad. I remember it as my first encounter with tragedy at close family level, and it left an indelible mark.

Max's boss was the Minister for Justice. He was an important man, but as soon as he heard of the accident he dropped all other business to come and comfort Max and Phil. He arrived into Garda Terrace. While the rest of us were trying to come to terms with the horror of what had happened, he took personal charge of many of the arrangements. Myko asked Phil to think about the burial plot.

'Leenane and nowhere else,' Phil said. 'I want her with the family and where people will know her.'

There was no phone in the house. It was the minister who made the phone calls; he contacted Leenane and the key people who needed to be notified. He was with them all that night, talking to the family members. Not doing much, but simply being there and sharing their pain. The following day, as Myko was lifting Bernadette in her tiny white coffin into the back of Jim Fitzgerald's estate car, because nobody wanted a hearse, the Minister was still there, comforting and supporting them. Then he got into his car and followed the saddest cortège to lovely Leenane.

I had never met that minister before, though I had seen his name prominently in the news. He had a reputation. For the following thirty years he was rarely out of the news or out of trouble. The political icon of his age. Always the subject of extreme views, his political career was a rollercoaster ride of peaks and troughs. Many times in later years I was among his harshest critics, even if I often also appreciated his positive contributions. Like so many political careers, his ended disastrously and he finished in a flood of vilification.

Through all those years, however, my view has been leavened by and filtered through that first impression of pure humanity that was Charlie Haughey during the tragedy of little Bernadette.

ANYTHING BUT
A SOCIALIST

My mother always remarked of my father: 'He was cute enough not to tell me he was Fianna Fáil until we were well married.'

Election time in our house was tense. Myko was a lifelong, unquestioning Fianna Fáil man. He supported them down the line. It was a recurring source of frustration to Teresa.

'For such a bright man in other ways,' she would say to her audience, and in his presence, 'wouldn't you think he would have seen through them?' No doubt, much of Myko's loyalty was rooted in memories of his father, Joe, who had been involved on Dev's side during the Civil War and had also been on the run from the Black and Tans during the War of Independence.

The Moriartys, on the other hand, were pro-Treaty to their core, Fine Gael all the way. The family would always be active at election times and some of the Moriartys of my grandfather's generation were county councillors. When politics and the state of the country were being discussed in our house, every excuse was found to place the blame for any catastrophe at the door of the 'Long Fellow', Eamon de Valera. In the Moriarty interpretation of politics, Dev was the source of most that was wrong with Ireland. The only non-Fine Gael beneficiary of a Moriarty vote was Dan Spring. At that time, the Dingle peninsula was part of the North Kerry constituency and Dan was the Labour Party TD. The Moriartys always gave him a scratch at general elections. The 'scratch' would have been a third preference, having already voted for the two Fine Gael candidates. My mother would explain the vote for Spring on the basis that he was a decent man. He was that, but I'm certain that the vote was directed more at keeping Fianna Fáil out than with keeping Spring and Labour in!

When our near neighbour and one of Teresa's customers, Michael Begley, was elected as a Fine Gael county councillor and later as Dingle's first Fine Gael TD, there was jubilation. Michael was not a man to take prisoners, and he had many a heated argument with

Foxy John and Uncle Patty. Nonetheless, they supported him loyally and canvassed for him for years.

So it was in this maelstrom of blueshirt politics that Myko found himself, and, fair dues, he fought his corner well against all the odds. Though the Moriartys always pushed the Fine Gael case, Myko approached things differently; he never proselytised for Fianna Fáil and never consciously tried to change a person's mind in that direction, but he left you in no doubt as to his views. He had one minor but continuing victory and that was in the matter of newspapers. The Moriartys read the *Irish Independent* only; the *Irish Press* was de Valera's propaganda machine and had no place in a Fine Gael house. Except that Myko was the one who bought the newspaper every day, and he chose the *Press* every time.

'You bought that old paper again,' Teresa would say in disgust. But it didn't stop him. It provided me with a choice of reading: Rip Kirby and Denis the Menace in the *Indo* at my grandmother's, and Captain Mac and The Phantom in the *Press* at home.

Despite his own pronounced and unremitting party political bias, Myko's general position on political activity and the furtherance of democracy was well thought through and admirable. He absolutely refused ever to discuss the pros and cons, or the events of the Civil War, taking the view that it was a black period of our history that was best left alone, not to be examined or discussed until all participants were dead. Even then he felt that it should be left to academic consideration and interpretation by the historians of the day.

'Politics should concentrate on events of today. Leave history to the historians,' was his credo. It was not bad advice, and Irish politics might have matured much more quickly if prominent politicians had taken a similar view earlier in the history of the State.

One day, when I was in my very early teens, Myko brought me home a rolled-up piece of newsprint. It was torn at the edges and not very clean; the print was smudged in places and the paper was yellowing and dried out. He handed it to me in the most matter-of-fact way and I took it from him without any show of appreciation for what became, in time, the most invaluable material gift of my childhood and one which I treasure to this day.

'Con Lucey was cleaning out his sister's house – she died recently in Cork – when he came across this,' he said. 'He was going to throw it out because he felt it had no place in a Cumann na nGael house, but he asked me if I had any use for it.'

I could sense Myko's excitement as we unrolled the paper. 'It's the 1916 Proclamation of the Republic,' he announced. 'Probably the most important document of its day, and it's an original.'

Big deal, I thought to myself. Maybe the fact that it was on its way to the dump convinced me that it was not worth much.

'Apparently, on the day of the Rising a large number of the Proclamations were sent down to West Cork,' Myko went on. 'It has been in the Lucey house ever since. But they took Michael Collins's side in the Civil War, so they don't have any value in it now. I don't know that the Civil War position should make any difference to the Proclamation, but people are people!'

To my shame, and, I'm sure, to Myko's disappointment, I was less than impressed with his gift. In my defence it could be stated that it did not look like any copy of the Proclamation I had ever seen, all of which were a half-page in size. I did, however, keep it and took it with me whenever I moved. It was stuck on the wall of my bedroom at home and again in my room at college. I valued it for sentimental reasons, having received it directly from my father. But apart from using it once or twice as a teaching aid in classroom history lessons, and being impressed by the breadth of vision of its creators on matters of equality and social justice, I never paid much heed to it and never thought that much of it or about it.

Never, that is, until my election to the Senate in 1987. Framed in the main hall of Leinster House I saw something that looked absolutely identical to my own copy of the Proclamation, except that this one had a signed inscription by former President Seán T O'Kelly, confirming that it was an original. For the first time I felt a sense of excitement about the old rolled-up document. Like meeting an old friend in a faraway place.

I examined in detail the Leinster House copy. The size, paper quality and print smudging looked the same as mine. I made a note of the various little print errors – where a letter was out of line or where there were other print marks – and then compared them with my own one at home. The lettering and text were the same in every way, but the print marks and smudges were different. I was thoroughly disappointed to find that it was not an exact copy. Some months later I mentioned it casually to a printer acquaintance.

'No, no,' he said, 'of course yours is not an exact copy. If it were then it wouldn't be authentic. There were no copying machines in those days. They were printed off like news sheets, each one coming through the machine individually. The marks of the casings around the print lead and the ink smudges could not be the same on every sheet. Even though they would all be very similar, it is unlikely that any two would be exactly identical.'

After a bit of research, I came across a pamphlet on the Proclamation which gave the story of its printing. The Proclamation was produced by two printers from Capel Street. They used a printing press in the basement of Liberty Hall. The account related how they ran short of some letters and had to make do in some cases with different fonts; how they ran out of the letter 'e'; how they only had enough type to set half of the Proclamation; how they did that, then turned it top to bottom and, having set the second half, ran it through again. For that reason all original Proclamations have a misalignment between the top and bottom halves. A second run was printed some months later, but these had none of the flaws of the original. I could see immediately that in my Proclamation the top and bottom were slightly out of line. I went through the other checks with the printer and he confirmed its authenticity.

It was a tremendous discovery and even more so when I established that there are now only a dozen original Proclamations intact. Today that rolled-up piece of paper I received so ungratefully from Myko is one of my most valued possessions. Many in modern Ireland tend to dismiss anything relating to 1916, but the fact is that the Proclamation is a most progressive document in many ways, reflecting the most worthy principles of equality and interculturalism. Though most Irish people have never read the Constitution, many of them, including senior politicians, believe that the imperative about 'cherishing all of the children of the nation equally' is in the Constitution. It never was. The only place it has ever been enshrined is in the Proclamation. I still regularly read the fourth paragraph of the Proclamation that guarantees, *inter alia*, civil and religious rights to all our citizens. A bit like Christianity, it was never given a fair chance by the vested interests.

Hilda Moriarty was a close friend and cousin of Teresa's in Dingle. She was a most popular and strikingly attractive woman. Apparently, she broke hearts. But she was forgiven. While studying medicine in Dublin, she had a flat in Raglan Road. A penniless poet who lived in the area befriended her. According to Teresa, Hilda did not have too much time for him. When she was moving to better accommodation down the road, the poor poet helped her move to the new place by carrying her stuff down the road balanced precariously on his bicycle.

'Sure, Hilda used only laugh at him,' Teresa would say, but from my own experience of Hilda, I could not imagine her ever being anything other than nice to people around her. She was a lovely woman in every way.

Anyway, the poet's name was Patrick Kavanagh. He expressed his love for her in the beautiful ballad 'Raglan Road', which he wrote about her and as a tribute to her. I studied Kavanagh and even met him once, but unfortunately knew nothing of his association with the family at the time. What a missed opportunity! As if that was not enough claim to fame, Hilda then went on to make a match that caused consternation in the family – she became engaged to a handsome Limerick solicitor named Donogh O'Malley.

The problem from the Dingle perspective was that the prospective bridegroom was Fianna Fáil through and through. How would the Moriartys cope with this? Donogh arrived to meet Hilda's people in Dingle. Her father, Dr Paddy, had died by that time, so it was mainly the extended family. They met him; they poured drink into him; they would be proper but reserved hosts and then bid him goodbye. But they had not reckoned on one factor: Donogh was too damn like them.

A wild man, with no limits, he loved the drink, the *craic*, the arguments. They couldn't resist his personality. In no time at all he was one of them. They avoided, dismissed, or ignored his political atheism to the true Blueshirt God. He was forever welcome. Every summer they came back to Dingle for their holidays. Hilda would come down in July with her two children, Daragh and Deirbhile, her white Morris Minor packed with holiday bits and pieces. Almost every day she would call to our house in the Mall for a chat with Teresa; we thought she was lovely. Though we were slightly older than her children, she would often take a few of us to the beach. She loved Ventry beach, where her father had at one time owned a seaside cottage. It seemed to me that she went there every day.

Donogh, who was by then an up-and-coming TD, would join her in August. My memory of him is of a friendly, approachable and interesting man who had time for people around him and was full of the joys of life.

Some years later, in 1967, when I was a member of the student committee of St Patrick's College in Drumcondra, on the day of the formal opening of the new college buildings, the college authorities invited me to greet the President of Ireland, Eamon de Valera, and the Minister for Education, Donogh O'Malley in the hospitality room after Mass. It was my job to ensure that they were occupied and entertained for some minutes while the college clergy were disrobing after the church ceremonies and the official blessing. Donogh was in great form and had a great welcome for me. As usual, he talked openly and forthrightly about his plans. He was going to merge certain departments of UCD and Trinity colleges; in his opinion there was too much duplication. He was, for instance, going to locate the entire Engineering faculty in UCD. He had a plan that he felt was certain to work.

'How will you get agreement on it? Won't there be opposition?' I asked him because I knew enough of student politics to be aware of the tensions between the two Dublin universities.

He looked at me, somewhat askance. 'Well, I'm just going to announce it!'

Then he saw that President de Valera was on his own. 'Will you go over to that Long Fellow over there; nobody seems to be talking to him. Open up with a few *focail Gaeilge*, he likes that.'

I was very taken aback by Donogh's irreverence towards the founder of his party, even though I was well aware of the regular rows between them when Dev was Taoiseach and Donogh was constantly in public scrapes.

'Go on, fuck off over to him,' said the Minister for Education, heading for the corner of the room furthest away from his great leader.

Dev was, as ever, wearing a dark suit with a red Fáinne embroidered on the lapel. I was well accustomed to pictures of him with his wire-rimmed glasses and had read all the jokes about him being half-blind, so I was amazed by his striking, brown eyes and his clear skin.

Making conversation was difficult. We got off to a very slow start, with me making all the running, and hardly any response from him. He was relaxed, but not inclined to talk.

In some desperation I asked him what would he have liked most in life if he had never gone into public life.

'I'd love to have lived quietly, on an island of my own, where I could have lived life as I chose without interference and where I would be in charge.'

Unthinkingly I blurted out, 'Sure you got that anyway.'

In fairness to him, he laughed. After that he loosened up.

I often thought afterwards that he had set me up with his comment. Dev's sight was very poor at that time and it must have been most frustrating for him to be moving about in large groups when he did not recognise people.

I never met Donogh O'Malley after that day; within two years he was dead from a heart attack. People of all parties and none felt the loss and grieved. His progressive decisions as minister, particularly in the area of free secondary education, had touched every family in Ireland.

However, the proposal to amalgamate departments of the two universities, which he had so casually outlined to me that day in St Pat's, never happened. I think it was the churches that put a stop to the idea. I mean, how could we condone Catholics being exposed to the naked Protestantism of Trinity College?

The fact that Hilda was not chosen by Fianna Fáil as the by-election candidate to fill Donogh's seat after his death confirmed my mother's view of the party's undependability. Many years later, on the evening of Hilda's own funeral, Teresa rang me. 'That yoke Haughey never even came to the funeral, with all his old talk about his friendship with Donogh and Hilda. In fairness, Brianeen Lenihan was there, but I always thought he was the best of them.'

The importance of our participation in the democratic process was drummed into us by Myko and Teresa. No excuse would be tolerated by either of them as a justification for not voting in elections. Myko maintained that, apart from all other matters, the memory of generations of people who had agitated and fought for the right of the Irish to vote was insulted and offended by us not exercising the franchise. His core argument, however, was that people had a responsibility to contribute to the organisation and management of their country and should acquaint themselves with the policies of those standing for election in order to support those closest to their views. He was unshakeable on the issue.

'And what,' I once asked him, 'if there were no such candidate presenting?'

Myko had no doubts on that one. 'Then you have a responsibility as a democrat to organise that an appropriate person be identified and encouraged to run as a candidate.'

'And if that proved impossible?'

Myko's answer was devastating in its simplicity. 'Then you should stand yourself.'

The real irony of all this, and probably a major factor in forming his views, was the fact that as a member of the Garda Síochána he was not entitled to vote. That law was not changed until he was middle-aged. I well remember that he was like an excited child the day he cast his first vote.

Myko was forever philosophising on government and political life. A favourite theme of his was the nonsense of appointing a teacher as Minister for Education, or a doctor as Minister for Health. He would argue that to appoint as minister someone who was already an expert in the area was to misunderstand the process of government. The minister's function was to listen to the case from all sides, take and assess all the available expertise and then make a decision in the best interest of the common good. Putting in place someone who held clear views formulated from having been inside the profession simply ensured bias and was a recipe for trouble. Myko loved legislation and the legislative process. He enjoyed pointing out the illegality or incorrectness of ordinary things.

Take, for instance, the commonly seen notice: Trespassers will be prosecuted. 'They *may* or they *may not* be,' he would say. Proposed or pending legislation came in for particular scrutiny. One of his favourite sayings was that nothing devalued the process of legislation as much as the enactment of a law which either could not, or would not be enforced. Undoubtedly, he must have poured scorn on the Dog Muzzling Act and the Stray Horses Act.

Sometime during my late teens, Teresa and Myko began to worry that my interest in politics was pushing me down an unacceptable road. They had formed the impression that I was inclining towards Labour and the Left end of the political spectrum. This was too much for them. Both of them seemed prepared to put aside their own particular bias to ensure that my resting place would be either Fianna Fáil or Fine Gael. To be a Labour follower at a time when that party was proclaiming that 'The Seventies would be Socialist' was too big a worry. Labour-Socialism-Communism was the link that worried them.

They even went so far as to arrange for a political activist to talk to me and to convince me of the error of my ways.

I never joined any political party. That is nothing to cheer about and is, I believe, a loss to myself. All my life, while maintaining a strongly independent political line, I have admired those brave enough to compromise to the extent of becoming party members. I have never felt able to do that. I admire those independent politicians who take a strong view on broad societal issues. They have a significant contribution to make. On the other hand, I have never been able to take seriously those single-issue, supposedly independent politicians who claim that because of their independence they are somehow cleaner, more moral, more honest and more wholesome than any party members.

GOODBYE DINGLE, HELLO DUBLIN

Finishing the Leaving Certificate was a release. As we strolled down the Barrack Height after the last exam – I think it was Latin – the talk was all about how we might have done; how things had come up that we never expected; had we given the right answer to that trick question. But my feelings were that it was all over now and it was time to move on. I had no idea what was coming next, but I was looking forward to whatever it might be.

It was a lovely day. I grabbed my yellow-and-black drop-handlebar bike with all the gears that I was so proud of, and cycled west back towards Milltown bridge. Happy to be on my own and free. I didn't bother turning up by Farranredmond and the Hospital, but crossed the bridge and kept on through Cluais and Burnham and then the sweep of Ventry harbour and beach in front of me. Looking out across Páirc and the Bolg I could see South Kerry rising out of the haze. That June day Coumenole was crowded as I cycled around Slea Head, and the tourist cars were queued up outside Kruger Kavanagh's, but I had no interest in meeting crowds of people.

However, as I was going up the hill out of Dún Chaoin, the bike decided of itself to turn around up by Tigh Mollaí and into that familiar hamlet of houses, Carhue. A place of happy memories. It was here during previous summers that I had spent a few weeks at a time in the home of Eileen Lynch and Micí Shea learning Gaeilge at its source. Me trying to put a *snas* on my school Gaeilge and they, with infinite patience, gently correcting, explaining and encouraging. Then the *bothántaíocht* of the early evening when the neighbours would gather into the kitchen for a chat. And the raw fear the first time Eileen pulled down *An Seanchaidhe Muimhneach* and asked me to read one of the stories aloud in front of some of the most exalted of the community, including the famous 'Pound' who was an institution in himself and the standard-setter for all local vocabulary and dialect. Didn't I have the brass neck to do it at all, even at Eileen's bidding?

Later in the night it would be down to Kruger's pub to see who was there, what was new and who was new. Sometimes, on special occasions, there would be an invitation to the wooden chalet called Tigh na Cille, owned by Father Paddy Browne, brother of Cardinal Browne and uncle of Máire Mhac an tSaoi. The MacEntees were regular visitors and Máire was making a name for herself as a poet, but at the time I was less interested in poetry and more interested in the Ó Dálaigh girls, who were around my own age.

But back to that day and *bhí árd-fhailte dhom ó Eibhlín agus Micí.* How had the exams gone? Would I stay with them for a while? It was hard to refuse their innate hospitality and generosity. They were the best of people. They were the ones who gave me a most precious gift: a lifelong love of the Irish language and, in particular, of the Gaeltacht people.

In good spirits, renewed by the hospitality of Dún Chaoin, I made steady progress and shortly turned through Casadh na Gráige with the magnificent view of Clogher strand, Piaras Feirtéir's cave and the peaks of the Three Sisters against the skyline. I kept pedalling through Ballyferriter and didn't take a rest until I reached Riasc, where I stopped at Bricks'. The Bricks operated the school bus and picked up students at our shop every evening, so I knew them well. They were always friendly and great company.

Soon I was passing close by Gallarus Oratory; we were fierce proud of the fact that it was listed in the *Guinness Book of Records* as the oldest church in Britain or Ireland. It was an important place on Cosán na Naomh, the Saint's Path, along which St Brendan and others walked on their way to the top of Mount Brandon.

From the summit of Com Ga I freewheeled downwards to the Long Road. Donal Lynch was home in Kilfountain, just back from college in Baile Mhúirne, with his exams finished as well.

He was in great form and dying for the *craic* – cock of the walk, ready for anything. He thought he was going to have a great summer, but he was hardly home when he had been captured and sentenced to hard labour down the fields, thinning turnips. Donal was the youngest boy in the family and, of course, the others were only waiting for him to come home to land him with the dirty jobs.

'Desperate,' he said to me later when he was telling me the story of that day. Himself and his cousin, Danny Lynch, had to start into the field of turnips. They began at the top of a drill, bending over the plants and reaching down to thin out the extra ones to make room for the remaining plants to grow strongly. There wasn't enough space to kneel and the drills were too low to work them standing. Talk about awkward. It was back-breaking work all the way down the interminable length of the drill. And then at the end they had to turn around and face up the next one. According to Donal, it was 'pure penance' and they were there for the day, like headless camels with their arses stuck in the air, their heads down at the drills and their necks straining up so that they could look ahead of them. The hot sun beat down on them; their backs ached, they were dirty, sore and sweaty. This was not part of what they had planned coming on the bus from college yesterday. Muiriseen Granville, a farm worker of indeterminate years, was thinning the field with them. He was enjoying the discomfort of the college boys.

The day's work ended, they were sitting resting at the gate of the field. Muiriseen, none the worse for the work, was lighting up his pipe for a smoke.

'Did ye enjoy that lads?'

'Well, fuck that for a job,' said Donal.

'Unnatural,' was Danny's verdict.

'Well now, ladeens, let that there be a good lesson for ye.'

'What lesson is in it? A waste of time.'

'Remember what I'm telling ye, and that's that there's no future in any job where you're working with your arse higher than your brains.'

They never forgot. And when they got the call to teacher training they gave it deep and intense concentration for about ten seconds before accepting. And they did well, the pair of them. It's far from thinning turnips they are now.

By all accounts, the world was now at my feet. Well, it certainly did not feel that way. Apart from applying for everything, I hadn't given the slightest thought as to what I might really do next with my life, but I knew one thing for certain – I had no interest in being behind a counter from early morning until late night. I had had enough of that. In Dingle I was at the beck and call of my mother and my uncles; I liked them all but there was always work to be done and I wanted away from all that. The next move would be freedom.

Some of my classmates had left before the Inter. Cert. to take up labouring or non-skilled work. After the Inter. some more had gone to jobs in CIÉ and the Post and Telegraphs. A few of the lads started apprenticeships; Thomas Lyne began the four-year apprenticeship with the ESB to become an electrician. At that time, kids from families with money were guaranteed a job in one of the banks. Others who were comfortably off had decided to study law or medicine.

For those of us in the middle of the social spectrum, our options would be determined by our Leaving Cert. results. The question of staying in or leaving Dingle never arose. Choices would be limited, but none of them would be in Dingle. We knew what the possibilities were and had applied for a lot of them. All of our parents were keen on the Junior Executive post in the Civil Service – great security and great opportunities for promotion, we were told.

A position as Executive Officer in the Electricity Supply Board was also encouraged. 'Sure, didn't Paddy Moriarty from Doonshean go there and he's one of the top men there now.' The Meteorological Service and Aer Lingus also had their supporters, and naturally everybody, as a matter of course, applied for primary teaching. If you did well in the Leaving Certificate you could expect 'the call', as the offer of a place in Teacher Training College was called. Getting 'the call' was a sort of badge of honour. I had no great interest in teaching, but neither had I in any of the other options.

At the time we knew a small number of Dublin lads of our own age whose families holidayed around Dingle. Their choices were much broader, but absolutely foreign to us. They would talk of a getting a good job with a company. Quite frankly, we had no concept of that or of what it might mean. They would also talk about maybe enrolling in UCD for a degree. For them, it was only down the road, and apparently great *craic* altogether.

I wasn't really bothered and didn't give it much thought. As we waited for the results of the exams, we had a great last summer in Dingle. Pat Neligan, who had done his Leaving Certificate the previous year, had taken 'the call' and was now in St Patrick's Teacher Training College in Drumcondra in Dublin. According to him, life was great there. There was a mighty crowd from West Kerry in the college: as well as Pat there was Micheál Moran, Liam Connor and John Michael O'Donnell. In fact, all of our gang was there. From Drumcondra it was an easy walk into the city centre to cinemas, clubs and dances. He was loving it. It sounded great, especially the freedom of it, except that I had never considered teaching as a career.

My results came in August. They were good. The next day I was delivering bedroom furniture back west for Foxy. Usually I went on my own, and after the tension of waiting for the results and the previous night's celebrations I was looking forward to the drive by myself in the old Hillman Estate. Foxy always saw me off from the yard after a session of questions and answers about what was going to whom and where they lived and who they were related to. But on this occasion Foxy came with me. He was all chat about the exams. Delighted with my results. Then he got straight down to it. What college course was I interested in pursuing? Would I have any interest in coming into the business with him after college?

No chance. I wanted away from the hassle of a business where you were on call at all hours of the day and week. I had done enough of that to keep me going for the rest of my life. Now I was intent on a private, easier kind of life.

We had the furniture delivered and were back in Dingle, passing the Provincial Bank on Main Street, when he ordered: 'Pull in here outside the bank.'

I parked. He turned to me.

'What course will you do?'

'I haven't decided.'

'Will you go to university?'

'I don't know. I don't think so.'

'Do you know what we'll do now? We'll go into the bank and sort out the money for your university course.'

I was puzzled. 'How do you mean? Some kind of loan?'

'No loan. I want to arrange for you to have the money you need. We'll go in here now; nobody will know our business. We'll do it all now, and even if we fall out, the money will still be there for you. I'll sign over money into an account in your name so that you will be able to withdraw enough for your fees and some more every year. I don't want it back and I don't want anybody to know. I'll only ask you to do two things for me. Don't drink whiskey and don't do medicine at college. We have a bad record with those two!'

I was completely taken aback.

'No thanks, Uncle John!'

'Won't you be said by me?'

'No, I won't, and that's for certain.'

'Don't be a fooleen. I have no children and more money than I need. Will you let me do this?'

'No. I'll pay my own way.'

'You were always stubborn. Will you not do this for me? '

'NO.'

'Come on, so. We might as well go home.'

That was it, we went back to work and it wasn't mentioned again. On reflection, I know I was wrong. I think it hurt him. It was something he wanted to do with the money and I should not have resisted someone of such extraordinarily good intentions.

I duly got 'the call'. Teresa wasn't impressed. She was strongly opposed to my becoming a national teacher. 'You could do better for yourself.'

Myko, on the other hand, was all for it. Me, I didn't know what to do. Pat Neligan was pushing strongly for me to go; Micheál Moran was really enjoying it. A lot of the class were going: Jim Lundon, John Martin, Tommy Dowd. Donal Lynch was going too. It was going to be like home, and it didn't sound like hard work.

Why not? I decided to give it a shot.

Teresa was disgusted, but gave in and, in typical fashion, began to have big notions of the possibilities that would open up for me.

'Sure, maybe you could do as well as that Brosnahan man from Tralee. He's a big man in the INTO and a senator now as well.'

Some chance.

See you.

Hello, Dublin.